✫ Contents ✫

☆Scream of Eagles ☆

The Creation of Top Gun—
And the U.S. Air Victory in Vietnam

by Robert K. Wilcox

JOHN WILEY & SONS, INC.

New York ☆ Chichester ☆ Brisbane ☆ Toronto ☆ Singapore

To my father, Lt. Col. J.G. "Jake" Wilcox, who inspired this book
with his stories of the 8th Air Force in World War II England.

Recognizing the importance of preserving what has been written, it
is a policy of John Wiley & Sons, Inc. to have books of enduring
value published in the United States printed on acid-free paper, and
we exert our best efforts to that end.

Copyright © 1990 by Robert K. Wilcox

Published by John Wiley & Sons, Inc.

Library of Congress Cataloging in Publication Data

Wilcox, Robert K.
    Scream of eagles : the creation of top gun and the U.S. air
victory in Vietnam / by Robert Wilcox.
        p. cm.
    ISBN 0-471-52641-X
    1. Navy Fighter Weapons School (U.S.)—History. 2. Vietnamese
Conflict, 1961–1975—Aerial operations, American. 3. Fighter plane
combat—United States—History. I. Title.
    VG94.5.N65W55   1990
358.4'14'071173—dc20   90-38152
                                                        CIP
Printed in the United States of America
90 91 10 9 8 7 6 5 4 3 2 1

☆ Preface ☆

In 1968 American Air Force and Navy fighter pilots found themselves losing the battle for the skies over North Vietnam. Their kill ratio from engagements was a dismal 2-to-1, which meant that for every two enemy MiGs that Americans shot down, the North Vietnamese, virtual newcomers to dogfighting, shot down one American plane. American fighter pilots had never suffered such embarrassingly low kill ratios in American air warfare history.

In actual numbers—approximately 25 American fighters had been shot down—the losses were not critical. But they could be if such ratios continued. Fighters after all, were the primary protection for the bombers on their runs into Vietnam, as well as for the U.S. fleet off the coast.

In 1968 the North Vietnamese Air Force was just gearing up; its pilots were still learning. In the future, they could be expected to increase their number of attacks and cause havoc in the air. Since air superiority is a prerequisite to victory in modern warfare, not only would more American pilots and planes be destroyed, but also the outcome of the war could be affected. And what if we got into a larger, global war?

Air Force leadership did not react to this threat during the Vietnam War. But the Navy, to its credit, did. Pooling its fighter pilot expertise, a small cadre of instructors assigned to Miramar Air Station, California, were charged with correcting the problem. At the time, none of those involved—instructors or students—realized the long-term significance of what they were being asked to do. They were simply responding to a war emergency. Eventually, however, they were to change the course of the air war by forging the only clear victory America was to win in the Vietnam War. Their largely secret efforts would change fighter training and tactics in the decades that have followed.

This is their story—the story behind the creation of the Top Gun fighter pilot school.

☆ Acknowledgments ☆

The book could not have been written without the cooperation of those written about, especially the principals. I told them when I started that I wished to tell the truth about what I considered to be a great story, warts and all. Most of them I believe, would have been content to have left the story untold. They had lived it and that was enough. But I thank them for their patience, candor, and helpfulness.

That goes for those I talked to who are not mentioned in the book as extensively as the principles, or not at all. Their interviews also helped, and I thank them for the time they gave me.

I was lucky to find Ralph Platt, a man of many talents. Ralph had been an Air Force F-86 pilot and is now a computer expert, who not only transcribed the interview tapes and typed the manuscript, but who also acted as an expert advisor who was always ready to answer questions.

Early on, Frank Baldwin, a friend of my sister-in-law, Iziar, was gracious enough to introduce me to J. D. 'Doug' Smidt, a former Navy pilot, who steered me to Dan Pedersen. That got the book rolling. Ms. Anna C. Urband, of the Navy's Office of Information in Washington, was always helpful in locating documents and former Naval officers; as were official Naval historians and archivists Roy A. Grossnick, Wes Price, Ed Miralda, Bernard F. Cavalacante, and Celia Rakestraw.

Top Gun at Miramar, although short on archives, provided requested documents and answered questions. In particular, I'd like to thank skippers Chris Wilson, Ric Ludwig, and J. S. Daughtry, Jr. At the Pacific Fleet's headquarters on North Island, LCDR Tom Jurkowsky, Public Affairs Officers, aided with initial ground work; as did George Haering, a civilian analyst in the Pentagon, and Ed Rouen and B. C. Reynolds of the San Diego Aero-Space Museum.

Also giving variously and graciously of their time, knowledge, and/or resources were: Capt. R. Moon Vance at VX-4, Capt. Ernie

Christensen at Naval Air in Washington, USAF Col. Peter Dunn and Navy Capt. Dave Hill, both at the University of Missouri-Columbia; Billy P. Hill at Information Management Inc., Las Vegas, Nev., and Bob Lawson, editor of *The Hook*. In particular, I'd like to thank John D. Gresham for his help in analyzing the events of May 10, 1972. John is an astute researcher and expert in his field.

Finally, I'd like to give special thanks to my literary agents of nearly 15 years now, Jim and Liz Trupin, Jet Literary Associates, Inc.; good friends who contributed greatly with their support and by selling the book; my editor at John Wiley, Roger Scholl, for his excellent contributions in editing; and, of course, my wife, Bego, for her steadfast backing of what finally has become for both of us a rewarding profession. Onward and upward.

☆ PART I ☆

The Men Who Would Be Eagles

☆ CHAPTER 1 ☆

Dan Arthur Pedersen could see the contrails of two jet engines as far as eighty miles away, at the edge of the high desert east of Los Angeles. The vapor streaks led up, and then curled back down. Nothing horizontal, as you'd see in airline flight. Those jets were fighting—hassling—he was sure of it. He banked his jet, and accelerated toward them.

It was a week before Christmas, 1958, one of those cold, clear winter afternoons when visibility was unlimited. Pedersen, 23, who would, almost a decade later, create and command a brand-new Navy fighter-pilot school known as Top Gun, was just a green ensign, not yet two years out of flight school, tooling around in his hot F4D Skyray.

☆ ☆ ☆

The Skyray was one of the Navy's first supersonic jet fighters. It flew faster than the speed of sound, setting a world record of 753.4 miles per hour in 1953. What distinguished the Skyray from other fighters was its swept-back full-delta wing—an innovation influenced by World War II German Luftwaffe planes—and a powerful 10,000-pound thrust Pratt and Whitney engine with afterburner. Dubbed "manta-like" and "batwinged," the Skyray, with its afterburner kicked in, could shoot to 10,000 feet in fifty-six seconds; 50,000 feet in two and a half minutes. Ensign Pedersen was driving a rocket. And the plane's aerodynamics, especially the delta-wings, gave it great maneuverability.

☆ ☆ ☆

Born in Moline, Illinois, the grandson of Danish immigrants, Pedersen had all the attributes of a good fighter pilot: keen eyes, good eye-hand coordination, split-second judgment, love of flying, the body strength to handle the incredible physical forces his plane encountered as it roared and churned through the atmosphere, and the mental toughness to steel himself against the fear and stress that were always a fighter pilot's enemy. At 6′3″, he had the big-boned frame and rugged good looks of a young Johnny Unitas. His size also gave him a certain swagger; it wasn't so much cockiness as a way of standing forthright, sizing you up with a steady, measuring gaze, a hint of challenge on his face. The stare was usually followed by a big, lip-curling grin. And a voice that sounded at times like John Wayne's.

Pedersen had earned his jet fighter wings in the midst of a revolutionary era in fighter techniques. Missiles were replacing guns, especially in the Navy. Gone were the days, said experts in the Pentagon, of close-in, turning fights—what were commonly called "dogfights"; planes swirling at each other's tails, looking for a deadly "six o'clock" shot (a shot of an opposing plane's six o'clock position—his tailpipe). Korea had seen the last of the dogfighters, went the conventional wisdom. Jets were now too fast and too sophisticated for swirling, close-range machine-gun battles. This new era would see supersonic jets firing air-to-air missiles at bogeys that were often so far away they could be seen only on radar scopes. You didn't have to be close. In fact, you had to be far enough away for the missile to track and arm its target. Once the missile was launched, the "interceptor," as some fighter planes were now being called, would most probably streak away and its crew watch impact on a tiny on-board screen, or hear about it from a ground control center. Air combat maneuvering, or ACM, as they later called a high-speed turning fight in the textbooks, was nearly dead, relegated to a few approach-and-retreat maneuvers.

"Air defense tactics" was the new doctrine, the new aerodynamic gospel, preached above all by the aircraft and armament manufacturers who were closest to the new technology.

While many veteran fighter pilots were skeptical, all of the armed services were racing into rockets and missiles. Sparrow and Sidewinder were the fighter weapons most talked about at the Pentagon—small "air-to-air" rockets made to be fired from airborne interceptors at approaching bombers.

Pedersen's Skyray was one of those interceptors. It had guns, but it also had rockets, two pods under each wing. Pedersen was in the thick of the new tactics, flying daily intercept missions out over the Pacific, or inland toward the deserts and mountains. The mission was an intecept flown by an "interceptor."

Most of the time, Pedersen, like the other Navy pilots flew strictly controlled intercept missions. Out to the target and back. Radar monitored all the way. But on days off, he could go over to maintenance control and pick up a newly-fixed or spare Skyray and take it up. He could cruise to a relatively untrafficked area over the ocean or desert, and push his machine to its limits, hopefully test it against another pilot.

Close in dogfighting was not only being phased out of the training syllabus, it was illegal. A pilot could get in serious trouble for doing it, even on his own. Those airplanes cost money, it was explained, and a dead pilot is *not* a Navy asset. But the more aggressive pilots did it, those who thought of themselves as one of the elite. Fighting, hassling, was the way to perfect your ability. It was also the way to establish the fighter pilot pecking order.

A fighter pilot was a mathematician riding a roaring, mammoth blowtorch; a bucking, snapping, multi-ton package of explosive metal and circuitry, whipping around as deftly in the air as the lure on a fisherman's line. The crushing G forces in the high-speed turns could flatten a pilot's face, dim and narrow his vision, cause the blood to rush so quickly from his brain that if it wasn't for his G-suit, he'd blackout forever. The stakes, the consequences of being less than best, of being second best, could be fatal. Hassling helped to perfect one's skills. It forced a pilot to be alert. Intimidation and unpredictability were part of the point behind such fights. An adversary sometimes swooped so close that you could see his helmet markings. Anything less than perfect execution, total mastery of aircraft, and mastery of fear, would send your airplane into a sudden, uncontrollable spin, a loss of aerodynamics from which only the highest degree of expertise could pull you out. And there was always the danger of equipment malfunction. Yet, in spite of the rigors and dangers involved, there were fortunately few accidents in these sporting jousts, probably fewer than in normal operations.

☆ ☆ ☆

Pedersen was now approaching the high desert and could see clearly the two hasslers he'd spotted earlier. One was an F-8 Crusader, one of the newest, fastest planes in the Navy at that time. Silver and sleek, with a round-mouthed airscoop under its nose, swept-back, eagle-like wings draped from the top of its fuselage, the F-8 was the Navy's last "gunfighter." Although it would later be fitted with rockets and missiles, it now carried only 20mm cannons. The Crusader was the first operational carrier plane able to exceed 1000 miles per hour, approaching a sensational Mach 2. But the Crusader was getting beat!

What was out-maneuvering the jet, the surprised ensign realized, was an old F-86 Sabre jet. The Sabre was a classic dogfighter; small, maneuverable; the scourge of "MiG Alley," the best jet fighter plane, pound for pound, in the skies of Asia during the Korean War. In the last seven months of the Korean conflict, it had chalked up a terrific 17-to-1 kill ratio against the MiG—seventeen MiGs shot down for every U.S. plane lost. But the plane was no longer operational in the regular services. It was considered outdated, not part of the new missile-interceptor force. This one, he could see from its markings, was an Air National Guard bird, probably from Van Nuys, where he knew there was a Guard fighter unit. Guard pilots, usually former Air Force, might have blazed a trail of glory over the Yalu River in Korea, but now they were just "weekend warriors," pot-bellied, gray-bearded old men who took the old jets up once a month to keep themselves and the airframes from rusting. Or so that was their image among the younger, active pilots. This Sabre was eating the F-8 alive. The F-8s were fleet "air superiority" fighters, the "hottest" of the new jets. There was a big rivalry between the F-8s and the other squadrons.

When the F-8 had had enough, Pedersen, figuring he could gain some points, jumped the Sabre himself. There's a certain etiquette to observe in such fights: after coming alongside of and getting the F-86's attention, the two raced off in opposite directions, like pistol duelers, only putting miles instead of feet between themselves. Then, like knights of old, they turned and charged each other, hell-bent-for-leather, flat-out, head-on at each other's noses. They call it "making passes." Then comes the jockeying for position. The object is to get on the other's tail, and into a "valid firing envelope." In order to maneuver into such position, the planes turn in to each other, each trying to gain the advantage. When a pilot turns, his airspeed goes down—he usually loses energy and altitude. Inevitably, in a good-turning fight, speeds get slower and slower. The advantage of high speed in a straightaway gives way to quickness and maneuverability while turning. A smart fighter uses his advantage. This is what the F-86 pilot did.

While the Skyray was faster, the Sabre's turning radius, or arc, was smaller, which meant it could turn within a smaller space. When Pedersen tried to brute-force his slower adversary, literally scare him into a bad move with a locomotive charge, the F-86 pilot cooly held his ground, then executed a maneuver Pedersen had never seen. It flipped the aircraft 360 degrees underneath Pedersen and turned it into Pedersen's wake quicker than the startled ensign could turn the Skyray into his.

This didn't automatically give the F-86 a tail shot, because Pedersen quickly turned again. But every time Pedersen turned, the Sabre turned too—and quicker, in a tighter arc. The distance between them, the distance that would finally give the Sabre the theoretical killing shot, was closing. "Two or three turns, and he was all over me," recalls Pedersen. "I was saddled. I couldn't shake him."

Pedersen decided to go up, to use the Skyray's afterburner to climb and gain some maneuverability. Hopefully, the climb would also cause the Sabre to lose sight of the Skyray in the high sun. It's hard to keep track of somebody above you. And when a pilot loses sight of his adversary, he's in big trouble.

But the Sabre didn't fall for it—just as he did not fall for it from the earlier F-8 Crusader. "He'd seen all these things." Like a fox, he just hung below, keeping Pedersen in sight. When Pedersen came back down—and you always have to come back down—he drove right to a spot behind Pedersen's wing and stayed there. It was smart fighting. He just didn't fall into the trap Pedersen was setting. He knew the F-86's strengths, and he stuck with them.

"He kept working the inside arc," Pedersen recalls, "You eventually have to run, or he gets you."

The young ensign finally pulled up and leveled his wings in concession. He was beaten—there was nothing else he could do. He'd underestimated his adversary.

Later, the pilot of the F-86 called Pedersen. The Major had over 3000 hours in the Sabre, 2000 of which were in Korea. He was an ace. He knew the F-86 inside and out, and he knew the Skyray. "He pulled my chain something fierce, telling me what I'd done wrong and how he'd exploited it. He was an aerodynamist, and I was brute strength and awkwardness. I was eager and aggressive, but I didn't really know the first thing about fighting my airplane. I hadn't seen anybody that good yet."

It was his first realization of the difference in aircraft and pilots; what different planes could and couldn't do, and how pilot knowledge and skill—not the airplane—were really the crucial factors in victory. According to its manufacturer, the Skyray was the best turning machine in the sky. But the pilot he was talking to had made mincemeat out of that claim.

Pedersen realized he'd better learn a great deal more about his airplane, what it really can and can't do—the things they weren't teaching in flight school. He realized he had been stupid to jump in like that without knowing the first thing about who and what he was fighting. "Those contrails had looked inviting, like honey to the flies. But you've got to be prepared for the best. You can't be guaranteed the guy's going to be [as pluckable as] a grape."

It was the germ of perhaps the most important flying lesson of Pedersen's career: experiment with your airplane. Find the ends of its envelope. Learn all you can about your potential adversary. And practice, practice, practice.

The Vietnam War was still several years off. Pedersen had no inkling of what was ahead, or how important the lesson he'd learned would prove to be.

☆ CHAPTER 2 ☆

Joining the Navy at a time when there was an excess of pilots, Mel Holmes —"Rattler" as his call sign would later become at Top Gun, and a pilot who was to become one of the best F-4 Phantom pilots in the world—had been remaindered with a lot of other young fighter hopefuls to a backwater, Utility Squadron 3—"VU3" in official designation. It was a kind of service unit to the fleet. The fleet, Holmes knew, was where the action and prestige were. If fleet ground control intercept (GCI) trainees needed practice vectoring fighters to bogeys, VU3 pilots were sent to simulate the exercise. If they needed gunnery work, VU3 hauled the targets and drones. The squadron was a lackey, a nowhere unit from which Holmes, an ambitious, highly regarded pilot used to speaking his mind, was doggedly trying to extract himself.

"I fought like the Sam Hill to get out. Can't remember how many letters I wrote to the bureau [Navy Bureau of Personnel] to get into a fleet squadron. But I think in the long run it was good for me. We had the flexibility to basically do what we wanted in the airplane, where in the fleet you had to do the training the way it was programmed."

Based on North Island, VU3 was run by World War II and Korean War era officers who were nearing the end of their careers. "We didn't have a lot of supervision." But they did have a lot of Skyrays, and fuel. Consequently, once they'd completed the day's work, they were usually free to roam "Whiskey 291," the huge piece of military airspace off the Southern California coast (off limits to civilian aircraft), and jump any plane they found. They didn't have to worry about COs grounding them or using too much fuel. "We fought our brains out," remembers Holmes.

9

As he looks back on it, he was lucky to be flying the Skyray. Despite its waning future, the plane, which at one time had held so many official world records, *was* a great-turning aircraft, and one which wouldn't kill a pilot at the first mistake. "It was a tremendous learning tool for me . . . very forgiving. You could pull the hell out of it, and it always seemed to come back out of any maneuver." This was largely due to its big delta wing. While the wing offered resistance to the wind which would cut speed, its large mass—557 square feet, and at one time the greatest wing area seen on a Navy fighter—acted almost like a parachute if the pilot got in trouble. A pilot could take it to the edge, stall, even spin, and it would recover relatively easily. Says Holmes, "It gave me a lot of confidence I might not otherwise have acquired."

The freedom these pilots enjoyed helped too. According to Holmes, "In the fleet [the training program] was all intercept. Protect the carrier. Long-range missiles. That sort of thing. There was little air-to-air maneuvering. But we were completely away from that, out of contact with what was really going on in the Navy. We were just up there pulling our brains out and thinking that was the way it was in the fleet. . ."

In fact, as a result of the new intercept philosophy, the Navy had disbanded its dogfighting-bombing school, the Fleet Air Gunnery Unit, or FAGU. Only a dwindling number of fighter pilots, most of them in F-8 Crusaders, were left to pass on the tradition. More than any other single event, some were to feel, FAGU's decommissioning was the beginning of the dark days that were to come.

☆ ☆ ☆

A star athlete, Holmes set college basketball scoring records at Eastern Oregon College. Six feet tall, square-shouldered, quick to shake your hand, he was outgoing and purposeful.

A recruiter from the Navy had spurred his Navy aspirations, and he applied for a commission upon graduation. On a team trip to Alaska, he stopped off in Seattle to take the tests, but the taxi he was in mistakenly deposited him at the wrong door, and he ended up passing an aviation officer candidate test. "So instead of surface school, I was bound for Pensacola.

"We had thirty-three pilots in my class. Twelve finished. At that time there was quite an attrition rate. The Navy didn't need pilots. They had many more applications then. Pilots were staying in. The economy had a lot to do with it." The actual flying of a plane—at least at first—was difficult too. The math was tough. So was the coordination of hand, foot, and eye. There were a million things to do and remember. "It was difficult. But I think having been an athlete, and having the aggressive attitude that you don't like to admit or accept failure, helped me. Not so much the skills of an athlete, which you don't necessarily need, but the inner drive to excel and perform. That's how I made it through."

By the time he'd graduated and gotten his wings early in 1963, he'd been selected to continue in fighters. "He was an outgoing, leadership-type guy," recalls Royal Cherry, a VU3 pilot at the time. "He was real motivated. Could take charge, get things done."

Early on, Holmes remembers watching a more experienced pilot, Tom Rodgers, fight an F-8.

"I didn't actually participate in the fight," remembers Holmes, referring to a melee over San Clemente that cemented his coming of age as a cockpit strategist. "There must have been fifteen or sixteen fighters in the damn thing. We had demons [F-3 Hs], F-8s, a couple of A-4s. I just sat up there and watched. My God, Tom was aggressive. He just ate that F-8 alive." Because Rodgers knew he couldn't hope to out-speed the faster Crusader, he and the other Skyray pilots had developed a tactic of goading the F-8s down to a low-altitude, turning fight where the Skyray's big wing would prevail. He pressed his advantage. "He wasn't afraid to push the airplane, make it do everything short of going out of the envelope. He actually maneuvered until at the end of the fight he was about fifteen feet from its tail. When the F-8 finally gave up, he just moved up to its wing, looked at him and left. That's the type of thing that unfurls the aggressivness in you. It showed me I could be more aggressive and not worry about it."

It also taught him another important lesson—to use your airplane's advantages. And don't let your opponent use his.

"You have to understand who you are fighting. I discovered this later on in the war. You don't go down and start turning with a MiG-17."

Fighting another VU vet, Wayne Hanley, Holmes learned that "Your first move is your best move." Speeding toward Hanley, "I'd always get beat on the first turn. I'd wonder, what the hell's going on? I finally realized that your first angle is the best angle you're going to get." What Hanley was doing was cutting inside of Holmes' first turn, and doing it so well that he was able to zip right to Holmes' tail. "From a head-on pass, if you can get an angle on a guy and get so many degrees advantage on him toward his six o'clock [position], then you don't have to ever make up that angle. You've picked up some degrees that you don't have to give back . . . It's really reacting, out-thinking the guy . . . If you can anticipate what he's going to do and cut the angle, you're ahead of him . . . If he takes the move away, then you know what kind of pilot you're up against."

This ability to project an opponent's next move, to anticipate it before he actually makes it, is akin to a linebacker instinctively moving to a hole before it opens, or a second baseman moving into position for a line drive before it is hit.

"Exploding your eyes," was another phrase Holmes used to describe that increased sense of awareness and anticipation, borrowing the phrase from running back O. J. Simpson. "Instead of closing his eyes when he got hit, [Simpson] would say he'd 'explode' them open so he had even more peripheral vision. Well, a fighter pilot is looking to areas and trying to estimate distance and refocus his eyes and imagine where the guy's going to be next. Once you know the piece of sky he's going to be in, you point your nose to it." According to Holmes, to many, everything is happening too fast. It's a blur of spatial disorientation. "It's not the type of thing you can just pick up. Some guys have it, and some don't."

Holmes had it, a natural ability to make sense out of a three-dimensional chunk of sky filled with planes and missiles. He'd sit high in the cockpit, "as high as I could get so I could see off to the sides. I'd lean forward with my eyes up as far front as I could get them. I could handle myself a little better that way."

It was always a problem seeing out of a cockpit, especially to the rear where the wings and fuselage created a blind spot. The pilot had to twist his head back and forth to keep his opponent constantly in view. After a fight, he'd return to Coronado "wringing wet, sopping wet. And this happened every engagement I had—my right arm was physically tired. The muscles would be cramped because I'd be pulling so hard. My neck would be sore trying to hold it up under the strain."

Tom Rodgers remembers, "Mel was interested in making sure he did a good job all the time. Even if he lost a fight, he'd be right back, equally determined to win against the same person the next time.

By early 1964, Holmes was one of the squadron's ACM (air combat maneuvering) leaders. "I think it's the exhilaration. Your blood's pumping. . . . It's like a joust. You're going out against another guy to see who's better. My God, competing against another individual to see who's best. I can imagine what the knights of old thought. I haven't been able to find that kind of exhilaration anywhere else."

Occasionally, he'd run into the new F-4 Phantom, the plane that would be so much a part of Mel Holmes' future—the plane that would soon become the front-line fighter for both the Navy and the Air Force. "Biggest, meanest-looking airplane I'd ever seen. My God, the wings droop, the wing tips angle up. The stabilizers [tail fins] angle down. It had this big, ugly nose, and it sorta sits there on its haunches looking you right in the eye."

Resembling a prehistoric reptile, its two huge General Electric J79 engines bulging its sides, humpbacking its 58-foot fuselage, the "brute," or "monster," as the Phantom was sometimes called, was already the talk of the Navy. It was rewriting the record books for speed—1606 miles per hour (the previous record had been hundreds of miles per hour slower); and sustained combat altitude—66,000 feet (it could climb to 100,000 feet if necessary). With afterburners a pilot could slam in a combined 35,000 pounds of thrust with the movement of a throttle; the plane could climb at a stupendous 30,000 feet per minute. Its weapon load alone was twice that of a World War II B-17 bomber. "It was the best," recalls Holmes, "and everybody, including me, wanted to fly it."

Ironically—at least to Holmes' way of thinking—the F-4 crew members weren't much interested in fighting. "They'd just make a couple of passes and leave. They really wouldn't get into it." If

Holmes had been in the fleet, he would have understood the reason. The Phantom was being touted as the supreme interceptor. With the latest radar tracking system, and a second crewman—the radar intercept officer (RIO)—in the back seat to operate it, the fleet brass didn't feel the Phantom would ever need to mix it up close with other planes. So sure was the Navy brass of this prediction that they had made the unprecedented decision not to include guns on the plane, the traditional fighter weapon. The Phantom was to be the first U. S. "all-weather, multi-mission" aircraft armed solely with missiles: specifically, the radar-guided Sparrow and the heat-seeking Sidewinder, both newly developed for intercept.

As G. G. O'Rourke, in his book, *The F-4 Phantom II*, recounts: "Cocky F-4 crews were soon telling . . . controllers, 'Don't give me all that lead pursuit positioning jazz . . . just point me at the target and shut up. . . . If we don't get him coming through the first time, we'll honk it around and catch him from behind.' "

In other words, the pilots held the position that they would spot the bogey on their radar and destroy it with a long-range missile before the other plane realized the Phantom was there. And if they missed, they'd simply turn around, and get him on a second long shot. Everything would be head-to-head, with no-close in turning. ACM would not be needed.

Not everyone bought the Navy's strategy, but the F-4 tended to make believers out of doubters. The 44,000-pound jet literally shook the deck when it was catapulted off the carriers. Its fiery twin-barreled exhaust lighted up an entire carrier on night launch. It was the sort of new weapon that anyone whose job it was to wage war would love. And if by some freak accident it didn't actually kill its target, pilots kidded, it would scare the poor devil to death.

So impressive was the F-4 in so many ways that the Air Force, after much consideration, decided to order it as well—with slight modifications, including the addition of guns, for its *own* pilots, one of the few times the rival service had ever adopted to Navy planning. For the first time, the Navy fleet, long accustomed to being second best in the air because of carrier requirements, had the finest combat aircraft in the world.

Or so, at any rate, it seemed.

Holmes was well aware of the F-4's reputation, and continued to pester the Navy personnel bureau to assign him to the fleet, either to an F-8 squadron, or, hopefully, to the F-4s. Pilots were being trained for transition into Phantoms at nearby Miramar in San Diego, which had become the support base and home station for all West Coast fighter squadrons. They were beginning to call the base "Fightertown," as the U.S. military increased its readiness in response to the growing war in Southeast Asia.

In 1964, shortly after the Tonkin Gulf incident officially launched America into the Vietnam war, Holmes' wish was granted. He received orders to report to VF-121, the huge Replacement Air Group—the "RAG" for short—the unit that trained pilots how to fly the F-4.

☆ CHAPTER 3 ☆

On April 9, 1965, just five days after the first North Vietnamese MiGs challenged American planes in Vietnam, a Navy Phantom F-4 tried to dogfight with a MiG. It was shot down, and both of its crew members, LTJG Terence M. Murphy and ENS Ron J. Fegan, were killed.

Information on the dogfight, which is still classified, was sketchy. The Phantom was one of several VF-96 planes from the carrier U.S.S. *Ranger*. They were on MIGCAP (guard patrol) off Hainan Island in the Gulf of Tonkin. Four MiGs attacked; "the crew," says a Chief of Naval Operations document, "tried to turn against the MiG -17 . . . bled off air speed, and was caught in the MiG's gun sights."

The shootdown proved to be a dramatic example of the fact that the Phantom, the Navy and Air Force's frontline warplane, could not normally turn successfully with a MiG. The plane was too heavy; its wings were too small to propel it through turns without a great deal of speed, which meant that the F-4 could not turn as tightly as the MiG. But few at this point took notice.

☆ ☆ ☆

J. C. Smith radioed back "feet dry," indicating they'd just left water and were roaring over land. It was mid-morning, June 17, 1965. Smith was the backseater in the lead F-4 Phantom of a Yankee Station strike force from the carriers *Midway* and *Bon Homme Richard*; the strike force contained fourteen planes that were headed for the Thanh Hoa Railroad Bridge, later nicknamed "The Dragon's Jaw," because of its near invincibility.

16

The massive concrete bridge was located 80 miles south of Hanoi. The bridge spanned the Ma River, an important part of Hanoi's supply route to the south, which was becoming known as the Ho Chi Minh Trail. The fighters and bombers—mostly F-4s and A-4 Skyhawks—were part of Operation Rolling Thunder, the newly instituted U.S. strategic plan to move the bombing closer and closer to Hanoi until the North Vietnamese buckled under the onslaught and surrendered.

The planes turned north, jinking back and forth, gaining and losing altitude, presenting as unpredictable a target as possible, although they didn't expect much ground fire. Concentrations of antiaircraft artillery (Triple-A)—so heavy that they eventually would be described as comparable or worse than that over Germany in World War II—were mostly clustered around the cities. The strike force was speeding over green jungle, which was high enough to avoid small arms fire, but low enough to be safe from any surface-to-air missiles (SAMs), the deadly "flying telephone poles" that would later put so many American flyers in North Vietnamese graves and prisons.

SAMs weren't a major threat yet. They'd only recently been spotted being positioned in the North and hadn't been used. The strike force's main concern was the sleek little MiG-17, the maneuverable Russian fighter that, although relatively old now, had made its Vietnam debut over the North several months earlier, downing three Air Force F-105 Thunderchiefs over the very bridge they were flying towards, and causing the U.S. command to decide to begin giving their bombing missions fighter cover.

J. C.'s and five other Phantoms were flying TARCAP for the mission. When they arrived over the bridge, the six F-4s, in sections of two each—a leader and wingman—would take separate stations above and around the target and patrol for MiGs.

While the North Vietnamese didn't have much of an air force at this stage, even one unchallenged enemy fighter could wreak havoc on the bombers, whose pilots would be concentrating on the target. Even forcing the bombers to abandon their mission would be a victory for the MiGs. The F-4s were to act as the A-4's bodyguards; their state-of-the-art radars, the lookouts, would search the skies in 60-degree sweeps that could detect other planes as much as 100 miles in ideal conditions.

As a radar interceptor officer, or RIO, as the backseater was often called, J. C., a lieutenant commander, was busy operating the radar, giving navigational information to his pilot, CMDR Lou Page, and coordinating over the radio with the other RIOs in the flight.

J. C. Smith loved flying, but as a 21-year-old pilot in the VA-126 attack squadron, he'd almost lost his chance to fly forever. He found what he didn't like was VA-126's mission: bombing. Nuclear bombing. Repetitious maneuvers. Four-G boring, he called them. The attack syllabus called it toss bombing. You come in low, swoop up into a backward loop called a half Cuban eight, toss the bomb several miles out in front of you, and run for home. You couldn't just drop the bomb, because a nuclear explosion would destroy the bomber too. "Hell, it wasn't even dive bombing," he said.

In later years he'd become known for talking on the airways. He told tall stories on the ground. "The Mouth," "The Joker" they'd call him. It was a way of masking nervousness. Not fear of the risks or dangers of flying, but a fear of failure, of not measuring up to this great career of flying he had stumbled into almost by accident. Behind the earthy, quick-with-a-joke personality, beneath the fighter pilot brush-top and cool-under-fire attitude, J. C. was a very intense young man.

Born February 20, 1936, in St. Louis, Missouri, he remembers wanting to fly even before he could run. "I can remember sitting under the sink with a plunger stuck on the floor, using it as a stick," he recalled. His mother would drape the area like a cockpit. "The curved pipe was my gunsight. I'd fly that kitchen everywhere."

The family had moved to Belleville, Illinois, across the river from St. Louis, where his father was a millwright. J. C. inherited his father's aptitude with machines. But they didn't get along. He moved out of the house at age 17 and took a job as a mechanic at Brennan's Phillips 66. With the little he had left over after living expenses, he enrolled in nearby Belleville Junior College. Two years later he enlisted in the Navy. He had no idea the Navy flew airplanes. "I just wanted to get out of there." A Navy pilot told him about NAVCAD, a Navy flight program requiring only two years of college, which he had. He took some tests, and a month and a half later he was in a Greyhound bus on his way to Pensacola for preflight ground school.

After flight school, he was selected for jets, training at Kingsville, Texas. In late August 1957, he begrudgingly reported to Miramar's 126 bombing squadron. He considered himself a fighter pilot, and let them know it—which turned out to be his first mistake. After bombing practice, sometimes—if he could get away with it—even *during* practice, he'd jump out and start hassling. "This pushing that damn nose over in a forty-degree dive, holding it wings level, the ball perfectly centered . . . sucked."

He says none in the squadron could stay with him. "I was always fighting. They kept saying I was overstressing the airplane. I wasn't overstressing it. I was just beating them." He found himself in frequent meetings with the CO—at the CO's summons. "I bitched constantly about dropping bombs. My attitude was very poor. But I was where I didn't want to be."

Because of the way he threw the airplane around, pushing it to its limits, his planes were often "down," which put him in conflict with the maintenance officer and crews. As a result, the CO called him into his office again. "I knew what I was doing with the machine, but I was naive about rank. I felt I was better than this CO because I could fly better, which was wrong. He had more experience than me, and I ignored that. I failed to realize that he was setting the pace, that he was supposed to be the example that we follow."

The only reason things didn't come to a head sooner was the fact that J. C. was an excellent bomber. He was consistently one of the best in the squadron.

Picked to help represent his squadron at the intra-service William Tell bombing competition at El Centro, where the Navy had one of its chief bombing ranges. He delivered, he says, the bombs that won. The brass, including his CO, were sitting in the bleachers, and J. C. decided to do a victory roll before landing. "I came off the target and went out over the city." Unknown to him, he says, a squadron mate joined on his wing. "I wasn't supposed to have anybody with me, so I wasn't looking." He came back over the field and made a couple of fast rolls, snap rolls. The other plane couldn't follow and nearly crashed.

His CO was livid. J. C. was promptly grounded. Later, after a weekend flight that, because of a malfunction, resulted in having to scrap his plane's engine, he was summoned before an aviator's disposition board. A week later he received word that an admiral had overruled the recommendation of the board—that he be taken out of jets altogether and sent to a prop squadron—and had taken his wings. It was the lowest point in his life.

Sometime after that a friend on the air staff at Miramar had shown him a bulletin on the new RIO program the Navy was starting up. With the F-4s coming into the Navy, the service was going to need a new kind of officer—a naval flight officer (NFO). The F-4 was so sophisticated, went the thinking, that it would take two people to fly it—the pilot and the radarman in the back. The pilot would concentrate on operating the mechanisms of flight, while the RIO would concentrate on the radar, and radio communications.

In a combat situation, two heads were better than one. There was no way a single pilot could fly his plane, watch the bogey and radar scope, and operate the complicated new missiles. At least that's the way the brass explained it.

Most pilots were skeptical. Their basic attitude was, "I can handle it myself. I don't need a backseater to help me." But the RIO was the wave of the future. For J. C., it was a chance to get out from behind a desk and back into an airplane.

In August 1959, he'd reported to James Connelly Air Force Base, Waco, Texas, as one of the first Navy RIO trainees. The Air Force already had two-man crews in the F-80 Shooting Star and F-89 Scorpion. J. C. and a small class of about 19 others were going to learn the same operation and then become instructors to the Navy's RIOs and pilots who were assigned to the new F-4s.

Because Smith had been a pilot, he knew more about the work environment than the others, most of whom were enlisted radar operators commissioned upon graduation. Some of them had never flown before. He quickly became the leader of the group.

They started out in an old reconfigured B-25, which had a large radar scope around which six of them could gather while aloft. They'd practice picking out bogeys and plotting intercept courses. When he finished his training, he was sent to McDonnell-Douglas' plant in St. Louis to familiarize himself with new F-4.

The Phantom he'd come to learn about in St. Louis was the product of fierce airplane-building competition.

Since making the Phantom I in 1946 (the first jet-powered carrier fighter), McDonnell-Douglas had considered itself the Navy's fighter-supplier, a heady distinction. But in 1953, to its shock and surprise, it lost a fly-off to Chance Vought's then new F-8.

McDonnell-Douglas was suddenly outside, looking in.

Without a contract, McDonnell-Douglas set about to regain its previous position. Within a year, its engineers, after polling the Navy for its needs, had produced a zippy little fighter mock-up with guns. They called it Phantom II.

The Navy, recognizing McDonnell-Douglas' initiative, gave the company a letter of intent, but later requested changes that radically altered the new plane's design. They wanted a long-range, high-altitude interceptor for defense of the fleet. It would have to stay up for three hours at a clip, which meant much more fuel capacity (greater weight). It would have such an advanced radar that an additional crewman would be needed to operate it, and it was to be the first such plane with air-to-air missiles as its sole armament. The requirements meant that the plane was going to have to be much larger than the little mock-up—not a small, agile fighter.

McDonnell-Douglas went to work. Chance Vought got wind of the new Navy requirements and jumped in by beefing up their Crusader. In a 1958 fly-off, the new F-4 beat the new version of the Crusader and put McDonnell-Douglas back in the saddle.

Smith and the other RIOs spent three months in St. Louis and then headed for Miramar and VF-121, the F-4 training squadron. The 121 was to become the Phantom pipeline for the Pacific Fleet, the unit in which all the fleet's F-4 pilots and RIOs would be trained before joining fleet squadrons.

The Phantoms hadn't yet arrived, so J. C. and the others had to make a syllabus for the others who would follow. With two men in the plane, teamwork had to be developed. The pilots had to learn what the backseater's role was, and vice versa.

Despite his radio and navigation functions, the RIO's official job title was Weapons Systems Officer. The pilot had a scope in the front, but little control over it. He could do little more than glance at it. It was in the back seat that the radar was operated. Tweaking dials, using his own talent and hard-earned skills, the RIO sent a conish swath of energy pulses out from the F-4's bulbous nose into the sky ahead of it. If the impulses hit anything, their echoes returned to the Phantom, etching an image on the scope, which could be intensified by increasing the scanning swath brightness. He had to intercept it, decide if it was indeed a target, or something else— weather, a cloud, whatever.

Once the target was locked-on, the scope and its sides would come alive with vital information: position, speed, and course of the bogey. In the case of a Sparrow missile shot, locking the radar on the target was essential. The missile guided by following the radar beam between the Phantom and the bogey. If that beam was broken, the Sparrow would instantly stop following the target and go ballistic (straight, as if shot from a gun). In the case of the Sidewinder, the lock-on, although not essential, was still important. Although the Sidewinder didn't need the radar to track (since it tracked on the enemy's own heat radiation), the information being given by the radar—primarily the bogey's position and speed—could mean the difference between a good and bad shot. The pilot, who now had his hands full with an aggressive, nearby enemy, and needed his eyes outside the cockpit, could use the radar information relayed by the RIO to maneuver for the proper angle. If the Sidewinder was loosed at too much of an angle, the speeds involved might prohibit it from being able to make the high-G turn to the exhaust.

O'Rourke, commander of the Navy unit at St. Louis when J. C. was there, writes in *The F-4 Phantom II* that the RIO was "worth gold to the pilot: extra eyes, hands, another brain."

In the days to come, J. C. would fly with his share of pilots who resented RIOs. Often, it would take a scare, such as an episode of vertigo, or disorientation, to win the pilot over. Vertigo usually occurs in bad weather, such as in fog, or at night, when it's hard to tell what attitude the plane is in. "Your eyes or ears are telling you

you're in a bank or turn, when you're really straight and level. . . .
There's so many who've crashed, and you never know why."

One pilot he would fly with "was very good. But he had it bad.
I said, 'Pat, you got vertigo, tiger. Ease the nose up. Push your left
wing down.' I just talked it that way. I didn't tell him to go to his
instruments, because he wouldn't have believed 'em. He did exactly
what I said, and we popped up. And he said, 'God damn. That's the
closest I've ever come to dying.' We were in the soup. We would
have gone right into the runway."

Out at sea, approaching a carrier, it was easier to get vertigo.
It took guts to keep calm in a stickless backseat, with no way to
control what happened except a reassuring voice.

J. C. spent approximately two years at 121, becoming very proficient at intercept, preferring to play bogey in the training exercises
so he could talk exceptional young pilots into "pulling the airplane
around."

In early 1963, he got orders to report to Fighter Squadron (VF)
21 on the U.S.S. *Midway*. The *Midway*'s Air Wing 2 consisted of
seventy-five airplanes in six squadrons and two detachments, including Phantoms, A-4s, Crusaders, A-3B Skywarriors, and prop-
driven A-1 Skyraiders. Smith joined the carrier's 3700 officers and
men in "turnaround," the training time between cruises. Soon he
was off to Hawaii and Japan, with plenty of flying in between.

In turnaround before the second cruise, he'd met pilot Lou Page.
A veteran of combat missions in Korea, Page had replaced VF-21's
executive officer, who had crashed on a low approach to the carrier.
J. C. respected him. "He was the only one of us who'd seen flack.
And those silver-gray eyes, they'd just burn right through you."

Page thought J. C. the best RIO on the ship. "He was just extremely sharp, intense, knew the whole game." They became fast
friends. It wasn't always possible to fly with the same man, but they
managed it most of the time.

Smith was now in his third cruise; the Vietnam War had heated
up, and the *Midway* was in the thick of the action. It had been his
roughest cruise yet. The "Freelancers," as VF-21 was nicknamed,
were the only F-4 squadron aboard. With the best radar, they got
double, sometimes triple, duty. "We had the eyes. Anything they

did at night, we had to go with them. . . . Sometimes you'd go four days without taking off your flight suit. Many times I'd just go to the state room, put on a clean pair of underwear and go to a brief."

They'd been shot at almost every day. And now they were on yet another dangerous mission—the bombing of Thanh Hoa railroad bridge.

☆ ☆ ☆

The strike force approaching Thanh Hoa reached the bridge and J. C.'s and another F-4—manned by pilot Lt. Jack D. Batson, Jr., and RIO LCDR Bob B. Doremus—headed off toward the TARCAP position farthest west, the most inland. Once positioned, they flew a race-track pattern, the two of them about a mile abreast of each other in what was called "combat spread" —the two planes watching each other's six, as they guarded the strike force from MiG attack.

The racetrack's legs were about two minutes each—if flown at the same speed. But since the threat was to the north, they'd rush down the southern leg, make a quick turn back up, and then return at a slower pace coming back toward the north. The bombing target was about 20 miles southeast of them.

"We could see puffs of smoke. Every once in a while one of them would pop up, but you couldn't really see much of what was going on," J. C. said.

Everything below them was green. The two RIOs watched their scopes, sweeping the air space in front of the planes. The pilots kept visual lookout. They varied their altitudes from 9000 to 12,000 feet. Just above them, at about 14,000 feet, was solid overcast. They purposely stayed below it.

"All we're doing is guarding the fence," recalled J. C., "looking for bogeys to the north and west, checking on our own positions and fuel states, listening to the attack boys [the bombers]; if one of them is shot and goes down, we can go over for suppression until the Jolly Greens [rescue helicopters] are called in. We're all on the same frequency. Plus we're doing a lot of scanning, seeing what the other's got going. We're both looking at the same piece of sky. Sometimes he's got a cloud [on radar] and I verify, or vice versa."

They finally got a call from the bombers that they were "departing target." Since they were the TARCAP farthest inland, they'd be the last to leave. That meant several more orbits. As they heard "feet wet," meaning the strike force had reached the relative safety of the sea, they started to exit when J. C. got a strange feeling. "Lou, let's make one more quick orbit," J. C. said.

Since they had the fuel, Page agreed. "Roger. Let's make it tight."

They swung back up for one more northern leg. "We got just about where the radar was looking directly over Phuc Yen [a known MiG airfield on the northern outskirts of Hanoi]. I rolled the thumb wheel down slightly and picked up two contacts. They were about twenty-eight to thirty-two miles away, probably 2000 feet below us."

These weren't clouds.

"They were coming right at us. The sons of bitches had launched just as we were leaving. They had timed us so many times on our bombing runs that they knew how long we were going to be there, and when we were going out. They launched to come up our tails just as we were leaving, and we'd never known what hit us," recalled J. C.

This was the real thing. Somebody was going to be shot at and very likely killed in the next few moments.

"I was buried on the tube. They were off to my starboard side. I told [Lou], 'Steady.' " J. C. needed a few seconds to confirm. "Then I said, 'I've got contact. Ten right. Thirty-two miles.' "

To Batson and Doremus, he instructed: "Drop in trail."

"Roger," they responded.

Anticipating a problem most intercept planners hadn't foreseen, J. C. was setting up a "visual identification," or VID—a tactic he and Page had devised after many intercept practices. Although theoretically they could have fired a missile almost as soon as they got a radar "lock," the reality was that they didn't know if the distant blips were enemies or stray American jets. Despite the power of their new radar, it couldn't distinguish between the two. They were going to have to get close enough for a visual identification.

They wouldn't be able to see the planes until they were less than five miles away, and a MiG coming straight on wouldn't be distinguishable until it was less than two miles away, which was dogfight distance. Hence the maneuver: Once they're visually sighted, they would angle off a little from the head-on course. When the MiG saw this, they hoped it would turn into them, anticipating the Phantom passing it and allowing the MiG to get on the Phantom's tail. Once he turned, the MiG revealed its profile and other distinguishing characteristics.

J. C. and Page were the lead; therefore, they would make the identification and run the fight. Batson and Doremus would drop back about a mile and a half as the main shooters.

The two sides closed rapidly. The Sparrow needed a little over a mile separation to be effective. With the new formation, if the lead MiG was too close to the U.S. planes at the time of identification—which was looking more probable with each elapsing mile—they could still take a shot at the trailing MiG (the MiG behind the first MiG). J. C. informed their wingman he'd lock on the trailing bogey, or farthest target, and instructed Doremus and Batson to take the nearer, lead bogey—the plane they'd probably ID first.

"We were both 'Judy,' meaning locked on," recalled J. C.

They next activated their missiles. This was a crucial step in the combat scenario. The switches weren't turned on until the bogey was locked on. Once activated, the missile was hair-trigger. "I said, 'Select and arm.' He repeated it. 'Select and arm.' 'I have a select light.' 'I have a select and ready.' We were hot. We were ready to go."

They sped toward the target at "full military"—their fastest speed without afterburner. J. C. repeated the rapidly changing coordinates. One of the other retreating TARCAP Phantoms heard the radio traffic and asked to come back and help. But J. C. waved him off. "We had a helluva lot to do without having to talk to some airplane that was looking for us."

At about four miles, Page was finally able to see the bogeys with his unaided eye.

"Tally-ho!" he yelled. But there was a surprise: There were four bogeys, not two! They were in rough parade formation, the kind of very shallow V the Blue Angels fly—one beside the other, the leads and wingmen so close that they showed up as single blips on the radar.

The bogeys were still basically head-on, the two adversaries barely a minute apart from each other. J. C., behind Page, had a wall of instruments blocking his view, as did Doremus. J. C.'s eyes were glued to the scope. Only Page was looking at the bogeys, and he still couldn't positively identify them.

As planned, J. C. now gave him new course coordinates, which veered the two Phantoms to the right in an effort to get the advancing bogeys to turn into them and give Page a profile.

It worked. The bogeys banked, flipping up their wings. Suddenly, Page saw the distinct "yawning" intakes, bubble canopies, and rounded wing tips unique to MiG-17s. They had silver bodies with red and yellow markings.

"MiGs! MiGs!" Page screamed.

J. C., seeing they were still within range, yelled, "Shoot! Shoot!"

Page maneuvered the Phantom and squeezed the trigger.

"I heard the Sparrow go off our wing," remembers J. C. "Shhhhooooop. The next thing I know I see another Sparrow coming right across my wing tip." Bateson and Doremus had fired the second of the finned, arrow-like missiles. Their target, the lead MiG, was just now flying over J. C. and Page, not more than a few hundred feet above, preparing to turn down behind them.

At this stage in the war, it's doubtful that the North Vietnamese knew much, if anything, about the Phantom's head-on capability. Almost simultaneously, the MiG above them and the one they'd fired at exploded in fireballs.

Debris from the closest MiG, they believe, was sucked up in the intake of its wingman, and so a third was damaged or downed, though they weren't positive.

The final MiG broke hard across their belly, giving J. C. his first good look at one. He knew that in the next instant, the exiting MiG's tail would be pointing right at them.

J. C. said that he called for Page to turn right on the exiting MiG, but Page headed left for a split second, and then had to pull the plane up and back over, all the while flying in cloud cover, in order to come back to the right.

Page said that he was simply executing a practiced run-out maneuver in a vertical plane, where they'd have more energy than the MiG, to avoid getting into a horizontal fight.

Whatever the reason, they lost sight of the MiG in the clouds, and by the time they came back down, the only thing in the sky was a parachute holding a MiG-less pilot.

On the way back to the *Midway*, what had happened began to hit them: They had just gotten the first MiGs of the war!

"We were extremely excited," recalls J. C.

Their hard work and planning had paid off. The kills—among the few, as it turned out, by Sparrows in the war—had been classic, nonturning intercept. The MiGs had been shot down from a head-on, relatively straight-and-level, far-away position without any dogfighting. Unfortunately, the fight reinforced the attitude that dogfighting skills were no longer needed. Flush from victory, the two crews landed to a celebration. Without even a change of flight suits, they were whisked to Saigon to be special guests of Gen. William Westmoreland, commander of all U.S. forces in Vietnam. For a full day, their lives were a blur of press conferences and information officers cautioning them about what could and couldn't be divulged. They were the first U.S. heroes of the air war.

Behind the scenes, the Navy tried to give J. C. a lesser medal than Page because J. C. was only a RIO—an attitude that would undermine teamwork in the Phantom. J. C. told them to stuff it; he'd refuse anything but an equal award. The Navy was anxious to avoid negative publicity, particularly with regard to its newest heroes. As a result, all four eventually received Silver Stars, the nation's third highest military award.

☆ CHAPTER 4 ☆

Jim Ruliffson climbed out of the COD (Carrier Onboard Delivery Plane), his orange flight suit as out of place on the carrier flight deck, as the supply plane's propellers. The *Coral Sea*'s flight deck was greasy with the droppings of roaring, whining jet fighters and bombers. Flying daily over North Vietnam, the veteran pilots had abandoned the bright colors of noncombat zones to camouflage themselves in case they were downed in the jungle. Only newcomers or visitors wore orange. As a rookie, or "nugget," Ruliffson felt conspicuous and apprehensive.

Only three weeks before, he'd been practicing night carrier landings on a simulated deck at Miramar in San Diego, secure in the knowledge that he'd be joining another F-4 squadron that was in turnaround, and he'd have months to get oriented before shipping out to combat. But now, after a seeming whirlwind of events—a pilot destined for this squadron had been killed and he had to take his place—all that had changed. After qualifying for carrier landing three days before, he found himself being sent halfway around the world to join VF-21, his first fighter squadron, at Yankee Station off the coast of North Vietnam.

He made his way carefully—but quickly—off the deck, mindful of the hazards all around him: airplane chocks and tie-down chains; inferno exhausts that could incinerate a man, or blast him eight stories down into the sea; taut inch-and-a-half steel arresting cables that, if suddenly snapped, could cut him in half; live bombs and rockets, and volatile fuel being hurriedly handled by pressed and overworked crews. He ducked inside the giant, floating, 5000 man city, asking directions in its maze-like bulwarks to VF-21's busy ready-room.

Ruliffson was older than most nuggets—twenty-seven on this September day in 1966—having been a surface officer on a destroyer, the U.S.S. *Black*, before entering flight training. He had always been known for his maturity, as well as for his intelligence and industriousness.

With a short Marine haircut, and a neck and shoulders that *Life* magazine would later describe as a bull's, "Ruff" or "Ruli" as his friends called him, looked at a distance like an ex-jock tough guy.

"He was a very personable, articulate young man," recalls Vern Jumper, the wing LSO (Landing Signal Officer), who would grade him on recoveries. "I liked him from the start. He talked like he knew what he was doing. More mature than most guys we see who've just had their wings pinned on. He didn't come on real strong, didn't turn anybody off by trying to tell us how to do our job."

Graduating in 1962 from Iowa State, with a degree in business administration, Ruliffson had hoped to go on to flight training. But an astigmatism was discovered during his eye test. "They said go back and become an NFO. That's an up-and-coming program. You can still be in the air. But in my naivete, I said, 'Hey, if I can't go first class, I ain't going. Send me to destroyers,' which at that time was the premiere job for a surface officer, as opposed to being one of the thousands on a carrier."

But he soon decided he'd made the wrong decision. The *Black* was assigned plane guard. Since helicopters at that time weren't very capable rescuers at night, destroyers would follow the carriers for any after dark ditches. "I'd be a thousand yards behind it, watching all these guys fly over my head. Eighteen months of that, and I was ready for frontseat, backseat, any seat," Ruliffson recalled.

He put in for training as a backseater. And shortly thereafter he got his first upclose look at an F-4.

"We were chasing the *Kitty Hawk*," Ruliffson related, and the destroyer arranged for a liberty aboard the carrier. My A-4 pilot-guide greeted me with the question, 'Which party do you want to attend?' " The destroyer didn't allow liquor. Technically, the carrier didn't either, but it was awash with it.

Ruliffson got to sit in A-4s and Crusaders, and up on the flight deck Ruliffson said that, "these F-4s were on the catapult standing what they called 'condition one'—if anybody is coming at the carrier, it only takes them five minutes to be off and up on an intercept. Well, over by the catwalk were those four guys in full flight gear sunning themselves in lawn chairs. . . . I looked at them, and I looked at the airplane, and I said, 'That's my kind of job.' "

While still on the *Kitty Hawk*, Ruliffson had his eyes reexamined by the carrier's flight surgeon and got startling news: There was nothing wrong with them. Either there had been a mistake at the first test, or the astigmatism had been naturally corrected.

The flight surgeon suggested, "Wait 'til you get to Pensacola and walk in and say you want to switch."

That's what Ruliffson did. "I walked in," he recalled, "plunked my orders down on the desk, and said, 'I don't want to be a backseater. I want to be a pilot.' They fumbled around and said, 'You know, we can't do that.' And I said, 'Maybe *you* can't, but the guy above you can.' And I worked my way up to the admiral in about four hours and he said, 'Well, take another eye test, and if you're physically qualified, we'll look at your scores from before and see what happens.' "

Three weeks later Ruliffson was sitting in a classroom when somebody stuck their head in the door and told him that he'd been accepted. "I took everybody to the bar and bought a round. These brand-new ensigns had never seen anybody do that before."

Because of the top grades he received at the school, he was assigned to fly Phantoms. "Fighter aviation was my niche. I felt like I had arrived."

After a stint at the West Coast RAG, Ruliffson was assigned to a squadron scheduled for a full cycle of turnaround workup training— six to nine months—before they went back on cruise to Vietnam.

At the end of RAG training, while practicing night carrier landing, the last qualification before graduation, one of the pilots had gotten disoriented coming around. He had been farther out in the turn than he should have been, and way too low. The pilot hit a mountain east of Miramar, and both the pilot and the backseater were killed.

Since Ruliffson was a friend of the pilot, his CO asked that he and his wife accompany him to the pilot's home. He would also have to take the pilot's place in VF-21, which had already left for combat.

☆ ☆ ☆

Ruliffson was assigned to be Duke Hernandez's wingman on the *Coral Sea*. Hernandez had a terrific reputation. He had been a tactics instructor with the East Coast F-8 RAG back in the late '50s, before becoming one of the early pilots to make the transition to the F-4. In those days, if anyone flew ACM, it was the Crusader squadrons. Hernandez was one of the rare few who could fly the Phantom like a fighter plane. By luck of the draw, Ruliffson would have a good teacher.

His quarters were a cramped little room in the forward section beneath a flight deck, next to one of the steam driven catapults. The cat, utilizing steam from huge boilers, can accelerate a fully loaded, 60,000 pound Phantom to 150 miles per hour in two seconds during a launch. All Ruliffson had separating himself from the deafening surge was a single wall, hot from the steam. The entrance to his room was a curtain.

He had met his roommate, a RIO, just as he was heading out the door for a flight assignment. It turned out to be the last time he'd see the man alive. The flight was a night mission, and Ruliffson's roomate and his fellow crewman apparently flew into a mountain. His remains would not be returned to the U.S. until 1985.

"I was scared to death," Ruliffson recalled. "I meet this guy, and I turn around, and they lose him two hours later. I thought, What have I gotten myself into?"

Less than twenty-four hours later Ruliffson was launched on his first mission—the easiest they could give him, barrier combat air patrol, BARCAP, for short. His and several other Phantoms were placed between the enemy shoreline and the ships in order to protect the ships. There was little chance of attack—which the fleet knew; they were just breaking him in.

Had there been a MiG attack, it's doubtful he would have been able to handle it. The RAG had given him but ten tactics lessons, or hops, as they were called. A hop was one flight. He really didn't know what he was doing, yet. "I was flailing around in the sky," Ruliffson admitted. "I would maybe do something right, but I wouldn't know why.

"Later on, when I was teaching at Top Gun, I used to say that most guys can tell you in a fight what just happened. Some guys will be able to tell you what's happening right now to both of you; that is, what your airplane is doing, and what your opponent's airplane is doing. But what you're striving to do is project both aircrafts' positions and energy ten to fifteen seconds ahead. And it's those very few guys who can tell what's going to happen to both airplanes in those next few seconds ahead that are the true fighter pilots."

During his first days with the squadron the ship was primarily interested in how well Ruliffson could land, which was always a good indication of his ability. "Naturally, VF-21 had kept tabs on the guy I'd replaced while he was in the RAG—what kind of grades he'd made, how he'd done in various phases. But they didn't know anything about me," Ruliffson recalled.

In the ready-room was a chart called the Green Board. Beside every pilot's name was a long line of boxes. After each flight, the LSO would color them green, yellow, or red. Green meant well done. You had probably hooked the number three wire, the one everyone aimed for. Hitting the yellow wire was average.

Hitting the red wire meant trouble—the color usually was given if you'd hooked the number one wire, which meant you were dangerously close to smashing into the ramp, not only killing yourself, but also possibly strewing flaming parts and fuel all down the deck. If you received consistent reds, you could lose your wings.

Ruliffson did surprisingly well for a nugget, getting a green on his first landing and yellows and greens the next few flights after that.

"Jim was a damned good pilot right from the start," recalls LSO Jumper, who not only judged his landings, but also flew with Ruliffson. "I could tell that especially standing in the platform. He was rough, like all new pilots, but I could see he had the touch. Good scan. [A reference to the ability to assimilate lots of visual and audio information as he was coming down and translate it into the right adjustments in the airplane.] There was nothing dangerous about him. He could get aboard safely."

Very quickly they gave Ruliffson his first serious mission, a bombing run over the beach, meaning into North Vietnam.

"After launch we had to climb to 20,000 feet and get a drink from a tanker. I got up there," recalled Ruliffson, "and I remember thinking, boy, this airplane is really snappy . . . got a lot of poop to it."

Then someone reminded him he'd forgotten to switch off his afterburner.

"So I pulled it out of burner and started the transfer of the fuel that's in the belly tank up into the fuselage." But he hit the wrong switch and started dumping fuel from the wings. "Nervous? Boy, I was barely in control." But he delivered the bombs successfully, and within a few short days was experiencing the ultimate test: night landing.

During the Vietnam War, the Navy measured the levels of adrenalin in pilots during various high-stress activities. The activities included MiG engagements, flying through anti-aircraft fire, dodging SAMs, and night carrier landings. Night carrier landings had the highest adrenalin test levels, hands down. Day landing on a carrier has been likened to speeding through a narrow gate in a race car. At night, frequently in bad weather, it's like doing that in a hurricane wearing a blindfold.

Because of the speeds and motions of the airplane and carrier and the distances and rates of closure involved, the pilot's visual perceptions are often distorted. On a dark night, the patterned lights of a carrier below can look like oscillating stars in a faraway heaven. Pilots have become so disoriented that they've actually landed in water, and the deck has been perceived as a ghostly black hole.

Ruliffson's returning flight stacked according to gas, those with the least fuel remaining landing first. It was a precision, by-the-second operation: fifteen or so airplanes landing one after the other; the first and closest at 5000 feet, the second a mile behind at 6000, and so on. At a precise moment on their wristwatches, approximately one minute apart, each pilot would "push over" in succession into a prearranged glide pattern, starting a timed descent.

"You couldn't even be ten seconds off, because the guy behind you would close on you, or you'd close on the guy ahead," Ruliffson recalled.

On the deck they were preparing for fifty-second recoveries, giving each plane only a ten second margin for error. Anything over that would jam the operation, which was a near catastrophe. Pilots just couldn't make a mistake.

The closer Ruliffson got to the carrier, the harder his first landing became. "You descend at a fairly reasonable rate to get yourself down to 1200 feet, fly on in at 1200 to about three miles behind the ship, at which time you set yourself up in the rate of descent required for landing."

He'd been picked up by a controller, who would aide him, and he was beginning to make out the lighted centerline of the deck and the dropline going down from it toward the water. By aligning the two visually, he could help center himself.

At a mile and a quarter out, talking to the LSO and ship's radar controller, scanning his instruments, and watching the line-up lights, he could start to discern the "meatball" —a mirrored device reflecting a grapefruit-sized orange light, flanked on either side by a line of smaller green lights. By aligning the lights horizontally, he could tell that he was on the proper guide path.

"If the ball's low, I'm low. If it's high, I'm high," said Ruliffson.

He brought the lights together with precise movements of his stick and throttle, all the while hurtling closer, narrowing the margins to make such adjustments.

About a half mile—twenty seconds from touchdown—he radioed "ball" to the LSO, meaning the he had the ball visually in focus, and gave his fuel state, so they'd know if he had enough for a pass if he boltered.

Now he was on his own, given complete control. The only thing the LSO would tell him from now on was to bolt, if necessary, which would mean pushing ahead on the throttle to full power and accelerating off the deck.

Landing now became like threading a needle with a rocket. Ruliffson had to keep the rapidly descending Phantom on an exact glide path, at a precise speed, and in a level, unfluctuating attitude. Even a slight deviation in the last few seconds could kill him and cause a holocaust.

He hurtled toward the deck, rapidly scanning the cues with his eyes, translating them into split-second, hair-fine adjustments with his hands and feet until the final seconds. At that point, come what may, he had to hold the plane steady.

"It's instrument flying . . . that's what it is," Ruliffson states. "Very precise. Lights down the center, the ball over on the left. Right above the ball is the angle of attack gauge in the cockpit [showing the pitch attitude of his wings]. You're scanning these things. Making corrections."

The sudden impact on landing is always a shock.

"You know when it is going to happen after a certain number of times. But every time you land, it should be a surprise because you keep up your scan pattern to the last instant—meatball, lineup, angle-of-attack. . . . You go to full power in case you miss so you're ready to take off again even though you're caught in the wire. . . . You're thrown forward. I mean, you're going from 145 miles an hour to zero inside a second or a second and a half. It's really hard to keep everything right. You're working so hard. The adrenalin level is soaring . . . because you know what will happen if you don't do it right. Yet you know that if you do it right, everything's going to be fine. So you've got confidence in yourself. But I mean it is hard. The level of concentration. Day landings are like parking in a garage compared to it. You go out to qualify at night, and you get eight traps—you're a vegetable [by the time you're finished]. Exhausted. Drenched. You get used to day landings. You never get used to night. . . . "

And night landings were just the end of a combat hop.

Ruliffson completed his landing, and for him it was kind of a milestone. He got a green or yellow on the board—he isn't sure. "But I was already starting to relax," he remembers, "to feel more comfortable with the squadron guys . . . " And they were feeling more relaxed about him. He could tell.

"It wasn't one thing really, it was just that . . . they had been light-years ahead of me, and now I was pulling up to them. I had a bombing mission under my belt . . . a night hop . . . and I said, well, I think I can do this as good as they can. . . . I'd seen the tiger and survived."

It wouldn't be long until he'd be put on the first team: the night fighters, those who were sent out the majority of the time for the dangerous after dark missions.

He learned to hold his airplane in sixty-degree bombing dives, concentrating only on the target ahead and disregarding the flack bursting all around him; he learned to outmaneuver SAMs homing in on him by putting moves on them at the last second; break to one side when he was lucky enough to see the flashes of anti-aircraft guns on the ground, and then watch the radar-controlled rounds burst in the space he'd just vacated.

"Combat flying was a hell of a lot of fun and always a high," said Ruliffson. "You flew the airplane to its maximum. You were in an environment where you got to push the airplane instead of just droning around the sky. You felt like you were doing something for your country. . . ."

Coming back from a combat sortie, "Hernandez and I would always fight. We'd fight every flight. We'd actually throttle back in combat to save gas so we could have enough to fight. He was a great teacher.

"We practiced flying upside down in formation to learn more about our airplane. We had an air show that we practiced—we used to put it on for the ship. It was actually quite good."

Less than thirty days later—an eternity for most of them—when they were done with their first period "on the line" (in combat) and were heading back to the Philippines for a week's break, the deck housing the pilots would be locked off from the rest of the ship and the floors of the passageways would virtually run with liquor, as the pilots and RIOs celebrated their prowess—and the fact that they were alive.

☆ CHAPTER 5 ☆

Steve Smith, a nugget backseater with VF-213, and his pilot, a veteran Lieutenant Commander, readied for a hastily called mission on the U.S.S. *Kitty Hawk*. It proved to be a mission from which Smith almost didn't return.

They were to fly BARCAP off Haiphong Harbor as a large strike force went inland. Normally, BARCAP was a sleeper. But Haiphong, the chief entry point for almost all Hanoi's war supplies, was on the perimeter of the most devastating concentration of air defense in history: hundreds of clustered, radar-controlled, lock-on, Soviet-supplied anti-aircraft guns and SA missiles, and, according to sources like *The Vietnam War: An Almanac*, nearly 100 MiGs. The air war by January of 1967 was worsening. Over 200 U.S. airmen had been killed, captured, or were missing. Their sister squadron, VF-114, was in the midst of losing half of its crew to the enemy.

"Leading up to a mission I could be really edgy," recalled Smith, "I would go through all the things that we would face—the formidability of the opposition. . . . I'd look at the other guys, and they were just cool as hell. I sort of thought, they're so cool, and I'm all tied up in knots."

Of course, most were just as edgy as he was. Sometimes it would show in a sudden genuflection on the deck before climbing into the cockpit or in nervous laughter, or clipped silence.

Not until they launched would most of them, like Smith himself, calm down. "If you get afraid in the airplane, you are a danger to yourself. It might cause you to hesitate, and hesitation kills." Not everybody could suppress their fear. "You'd hear them scream on the radio. It wasn't a regular thing, but you'd hear it happen. Or you'd go up and be tanking and suddenly they'd have this mysterious mechanical problem and go back to the ship. But maintenance couldn't duplicate the problem. And you'd see other guys routinely have airplanes that never made it on certain missions."

The others called them "seagulls" —you have to throw a rock to get them to fly—and "sickbay flight." The Navy let them turn in their wings, or would take them. Smith flew with one pilot who was afraid of landings.

☆ ☆ ☆

Smith had flown his first combat hop over North Vietnam on December 4, 1966, after having been rushed to the front with only eighty-nine hours of training. "We were supposed to graduate with 120 hours of flight time, but I had all the basic blocks checked off. . . . I don't remember the date I left. It was just before Thanksgiving. Takes a month to get over there. I got to see Hawaii, Japan, the Philippines, and start finding out how naval aviators lived. . . . I was hot for it. . . . It seemed to me at the time that everyone knew what he was doing, where we were going, and what the right thing to do was. I just followed along. I didn't have a clue. . . ."

For awhile, Smith sweated getting a RIO slot in an F-4 because it didn't look like they were going to be available. Then, toward the end of his training, the slots opened. During his F-4 training at Miramar, he really started digging in, after an up-and-down indoctrination as a RIO. "I checked in early so I got to fly early. . . ." Where normally it took most people a week to qualify for carrier landings, he did so on a single weekend—twenty-five traps. Originally scheduled to leave in January or February 1967, his progress was noted and he was informed he'd be leaving in November.

The last part of his training was tactics. "We really didn't have any tactics," Smith remembers. The school taught basic intercept: One pass, maybe two, then get the heck out of there. "I knew if we got involved with MiGs it might be a hairy situation, and what we had to do is be prepared to get our shots and get out. We could not fight with them. We were not prepared to fight with them."

On the U.S.S. *Kitty Hawk* they broke him in at first with a young pilot, but before long he was flying with the veteran Lieutenant Commander.

The veteran pilot was one of the air wing's strike leaders. His approach to a RIO was, "I'll fly the airplane, and you do everything else. Direct me. Take care of everything. And give the orders."

"So here I am," Smith said, "a very junior ensign in the squadron, and he's got faith in me. How I got to be flying with him I'll never know. But he had been a RAG instructor. That's where he was coming from. He used the crew concept—the front and back seat as a team. We'd go out on an air strike, and I'd have [to direct and position] thirty airplanes . . . and the only thing I'd get from him was, 'What heading next?' and 'What altitude?' and 'What do you want me to do next?' And I'm yelling [they call it coaching] at those airplanes to get into position and do this and do that, and move over, and counting them off . . . leading the strike."

An inconoclast, Smith was impressed with the system—at least the one that reigned in combat. It had little pretension, bureaucracy, or petty rules. Ability and know-how prevailed. He became one of the junior officers known for his professionalism. Life to him became a kaleidoscope of drinking, sleeping, and flying. "We raised hell like crazy. . . . Flying was the highlight."

☆ ☆ ☆

As Smith and the Lieutenant Commander prepared for their mission going to Haiphong, the night deck was crawling with activity. It took fifteen minutes of preflight before the engines were started, and the planes began moving to the catapults. By then the noise was deafening and communication was only possible by radio or hand or body signal.

Next to recovery, launch is the most dangerous operation on the carrier. Their 25 ton airplane would be hurled 300 feet by the cat, at which point the plane had to be at flying speed. The few seconds after the launch were critical, when the plane's wheels left the deck, and the plane hung there ready to shoot forward or drop.

The plane had to be at exactly the right attitude or it *would* drop. It was only sixty feet to the water; 25 tons of metal can fall that distance in about a second and a half. Worse, the jet's engines would probably explode upon contact with the sea. If by some miracle they didn't, the plane sank so fast in water that ejections underneath the sea were generally impossible.

Smith's plane moved onto one of the waist cats on the short deck angling out from the side of the ship, next to the main deck. The Lieutenant Commander saluted. The yellow-shirted, mouse-eared flight director kneeled on the deck near them, looking forward—the signal to get ready. In a few seconds their wing would shoot dangerously close by him.

Smith and the Lieutenant Commander pulled their helmets back tight against the headrests. Above them were the hand loops they would reach up and pull should they have to eject. Their engines screamed at full power, brakes off, both burners lighting up the deck, the steel bridle cables, attaching the wings and fuselage to the cat, taut, the jet straining to break free.

The tremendous G forces they would experience on launch would dent their eyeballs, blurring their vision. At night there wasn't much to see, anyway, which made it all the trickier. They would only have a peripheral perception of deck lights meshed in an eerily blazing line.

The hard part for pilots was making any adjustment in the Phantom's attitude in the critical seconds following release. The Gs made it hard to see the instruments—the primary guide to whether the plane was at the right angle—or move the stick. Everything would have to be lightning fast and depended on the pilot's skill.

The cat exploded beneath them, hurling them forward in a cloud of hissing, night-dark steam. In two seconds they had accelerated to 150 knots and were off the end of the deck. But instead of heading up, the plane slid toward the ocean in an arcing turn.

"He [the pilot] either let go of the stick, or didn't properly rotate it," Smith said. "I yelled at him something like 'Pull it up! Pull it up!' I didn't even know if I got the last one out. I started to eject."

But then Smith saw that the ejection charge would propel him into the ship.

"We were angling toward it, not wings level. . . . I was scared shitless, realized I was going to die. . . . "

Smith remembers thinking, "I can eject into the ship, or I can fly into it. . . . "

Up top, the carrier was preparing to turn away from the plane, crew members preparing for the crash.

But the pilot made a correction and suddenly they were wings level, parallel to the ship, its huge walls hovering to one side of them, whitecaps churning inches beneath them.

"We were in the water—or on it," Smith recalled. "We were blowing water back up on the flight deck. And when you're [doing that] you have no right to get out of it. . . . But there's a thing called ground effect, and he woke up from whatever he wasn't doing, and the ground effect took effect [air cushioning], everybody is getting ready to look for our bodies and we started flying.

"The next thing I said was just hold it, take it easy and get it up. I went from shouting . . . to speaking very cautiously so that he wouldn't overreact."

They flew straight and then slowly began to climb. "I can't tell you how we got out of it," said Smith "Ground effect is a real thing, but it doesn't keep you from hitting the ground. Somebody up there put their hand down under us. I don't know. In the daytime you have no right to get out of it. At night, forget it. It just wasn't my day to die. But I'm really pissed. Immediately, I'm off with my mask, and he says something like, 'I'm sorry, but . . . ' I said, 'No buts, you son of a bitch! Don't talk to me. Just get to station.' I'm really pissed now."

They went to their BARCAP, flying in virtual silence. Smith recalled, "except for me taking care of checking us in and doing all that shit. The only way he gets my attention is when I say 'Roger' to a course or change of action. And then, instead of an hour-and-a-half flight, which was bad enough, they decided to come up and tank us and keep us up for another hour."

The Lieutenant Commander had been around for a long time and had landed on carriers before they'd gotten sophisticated. "He was what's called a deck-spotter, not the standard fly-the-ball-down and do-it-by-the-book guy." He liked to have the backseater call out his position, and when they were over the deck he'd "drop his nose and make a play for it."

Steve decided he wasn't going to help tonight.

"Think about that," the future Top Gunner said. "It's night, and we're really tired because by now it's two and a half hours in the airplane, and I'm not going to help. This man has taught me immense things. Made me very good at my job in that airplane. Extremely good. But I'm not going to help.

"So we come around, and he flies it with the LSO, and we bolter. The hook doesn't engage. It jumps over the wires, and we're back in the air. His [the Lieutenant Commander's] attitude is 'Screw you. I'll die before I ask you for help.' So we come around again, and they wave us off. Too dangerous. Now we have a fuel problem (not to mention what they're doing to the rest of the operation), and the weather's not too good. It's getting real serious. So on the third pass, I start talking to him. And I'm talking to the LSO, and we are going to get aboard this time. That's all there is to it. I said, 'We are going to land the fucking airplane! Got it?' He says 'Yeah.' 'Tell me that your hook is down right,' I say. 'Okay.' Now I go through the checklist and do everything I'm supposed to. And his responses are very mild. And I do exactly what I normally do, and we put the damn thing on the deck. It wasn't a very good landing. In fact, it was a very hard landing. But we got on board. And as soon as they pulled us clear, which was before I should have opened the canopy, I opened the canopy, got out of the airplane, went over the side and down to the ready room."

His pilot got down to the ready-room quickly too.

"He comes in the door at the opposite end of the room. I had my helmet in my hand, and I threw it at him. Across the room. Now I'm even more pissed. He tried to kill me—or so I thought. I throw a shot at him. He ducks. Maybe he tries to hit me back. People grab him and me, and they take him away. He's about to have other dispositions happen to him. But I'm not aware of this kind of stuff. I'm just mad as hell. The skipper says 'You're not going to kill him, or assault him. You're not in any trouble,' as if I should have thought about being in trouble, which, technically, I should have because we're both responsible for the airplane."

Later Smith found out the real reason for his pilot's lapse. He'd received a "Dear John" letter from his wife back in San Diego and had spent the previous forty-eight hours not sleeping and worrying about the situation, unable to talk to anybody about it. A pilot, especially a squadron leader, can't fly home in the middle of a combat cruise unless he wants to admit to what is usually perceived as emotional weakness and inability to control one's personal life, neither of which fighter pilots readily acknowledge. He couldn't just go to a pay phone either. He was out there fighting a war, and he had to go fly another mission. He got his disposition: he had to practice launches throughout their next liberty, which was not as bad as most of them expected. And Steve got a new pilot: John Nash, who would later join him at Top Gun.

☆ ☆ ☆

Born and raised in Hattiesburg, Mississippi, John Nash, 28 years old in January 1967, could have come from anywhere in the U.S. He had no southern accent, and his looks were undistinguished: medium height and build, an oval face beneath a receding brown hairline. He seemed older, but there was an intensity in him unmatched in anyone with whom Smith had ever flown. "I'd rather die than lose," Nash says, looking back on his career. "I don't know how guys can come back to the ready room day after day and look at guys who keep beating their brains out. . . . If I was exposed every day as being inferior. . . . I don't care how good I was. . . . I'd quit." He had quit golf after only five games, because his scores didn't recede.

He was not known for patience. "My Dad was . . . a perfectionist, very demanding," Nash related. "He and I were never close at all. . . . He had flown Jennies in World War I. . . . He wouldn't pat me on the back and say it was a good job even if it was."

He adopted his father's attitude. "Negative leadership. . . . You go to work expecting things to be right. If they are not right, you are critical. If they are, you tend to overlook 'em."

Nash was especially rough on those he didn't like. "If you are going to survive in a fighter squadron, you gotta be mentally tough. . . . I am a perfectionist. It aggravates me that I am not perfect, but, you know, every good aviator and naval officer is a perfectionist, in that [if] they couldn't do it 100 percent correctly, they weren't happy. The weak guys quit. They can't hack it. They can't hack it in the air, and they can't hack it mentally on the ground. They can't stand the needling. Needling to me, or kicking my butt, makes me work harder. I don't want to go back to the ready room and be the brunt. . . . There is no slack, I tell you, there is no slack at all. . . . "

Nash was one of those rare Phantom pilots who, against the trend, had been dogfighting in the F-4 since his squadron, the VF-213, nicknamed "The Black Lions," had transitioned to it in 1964. This was especially unusual since the 213 had previously flown "Demons" jet fighters, interceptors whose pilots generally were the last to want to learn air combat maneuvers. (The Demon was poorly powered and didn't respond well to aggressive piloting.)

"Flying the Phantom," said Nash, "is a lot more of an art than a science, because the airplane doesn't like to do what you want it to do." For example, it appeared to him to stall if he pulled it into too sharp a turn. It would buffet, bleed energy, and slow down, "which scared inexperienced pilots."

Other pilots would shy away from the sharp turn. But Nash couldn't—not if he wanted to beat other good pilots. So he'd pushed it through, regardless of the consequences, and found that it was "not only a beautiful aircraft, but handled well and recovered well. It wasn't prone to spin," which was the deadliest mishap. "You had to have confidence in it."

Nash would enter a fight like a boxer, "waiting to see what the guy's going to do, maybe give him what he thinks is a good deal, and if he takes it, then beat him in a hurry.

"By watching the guy's move, you know how good he is. . . . There are only a limited number of good moves, but there are a million bad ones. I never see a move that surprises me unless it's a bad one. . . . It's like playing checkers or chess. You make your move. You know what he should do. If he does it, you say, okay, he is at least as smart as I am. If he keeps making the right moves, you are going to have a fight on your hands. When he makes a mistake, you take advantage of it. . . . That's the soft spot. . . . I've seen some incredibly bad moves. Those are the only surprises in ACM to an experienced guy. . . . "

A veteran of one combat cruise prior to this one, Nash enjoyed the war and loved the flying. He found combat invigorating.

"When you go over, not having been shot at before, you wonder, What is it going to be like? How are you going to react?. . . . I can remember getting shot at for the first time. Teddy Roosevelt said: 'The most exhilarating thing in the world is to be shot at and missed' . . . You'd see the muzzle flash, see the little gray puffs and the orange balls come by. Hear them when they get close."

Nash's biggest shots of adrenalin had come from dodging SAMs. The first sites were being erected around Hanoi. "Of course we weren't allowed to bomb them," recalled Nash "because the Soviets were manning them. So we let them complete the sites and then they told us to go after them. . . . The specs on them were pretty good, and we thought we were going to get bagged every time they came up." He treated them like bogeys in a dogfight. "Try to keep them between your ten o'clock and two o'clock. Go fast, and do high G maneuvers. We found out they couldn't track if you did that. It was the ones you didn't see that were going to get you. . . . I was young. I didn't figure anybody was ever going to get me. . . . We had a lot of guys quit . . . a few who turned in their wings . . . a couple . . . who were scared to death. . . . It never phased me."

Steve Smith wrote home to his wife Karen: "John Nash is the best pilot I have ever seen." John regarded Steve as just another rookie RIO.

At that time, the tactic for night bombing was to come in high so you wouldn't run into the uneven terrain, then bomb under a flare dropped by a companion F-4. However, the enemy could see and hear you, and the U.S. had lost planes as a result. Nash and Smith decided to try something different.

While on day BARCAP they'd sneak off and reconnoiter a target. Then, when they got the chance, they'd zoom in at night alone using day tactics: Come in low, navigating the hills and mountains, pull up just before the target, roll inverted, which was the way they counteracted negative G, fire their rockets as they pull through, roll back over, and fly off.

"This was a very hairy maneuver in the daytime," remembers Steve. "Do it at night, and you're crazy."

One night in what was known as the hourglass, a funnel point for trucks just south of Haiphong, they caught a convoy with its lights on.

"We blew it up and caused a fire two miles down the road. They shot so much at us that the other planes we called in couldn't get in to throw more ordnance on it. You could see the fuel and things going up the road away from us. It was the most spectacular fireworks I have ever seen before, after, since, anywhere. . . . We just went off the coast and watched them. . . . We were sitting there saying, God, that's our Navy Cross. . . . Better than any movie."

Smith says they used the tactic until another crew tried it and crashed. He and Nash were then not allowed to fly together again.

☆ ☆ ☆

The Navy pilots and fighter crews were having a hard time against the North Vietnamese. The only U.S. fighter pilots establishing any kind of superiority over the North Vietnamese by the last day of 1966 were the Navy F-8 Crusader drivers, "the last of the gunfighters," as they liked to call themselves.

By January 1, 1967, the guns-only, single-seat F-8s had been credited with four kills. But one of the F-8 MiG Killers, Dick Bellinger, had, himself, been shot down by a MiG, reducing the F-8 kill ratio to 4-to-1, significantly inferior to the roughly 10-to-1 kill ratios maintained by various units of American fighter pilots in World War II and Korea.

There had been only one individual American fighter pilot in the Vietnam War with an outstanding record—the Air Force's dashing Col. Robin Olds. Sporting a handlebar mustache, married to a movie star, Olds was a young World War II ace, just now reaching his professional peak. By May 20, 1967, he had four North Vietnamese MiGs to his credit. The first ace of the war, however, was a North Vietnamese pilot, Capt. Nguyen Van Bay, who by May 1966, claimed his comrades, already had seven kills.

Overall, both the Navy and Air Force were hovering at a dismal 2-to-1 kill ratio, which meant that every time an American fighter pilot shot down two enemy planes, an enemy pilot would shoot down a U.S. plane. The North Vietnamese "peasant" air force, as American analysts liked to call them, was proving a tougher adversary than the Germans, Japanese, or Koreans.

If the Navy's MiG kills by Page-J. C. Smith and Batson-Doremus were left out, only one Navy F-4—the Navy's front-line fighter—had shot down a MiG through 1966. Even the Navy's propeller-driven A-1 Skyraiders were doing better, having shot down two MiG-17s on June 20, 1965.

As the air war went into its third calendar year, American fighter pilots had little beyond Col. Olds to boast about. Navy fighter pilots had nothing to point to. The seasoned among them were beginning to get worried. Why had we disbanded FAGU? certain Navy officers began to ask.

☆ CHAPTER 6 ☆

Jim Laing crashed through the jungle canopy, his parachute collapsing above him, his broken left arm flailing like a stick on a string. He had felt it snap when he'd ejected. "Next thing I knew I was on the ground trying to collect myself." The trees all around were huge, the foliage thick. "I couldn't see much further than about ten or fifteen feet." The sky was blotted out, but he could hear distant gunfire. Someone—probably the enemy—was close.

On May 21, 1967, Laing, a young RIO from Steve Smith's sister squadron, VF-114, on the *Kitty Hawk*, had been flying in a mountainous area on the inland border of Laos and North Vietnam, due west of Hanoi. The area was so remote that the military maps listed its relief as "incomplete." Its inhabitants were known to include Pathet Lao—Laotian communist guerrillas—whom he'd been briefed did not take prisoners.

Laing was in MIA country. Many who went down in it were never heard from again. Although he didn't know it at the time, his pilot, Denny Wisely, was hanging precariously upside down from his parachute in the top of a 100-foot tree on the other side of the mountain.

"I knew my arm was broken because it was dangling behind me," Laing remembers.

He was able to get out of his harness, and he gingerly tucked it into the donut-shaped Mark 3C life preserver around his waist. Disregarding the .38 pistol he wore, he pulled out a small, handheld radio and made contact with somebody overhead. "I told them I was okay and would give a beeper signal every thirty seconds or so. I only had one arm and I figured the radio was more important than the gun at the time, so that's what I stayed with."

At 21, Laing, a quiet, dark, and handsome man from Waterloo, Iowa, just a few years out of undergraduate school in engineering at Dubuque's Catholic Loras University, was just a "boot ensign." He had only been in the war since February, having been rushed through the RAG. He replaced one of the many crew members captured or killed in unlucky VF-114, which was suffering an inordinate amount of casualties. But already in that short, three-month span, he'd become one of the few MiG killers of the war. He was now facing one of the scariest situations for an aircrew member— the possibility of being captured, tortured, and even executed.

Just two days before, Gary Anderson, Wisely's RIO, flying with another pilot, had been shot down. As a result Laing had started flying with Wisely. Today was to have been their last mission—the combat cruise was over.

Laing, slipping into shock, steeled himself from panicking. "I don't think I was thinking about being captured. I guess more I was thinking of what I could do to make sure they [the Navy rescuers] found me. . . ."

☆ ☆ ☆

Somewhere in the skies above Laing, Darrell Gary, in the backseat of a returning Phantom, was listening to the rescue efforts. Since meeting in basic preflight, he and Laing had become close friends, so much so that at Top Gun they would be regarded as a pair: "Butch" and "Sundance" —or, more precisely, "Hawkeye" and "Condor," as their call signs were known. Gary, a former San Jose State football player, resembled a husky Robert Redford.

Attending preflight at Glynco, Georgia, together, Gary and Laing learned not only radar intercept, but how to handle inflated egos: "We were up in a T-39 trainer," remembers Gary, "a kind of small passenger jet, where a group of us could work on scopes. We had this Marine captain, a former F-8 pilot. Real salty. He allows as how real men don't have to wait through a flight if they have to relieve themselves. He had a plastic bag he was going to use. . . . So he took off his headset, went back and stood in the aisle and relieved himself. Well, the pilot had a real sense of humor. . . . He noses the airplane over, and it goes to zero G. Now this guy trying to hit the bag starts floating up off the deck for about three or four seconds, and then the pilot pulls it back and just plants him against the floor. All the stuff spills out of the bag all over him. He didn't try that anymore."

Following graduation, Gary and Laing had checked into the Miramar BOQ as roommates to begin their much anticipated schooling in the Phantom F-4. About a third of the way through, Laing had been paired with Southwick, a former F-8 pilot. It was a lucky match for the young ensign. Unlike most of the other pilots—largely first-timers or former intercept pilots—Southwick was a veteran fighter pilot. He was probably the only pilot in the entire training program who had gone through the Air Force fighter weapons school at Nellis Air Force Base, Nevada. It was the only school in any of the services at that time teaching even rudiments of dogfighting.

Southwick worked hard with Laing, seeing he had special talent. One reason was Laing's eyes. He would often spot the bogey before Southwick, who, because of his front seat, had a better field of vision.

Both Laing and Gary had the rare and prized (among RIOs) ability to project the flat, indistinguishable, drifting blobs on their radar screens into the three-dimensional air space in which they maneuvered. Then they could take charge and call fast and precise moves that would slingshot their plane to the kill. What made this ability rare was that a RIO had to do it in the tumbling, G-wrenching, air combat maneuver environment, while (in combat) keeping ever mindful of SAMs, Triple-A, and MiG traps—as well as moments of mind-bulging terror euphemistically labeled "the pucker factor."

Sitting in the infamous Cubi Point Officers Club their first night in the Philippines, Gary and Laing had watched as two junior officers had walked up to an obviously highly decorated senior officer, "spun him around and just kicked the shit out of him. . . . We couldn't believe it."

Later they were told, "that's CAG so and so—the wing commander. He got two of the young guys in the squadron killed. He was so intent on getting his medals that he didn't care about the team aspect and took his wingman into some pretty hot areas. They got scraped off by Triple A, trying to hang on for dear life."

What they had witnessed was an attitude they too would adopt: Watch out for your buddy. Police your own. After all, what can they do to you if they don't like it? Send you to the front?

Gary and his pilot replaced a crew in VF-213, while Laing and Southwick went to VF-114. Two months after arriving, on April 24, 1967, with the North Vietnamese Air Force finally starting to challenge in earnest, they found themselves in a large air armada on its way to the first administration-authorized attack on Kep, one of the five major enemy MiG bases, located thirty-seven miles northeast of Hanoi.

All hell broke loose as they reached the target. "The sky was full of SAMs," recalls Southwick. "I'd never seen anything like it."

Several of the Phantoms were hit and had to retreat. Southwick and Laing, who, along with Wisely and others, were part of the MIGCAP, took a "thump" on their underside, but continued to sweep over the target, keeping up their speed, trying not to get shot down. But the only MiGs they saw were on the ground in dirt revetments and stationary, and there were not as many as they'd hoped. The bombers—mostly bubble-faced A-6 Intruders and Scooter A-4 Skyhawks—started their runs. An A-6 burst into flames in front of Gary, its crewman ejecting through a furious fireball. Several more planes took hits, limping out. The bombers finished and started to egress, the target below them a mass of smoke and flames. Suddenly a warning voice came over the UHF: "MiGs coming up the valley."

Hearing the call, Southwick, already heading away, did a "fast 180" and saw "three or four" silver MiG-17 Deltas. He and Laing were at 1500-2000 feet, the MiGs out in front of them.

"We're meeting them head-on . . . the lead [MiG] to the right of my course," Southwick recalled. "I banked to the right and he banks to the left. We pass canopy to canopy, maybe a hundred feet apart. . . . I look at him and I am thinking to myself, Jesus Christ, this is just like in the movies. He's got on an oxygen mask. You can see in his cockpit." As soon as Southwick had called "Tallyho," Laing had started covering their rear. "He's responsible for everything forward of the wing line. I'm responsible for aft."

Going into the bank, they were starting to fight Gs. It was an effort for Laing to look from right to left, forcing his body around and craning his neck, simultaneously tweaking the radar in case they had to shoot a Sparrow.

The MiG went from its bank into a horizontal turn. But Southwick knew better than to try the same thing himself—it would be inside of him and on his six in no time. Instead, he reared the Phantom up into a climbing vertical "egg," dropping back down moments later into what Laing perceived as a "daisy chain" of MiGs circling horizontally, each MiG covering the other's six.

There was a lot of chatter on the radios as they dropped in— pilots yelling where the "bandits" were; who was about to kill, and who was about to *be* killed. Southwick remembers, "I saw a MiG off in the distance . . . out to the right" and then, "miraculously . . . from my left quarter . . . like my ten o'clock position, another MiG turning his belly toward me. Apparently, he didn't see me. He was maybe a couple of miles out in front."

It was a fighter pilot's dream.

They were entering the chain, or "wheel," not familiar enough yet with the tactic to realize there would be another MiG falling in behind *them*.

Only seconds had elapsed since they'd made contact. Clearly their position called for a heat-seeking Sidewinder missile. They armed the heat-seeker, kicking in afterburner to get closer. Southwick heard the low "growl" of the missile tracking, then the higher tone of lock-on. They were now roaring in faster than he wanted, so he throttled back to prevent getting too close. The missile needed a minimum distance or it wouldn't track.

"I guess I am about a mile behind him and I shoot the 'Winder, which does a barrel roll off the launcher and hits him on the right wing," Southwick recalled. "I see some . . . fuel and smoke coming out." Laing, still alternating his views out the airplane, saw the MiG's nose "go low," its wing dip, "smoke trailing out behind it." It was on its way down.

They were MiG killers—but they were in danger of being killed themselves.

Wisely, who'd been exiting the area, had returned to the target to find MiG-17s everywhere. The scene, he says, resembled "a giant inverted bowl, 5000 feet [high] and about four miles at its widest."

He saw an A-6 and an A-4 come through with MiGs chasing them. "The MiGs' afterburners . . . looked like sterno cans with flames lapping out. Normally the MiGs just slashed, but this was an "out-and-out have-it-all."

After chasing a couple, he saw a MiG sliding in behind a Phantom, which he later realized was Southwick and Laing's. The MiG was in their blind spot, readying to fire a Soviet Atoll, a Sidewinder-like, heat-seeking missile.

"Linfield, pull up," Wisely ordered, giving the squadron's call sign. Wisely was readying to shoot.

Hearing Wisely's call, Southwick realized "we'd been on the same course for fifteen seconds," which meant they were very vulnerable. He jerked the Phantom into a high-G barrel roll to the left and watched a missile shoot by. He thinks it was a North Vietnanese Atoll.

Southwick and Laing were now high in their pull-up to the left, their attacker following closely. Suddenly, the MiG reversed, rolling "very slowly back to the right, and in the process . . . just made it supersweet" for Wisely's Sidewinder, which, by then, had been loosed. It zipped right up the MiG's tailpipe.

"The airplane didn't blow up at all, but pieces started coming off the tail, and there was the classic black smoke coming out of the rear. He just went down into a shallow dive, looked like he was trying to pancake it into the flat terrain below."

Wisely, who'd earlier shot down at night what later was identified as a North Vietnamese bi-plane, was now a MiG killer, as well—the first Navy pilot with more than one confirmed kill.

Coming out of their evasive barrel roll, Laing, constantly scanning systems, saw a warning light, indicating they were low on fuel. Checking other gauges, they realized that while they had ample fuel left in the wing tanks, none of it was getting to the main tank that fed the engines.

They tried jostling the switches. Nothing worked. They had a serious problem, probably caused, they realized, by the "thump" they'd taken earlier over the mountains. They were soon going to run out of gas.

Rather than continue to chase MiGs, Wisely joined Southwick and Laing. "That was not terribly friendly terrain we were over," says Laing. They needed Wisely's help.

Southwick decided to try to make it to the water where they'd have a reasonable chance of being picked up. The two Phantoms lit out for the Gulf.

In Wisely's words, "It was quite a way to the coast yet, and it would take maximum fuel conservation to make it. . . . We coasted out between Cam Pha and Hon Gay, two very hot areas. Fortunately, we didn't draw any fire."

They got out five or six miles beyond the jutting, granite-walled coastal islands off Hon Gay as one of their engines flamed out. Southwick told Laing to eject. They couldn't eject together because the canopy came off in two sections, and Southwick's canopy would shoot back toward Laing. RIOs had been killed that way.

Anderson, who had a reconnaissance camera with him, got a picture of Laing just after ejection. He was tumbling thirty feet above the crippled jet, his chute about to deploy. It later ran in newspapers and magazines all over the world. All Laing was thinking about when he ejected was holding onto the handle that brought the face curtain to protect his head. The handle was usually discarded, but he and Gary had talked about which one of them would have enough composure to hold onto it when faced with such an emergency.

They were both in the water about thirty minutes—"enough time to get into a raft and kind of look around," recalls Laing. The North Vietnamese attempted to capture them, but a destroyer risked damage to herself by coming in close to the coastal batteries and shelling them.

They finally returned to the *Kitty Hawk* that night and celebrated. "The skipper of the ship met us, and there was a lot of picture taking and so on. Gary, who had been on the mission as a flak suppressor, remembers Laing wasn't as excited about the MiG kill as he was the deep water destroyer risking herself coming in. "You feel honored," said Laing, "but you really didn't feel like part of an elite group [of pilots who had shot down MiGs] until several years later when you found out there weren't that many shot down."

Hours after returning, Laing had been informed that he'd be taking a new backseat. A new lieutenant commander was coming out, and he'd be flying with him, giving up his old seat behind Southwick to a veteran RIO. The implication was that Laing had been getting to see too much of the action for such a young RIO. Honor and promotion were based on combat records, and others wanted opportunities.

It turned out to be a lucky move. On the very next mission, Southwick and his new backseater were shot down over the Thanh Hoa Bridge. They spent the rest of the war as POWs, an experience of torture and hardship Southwick still has a hard time relating.

On May 19, only three days before they were to end the cruise, Wisely's RIO, Anderson, taking the place of another RIO who had been seriously wounded the day before, was shot down with Charlie Plum in a raid on the heavily defended Van Diem truck repair depot four miles south of Hanoi.

With his own pilot unavailable, Laing was crewed with Wisely. On May 21, they were back over Van Diem as TARCAP embarked on a fateful mission. Before long, they would be lost in the jungle, fearing for their lives.

☆ ☆ ☆

"No sooner had our section turned north to take our station," Wisely recorded, "than they started firing SAMs at us."

They had an electronic "warbler" in the cockpit which sounded when SAMs were launched and changed pitch when they locked on. "If you don't see them, the sound scares the bejesus out of you."

Wisely dodged two, getting very low, then had to swerve to avoid flying through a wall of automatic weapons fire. Another SAM started tracking them, and they dove for their lives.

"We got down to a couple hundred feet, pulling for all we're worth with the warbler going off, and we went across a little hamlet that hit us with ground fire." Laing could see the tracers. "It could have been shoulder-braced [or] a real small fixed-mount on the back of a jeep or something."

They were hit on the wing, tail, and engine area.

"The stick just went limp like a piece of spaghetti," says Wisely. "I told Jim . . . we might have to get out. He said, 'Keep it going . . .' Neither of us wanted to spend the night at the 'Hanoi Hilton.' "

Overhead, John Nash had been popping up to begin his bombing dive when he'd heard a familiar voice saying, "I've been hit! I've been hit!" It was Wisely.

Nash continued the dive, delivering his bombs, and then "came back hard left to see this airplane down about five hundred feet . . . in the rice paddies." It was on fire.

Unable to steer and thus turn back toward the water, Wisely had simply lit his burner and rocketed off in the direction they were traveling—toward Laos and the unpopulated areas—steering with the feet-controlled rudders.

"Fortunately, the stabilator froze in a level position, so we had level flight," said Wisely.

What neither he nor Laing could see, however, was that fuel was leaking from a large hole at the base of one of the wings and the burner was igniting it along the side of the fuselage.

Nash plugged in his burner to join them and told Wisely to switch his burner off. They climbed slowly, but with good speed. There were high mountains ahead. They'd have to steer clear. Wisely flew the damaged jet by brute force, trying to keep the plane level.

Suddenly his missiles started firing themselves from the wing. An internal fire was burning through the wires.

They made the mountains by about eight hundred feet. But the Phantom started trying to roll to the right. Wisely fought it until it "got to the point where I couldn't hold it anymore. I looked at Jimmy in the mirror. I could see his face the whole time. He was waiting for me to just give him the signal, and I said, okay, better get out of there. I couldn't slow it down. . . ."

The Phantom started to roll over when Laing punched out. They were going faster than they wanted. The sudden violent collision with the wind turned Laing's body into a rag doll, extremities smashing against the metal seat he was still in. "My arm snapped, just as if it had been a stick I'd broken over my knee," recalled Laing. His other arm and his knees were jostled so violently that they were sprained.

Wisely punched out a few seconds later. Coming down, he'd seen a village "and the fireball from my airplane not far away. Fortunately, the wind was blowing me away from both of them." He landed upside down in the treetops, unable to move, but thankful to be alive. He loaded his .38 revolver with ammo in case the Vietnamese arrived first.

Laing, having reached the ground and removed his parachute harness, couldn't move. "My legs were really starting to stiffen up, and my right arm [his good arm] was in bad shape."

He picked splinters out of his body, keeping his mind occupied with what he had to do to make sure he'd be rescued. Eventually, he became thirsty. There was a little stream about ten feet from him that he could see behind dense foliage.

He started to crawl toward it.

"I don't think I got more than three or four feet . . . pushing things away and trying to [get his legs to work]." He says he wasn't worried. "If I hadn't been in contact with anybody, I think it would have been a different story. But I had something to do."

Time, he says, became both fragmentary and endless. His friend, Darrell Gary, offers this insight:

"Events are so compressed in time, so confusing, that sometimes you tend to shut down and fall back on instinct. . . . It starts back in the cockpit. . . . You are trying to deal with the first emergencies and you're very reluctant to admit that, goddamit, you're going to lose the airplane. . . . Guys try to struggle to keep the thing going, and by the time you make the decision [to eject], it is very traumatic, because here you are in your secure cockpit with familiar noises and everything, and all of a sudden . . . there is a 75mm shell and huge explosion. You're being thrust, slammed around, the noise of the wind is just an awesome cacophony of sounds, and then all of a sudden you're swinging in your chute. It's quiet. It's just such an eerie contrast. . . .

"Then you begin to think, 'Oh shit. What do I have to do?' Finally when you hit the ground . . . then you're probably in a state of shock. Kind of hyper . . . the whole shock all comes crashing down on you. That's when the guys always say they get cottonmouth. They never have been so thirsty in their life. Definitely a state of shock . . . then you gotta cope with some real important decisions. It's the kind of emotions where fear and everything just come rushing in on you all at the same time."

Wisely, relatively uninjured, was more alert.

He was perched on top of a 200-foot tree that only "branched . . . at the top. . . . It had hundreds of vines . . . which made it like a nest." It was a good hiding place, "so thick that the only way anyone could see me would be to find my tree and look straight up."

Above them, Nash was trying to get Air Force rescue helicopters in. "This was their territory. [They] had a couple of supersecret recovery sites in northern Laos they used for flying helos out of during their big strikes." But he'd had no luck. He was also getting low on gas. He decided to go out to the water and get a refill from a tanker. While there, a Navy helo requested permission to go in. "We said it was too far . . . the admiral . . . told them not to come. But they came anyway."

The helicopter, a "Big Mother," was joined by two A-1 Sky-raiders (also known as "Spads") for protection, one of which was piloted by Mike Guenther. "Nash was hollering . . . on the radio," remembers Guenther. "We sorted out where his guys were and said 'Let's go.' "

Back at the crash site, Wisely heard an HH-3 "Jolly Green Giant," an Air Force helicopter arrive, accompanied by Air Force Spads. He tried to direct them in, but wasn't sure exactly where he was.

They, in turn, were leery of approaching. Ten days earlier they had been tricked, and at least one of their helicopters was shot down in a similar situation. They wanted radio answers to code questions that Wisely couldn't immediately supply.

When the Navy helicopter, damaged by ground fire on the way in, couldn't effect the rescue because of a broken hoist, the Air Force, which had been raking the area with rockets and gunfire to keep the North Vietnamese out of the area, stepped in.

The Air Force helicopter swooped down to pick up Wisely, who was closest, first. The Jolly Green's downwash nearly blew him out of the tree. He didn't care. "What a great sight," he recalled. He got on the jungle penetrator, a metal tube with a hook-shaped seat inside, and rode it up. "What a feeling to get inside the helo. . . . I was really exhausted and just lay there for a minute. Then I got the jug of water and downed a quart or so. It was amazing how thirsty I was from the very moment I landed in the tree."

They next searched for Laing, who heard them coming and managed to talk them in. The downwash spread the tree-top canopy so they could see him. They spotted him 150 feet below. The penetrator came down through the branches and vines, and he was able to grab it. "I opened it, climbed on, and they started hauling me up." He could only hang on with one arm.

About halfway up, the cable started shredding and unwinding. It was about to break. All Laing knew was that he was starting to spin. "The more it spun," he remembers, "the more centrifugal force was created, so I was basically driven away from it. It was similar to a merry-go-round." Luckily, they grabbed him just as he was about to fall. Unfortunately, the crewman had hold of his broken arm. "I passed out there for a little bit, but came to and remember getting a shot of morphine."

Back on the *Kitty Hawk*, Darrell Gary was as animated at the news of his friend's rescue as flyers like himself allowed. "The guys are, you know, reluctant to use words about each other like love or respect . . . there are certain things they just don't like to say . . . but the feelings are real deep," Gary recalled.

He and Hawkeye, he now knew, would soon be celebrating.

☆ CHAPTER 7 ☆

At six-foot-three and cramped in the cockpit, Jerry Sawatzky—"Ski" or "Big Ski," as his friends called him—didn't have the flashy good looks of some of his fighter pilot contemporaries. He looked something like a tall, lanky Peter Lorre, except that there usually wasn't anything sinister in his appearance—except when he got aloft. Quiet and gentlemanly on the ground and quick to smile at his own cagey wit, he would become a terror in the sky. Talented and tenacious, he could take on anyone.

"I used to exercise to help myself keep Gs on the airplane." In a high G turn, the force restraining him could reach 1400 pounds. "I'd work with weights and things, mimicking what I had to do with my hands and head. Some people made fun of me because I'd be breathing so hard in the airplane, but it was like a wrestling match." He'd do practically anything to keep his opponents in sight. Not only was he afraid to lose them, but keeping them in sight helped to spur him on. . . . "You ever watch a guy on the golf course looking for a golf ball? You can always tell when he finds it. He speeds up. He has a direction to go."

During a fight, he looked like a contortionist. "I'd be pushing and pulling, stomping and craning," he said. Because of his height, he once got his helmeted head stuck in the small space between the canopy and seat, unnerving his backseater who kept asking, "What's the matter?"

☆ ☆ ☆

Speed and tight turns were the guts of Sawatzky's game. "I tried to quickly but smoothly get the maximum G allowable for the airplane." That meant "unloading" (accelerating) in straight and zero-G (level) flight until he'd regained his speed and could turn easily again.

"You want to avoid making in-between maneuvers. . . . If you're erratic or get in big arcing turns, planes can join on you. . . . You want to eliminate any excess that might give your opponent extra time to maneuver on you.

"One of the things I liked to do was fool people about my energy state [speed], or my ability to make the turn." Bending with a bogey that he couldn't get his plane's nose on, he'd "simulate wing rock, which is an incipient stall phase." Stall signaled he was running out of speed. "In an F-4, when really I had plenty of energy left . . . I would just rock the wings and [give it] a little less G [turn] and create artificially what looked like an overshoot. Then, as I got to his [blind spot], I'd slap on the G. . . . Hopefully, he'd reverse . . . stop pulling hard in his turn," try to come back for the tail shot he thinks is materializing for him. "Now he's solved my firing problem."

If he was zooming up and needed to reverse fast, he'd think nothing of executing a wrenching "Hammerhead," rocketing the plane straight up to near-stall, and with a quick combination of rudder and stick, whip it 180 degrees to either side on its wingtip, and roar back down. If someone was chasing him he might suddenly rear his nose up in an incredible G-pulling climb, swooping back over the top on the surprised attacker and pulling in behind his six.

"It's the power at your fingertips, the responsiveness of the machine to what you want . . . you're not just looking at gauges and responding to numbers."

Sawatzky's concentration was so intense that while asleep at night he'd sometimes find himself "sitting up in bed and flying." Once, during combat, he'd actually sat down at mess and started to strap in. "People don't appreciate how much you have to give of yourself." One night in his dreams "somebody was coming at me and I did a barrel roll underneath them and actually fell out of bed. . . . "

Ironically, Sawatzky's closest call wasn't while dogfighting, but simply taking off. He was in the backseat of a two-seat training A-4 in 1974 with a pilot who had been a former POW. As they were lifting off, a warning light flashed. From past experience, he knew he could disregard it, but the pilot hadn't flown an A-4 for seven years. Sawatzky was looking down in the cockpit, changing radio frequencies, when "out of the corner of my eye I see the runway coming back. He was putting us back down but had forgotten the wheels were up—full fuel load, 170 knots, almost 200 miles an hour. Well, of course, the first thing that happens is the wing tanks burst. I forget how many thousands of pounds of fuel were in them but we're talking serious flames. I'm getting out of there."

He was sitting on an ejection seat that could shoot a 185-pound man 300 feet in the air, which was enough height, with any luck, to deploy his chute. But in the sudden deceleration, the ejection handle had gotten tangled in the instrument training hood and he couldn't get a hold of it.

He went for the alternate handle between his legs. But before he could pull it, he saw the thick arrestor cable, stretched across the field for practice carrier landings, rapidly approaching.

If the cable caught him ejecting, it could cut him in half. If it caught the plane's long refueling probe, it could flip the plane over.

"You can go skipping down the runway," which was a "quick way to get peeled." Or, worse, eject upside down. "This was a rocket I was sitting on. . . . I've seen people eject into the runway. It's not pretty . . . so I kind of ducked, but we didn't catch [the cable]. So I got my head up again to see how we were doing, and we weren't doing well at all, because now we're starting to skid sideways and we're going toward the dirt."

Another possibility of flipping over. "Not only is it going to squish your cockpit, but do you know what it takes to turn a plane [back] over? A crane You know how long it's going to take them to get a crane there and hook it up? If we're lucky, thirty-five to forty minutes. You know how much of the airplane is going to be left then? Nothing. I am dead. If that airplane flips over sideways, I am dead. So I said, no way. I'm getting out of here. I've got this handle to pull, and I tried to pull it." But the force of the slide sideways prevented it. "I could barely get my hands between my legs because of the sideways G forces. I drove my hand in between my legs and I actually got my hand on that handle. But there was no way I could separate my legs enough to get that handle through them. I could not do it, and I'm not a weakling. . . .

"So finally we're getting so close to the dirt that I no longer want to pull it because here again if it flips over I am going to go skipping across and . . . hitting something."

Or punching a hole towards China.

"The ground's coming and finally I say, heck, you know, it's no good from now on for me to jump out. I am here for the ride and I just sort of mentally shrugged and said 'We'll go see if I am going to flip over and die or we'll see if I am going to stay alive.' "

They slid into the dirt and "darned if we didn't stay upright. [There were] serious flames all over . . . He called [back to] me . . . 'Blowing the canopy.' I said 'Fine'. . ."

☆ ☆ ☆

Sawatzky had grown up in Fort Worth, Texas. Skinny and awkward as a child, he'd made up for it with desire and brains. He'd always wanted to be a Navy pilot. "I used to ride my bike out the longest way just to watch the airplanes take off and land." In 1962, after cruises as enlisted sailor, he finally got his chance in the NavCad program.

He graduated fifth out of a class of sixty and was one of the first ensigns to be assigned Phantoms. Until then, protective of their new bird, the Navy had only been sending experienced pilots to 121. Now they were beginning to admit the promising younger pilots. The first time he had to preflight an F-4, he thought to himself, looking at the awesome jet fighter, "I'm going to control that?" But in the end, he just got in and did it.

Despite his later predilection to air combat maneuvering, he was taught little about dogfighting. Naval fighter strategy was still based on the concept of the intercept. While training went smoothly, Sawatzky discovered he still had a lot to learn about the Phantom. His first landing approach on a carrier showed him just how raw his flying skills were.

It turned out to be a real crowd-drawer. Sawatzky realized immediately that he was in serious trouble as he began to make his descent. "There are all these little techniques I wasn't aware of. I was overcorrecting . . . I didn't realize where I was. A little high? Steady? Climbing? Holding the glide slope? Coming down too rapidly? I just didn't have any feel for what I was doing. I was what they call 'behind the airplane'. . . ."

He got a wave-off, but touched down anyway, just past the ramp.

"I didn't miss it by much. I actually taxied over the arresting wires without catching one, so I darned near killed myself there, and then I didn't appreciate on a bolter that the Phantom's nose is kind of heavy. You have to have the stick in your lap when you go off. Well . . . I was slow getting the stick back because there again this was a technique I did not understand. As I went off the end of the ship I didn't have enough [lift], so I actually settled off the ship so low that the guys on the deck lost sight of me. Well, the flight deck's only about seventy-five or eighty feet above the water. The airplane's what, twenty feet high?. . . . I could see the waves going by underneath me. But what did I know? This may be the way they fly. I was scared, but, heck, I thought, I'm learning."

He finally landed, but as a result of his near mishap was sent home as unsafe. If he didn't qualify his next chance he'd be through as a pilot.

"It was probably the lowest point in my life. . . . In preflight I'd been number five in a class of sixty, competing with some pretty sharp dudes. [Being sent home] was saying I wasn't performing up to standards. To find that you did not make the grade after going through the Navy for years, throwing yourself body and soul into it. . . .

"I went [back] out with a different LSO the next time. We had better communication. . . . He understood my questions better."

He finally qualified and was sent to VF-21 on the *Midway*, becoming a squadron mate of J. C. Smith and Lou Page, and was on hand to welcome them home following their historic MiG kill.

Combat, Sawatzky discovered, was very different from flying in the States. "In the States, there are all sorts of restrictions on what you can do," but over Vietnam he could fly with abandon, "as long as you played within your abilities." Being shot at, he discovered, was terrifying, "but in a constructive way. It made me think about what I was doing. . . . I wasn't just moving around in some blind funk. I was doing reasonable, calculated things under duress. . . . "

One of his worst moments occurred when he flew over Vinh one night and got caught in radar-guided anti-aircraft fire.

Vinh was a heavily fortified city in the southern part of North Vietnam that had a MiG airfield, little of which Sawatzky had been briefed on at the time. "[The Vietcong] locked onto me apparently with radar, shooting 57mm guns at me. We didn't know they had [them] then—at least the aircrews didn't. . . . I'd never even seen tracers at night, particularly that size. They looked like flaming tennis balls, and what really alarmed me was they were coming by both sides of the cockpit.

"I remember thinking, 'I'm in the pattern!' It's like a shotgun blast all around a bird—it depends upon ballistic dispersion whether or not I am going to have one of those things coming up through my fanny!"

He yanked the Phantom "up and down and around into the clouds. . . . They actually had searchlights on me too." He could feel concussions from the shells going off around him. In the clouds, he had to maneuver on instruments, yet they still chased him. "You could see this hazy fire going off all around."

Miraculously, he wasn't hit. "I guess it was because I was maneuvering so hard. Finally, I broke loose and somehow got free. But it terrified the heck out of me."

Another time, Sawatzky and his leader had left their assigned BARCAP to hunt for MiGs. This was unauthorized, and in fact prohibited, but, as Sawatsky says, "the real chargers did it." A pilot could always say he saw unidentified bogeys on his radar and was chasing them. "You're a fighter pilot. Those airplanes are shooting down your friends." It was also a chance for some glory—and a way to negate some of the enemy's advantage by surprising him.

"I had Barry Scott in my back seat. We were up over the railroad that went north of Hanoi into China. It was very heavily defended."

There were high mountains on either side of them, forcing Sawatsky—if they were going to scare up anything—to stay in the valley. There happened to be a low-ceiling cloud cover of about 4000 feet, meaning that they'd have to stay under that to spot any MiGs.

It was a risky business. "Heck, we didn't know what to do [if they saw a MiG] other than lock up and fire. But that didn't matter. This was what it was all about."

They'd surprised the Vietcong coming through and had made it over Yen Bai, north of Hanoi, without being shot at and without seeing a single MiG. "Unfortunately, we came back the same way. . . . They were loaded for bear." And the clouds gave the North Vietnamese a reference point.

They came back low again but the ground fire this time was intense. "My leader pulled up and they got him going into the clouds. I started to follow him but there was just this ceiling of bursts going off. It looked almost solid—just a maelstrom of metal up there. I immediately flipped the airplane over on its back and yanked down, spoiling their solution. . . . I actually pulled down into them on my back, and got low enough that Barry—to show the caliber of those old RIOs—on his back, upside down, he took a picture of one of the gun sites. I don't know what happened to it. I think I loaned it to somebody. But you could see the guys in tee-shirts and khaki pants. You could see the gun barrels looking at you, and see them running the gun and looking up."

Sawatzky got around the corner of one of the smaller mountains and was able to escape. But radioing the leader, they got no response. "Barry and I talked about it a little bit. We were kind of circling around. . . . What if he's down there? Well, we had to know, so we both agreed we'd go back. We weren't wild about it, but we were going to do it."

They went back, "and I am telling you we were going fast. We took a quick look around there and I think it surprised them so much that anybody would return after that, that I don't think they fired a single shot. They weren't ready. . . . "

There was no sign of wreckage, so they decided to call rescue—a step that would make them justify their presence in the area. "We gave them the coordinates and they came back and I think said, 'Let's have those again?' It was considerably north of our station and they said unless we had confirmation of a person down there they weren't going near the place. It was suicidal to get that far in the heart of Vietnam. They were very, very angry . . . that was an off-limit area.

They were ordered home. "On the way we heard a radio warning to an airplane [from the Marine airfield at Da Nang], 'This is your last chance to identify yourself. We'll shoot you down.'"

Thinking their leader's radio might have been knocked out, they thought it might be him. When we landed, the crew chief looked up at me and said, 'Where's number seven airplane?' I just shook my head and said 'I don't know.'"

Sawatzky was told to report to the war room. The admiral was waiting to hear what happened.

"The CAG caught me in the passageway before I went there. . . . We took off our helmets and threw them down. He asked me, 'What happened, Jerry?' I'd already worked out a story with Barry. I told him we'd gotten a radar contact. 'Why the hell were you way up there in a restricted zone?' I told him we were in hot pursuit. 'Hot pursuit.' That was the magic word. You could chase someone in, but 'trolling' for MiGs was forbidden. He kind of looked away for a second, then back at me. 'That's not a bad story, Jerry. Stick with it.'"

Sawatzky went down to the war room. "The Chief of Staff himself interrogated me. . . . I mean that's the only word I can use. Interrogate. I stuck to my story. I was scared to death but, you know, what can we do to me? Send me to war? Shoot me? I've already had a ton of lead shot at me. . . . He was glowering, which might have had more effect had it been in calmer circumstances." The confrontation centered on the bogey Sawatzky said they'd seen on the scope. "I was an electronics technician, you know," said Sawatzky. "If you want to BS about CRTs, man, I can do that all day long."

A short time later, they heard that the other plane had landed at Da Nang. "I real quick ran and wrote down my whole story and titled it 'Ensign Sawatzky's Statement to the Admiral in the War Room,' put it in an envelope, and addressed it [to the squad leader] Urgent, Personal, Confidential." Sawatzky gave it to the helo pilot who was going to pick the other crew up, and told him to not let the two of them talk to anybody until they'd read Sawatzky's letter.

Upon arrival at the ship, the flight leader and his RIO were brought to the war room for questioning. Fortunately, their story matched Sawatzky's, and all four of them were off the hook.

By the end of his first cruise Sawatzky was a seasoned veteran, an expert at all the special skills of carrier bombing in a hostile land: launching, recovery, instrument flying, conserving fuel. He was an expert in everything but ACM.

"I could squeeze that fuel tank so hard that you'd think I was using my fingers."

But he'd also become somewhat of a loner, partly because of his personality, and partly because of what he cynically began to see as a disregard for front-line combatants by the people running the war.

He came off the cruise in 1965 thinking, "Your best friend was yourself. Your second best friend was the guy behind you, because if something happened to you, it normally would happen to him too. Everybody else was the enemy."

The Navy recognized his experience and skills and sent him to LSO school in San Diego, a distinction given only to the best carrier pilots. Then, in a special exchange program designed to give East Coast fleet pilots combat time—and thus an equal chance to garner recognition—he was sent to VF-74 on the U.S.S. *Forrestal,* an 86,000 tonner based out of Norfolk.

"[It was a] different kind of Navy . . . a lot stricter . . . super conservative, super cautious." If you were caught hassling, you were grounded.

"I wasn't very popular there," recalled Sawatzky. "They started calling me an angry young man." He felt his flying skills were suffering. "I would say things like, 'When are we going to start training? I didn't extend my sea tour for this war to come out here and orbit over a destroyer.' "

They didn't give him much LSO work either. "Most of the work was done by the staff, the Air Wing LSO. They didn't like to hand over that pickle. . . . I was desperate to get back to the West Coast."

Then, in the continuing war buildup, *Forrestal* was ordered to the Gulf of Tonkin. At least, he thought, he'd be back in a combat environment. He had no inkling of how catastrophically short the cruise would be.

July 29, 1967, was the beginning of the worst period of the war for naval aviation. Sixteen Navy planes were shot down over the next month, most by anti-aircraft fire. That morning, the *Forrestal* was readying to launch the second wave of a big Alpha strike and to recover planes from the first. Sawatzky was to be one of the LSOs, and he was waiting just below the deck for the launching planes to take off.

"I was near the ready room and I heard the bells ring. . . . Then the bo's'n called 'Fire! Fire on the deck!' We have a lot of fires on board, but what caused me concern was he didn't say where. Usually they'll say fire in front, or fire amidships. Then fire-fighting crews that are responsible for that area can run there. But he just said, 'Fire on deck!' That meant anywhere you can get to on the flight deck we've got work for you."

As Sawatzky later found out, handlers had connected wires activating the firing switches of Zuni air-to-ground rockets on an F-4 in the taxiing area. There had been a short in one of the wires, and the rocket had fired. "Nobody on the West Coast would have ever connected pigtails on rockets back in the pack. You plug those things in when the airplane is on the catapult and if it goes off it doesn't hit anything."

But the *Forrestal* had only been on line for four days. Those responsible didn't have the combat experience. The rocket shot across the deck and hit the centerline gas tank on an A-4. Burning fuel spewed out over the aft deck, which was littered with other bombs, rockets, and fuel tanks. A river of fire engulfed the deck and waiting planes, their crews screaming in the holocaust. The fire began to set off bombs and other fuel tanks, opening holes in the steel deck through which the flaming river boiled into the ship's lower interior, trapping others.

At first Sawatzky and those with him started up on the deck, "but then everybody dove back" because some "anti-radar missiles [with] a lot of small hard steel cubes in them . . . started going off. After the fire, you could walk on the flight deck and just scoop up handfuls of them." When he got back in the ready room, the video

camera used to monitor flight operations—which had been abandoned, but was still trained on the worst area—showed one of many
incredible acts of bravery during the fire.

One of the firefighters, later identified by *Life* magazine as Chief
Aviation Boatswain's Mate Gerald F. Farrier of Batesville, Arkansas,
walked directly into the flames spraying CO2 from an extinguisher
in front of him trying to get to a 1000-pound bomb that was being
enveloped in flames. He was trying to put the flames out before the
bomb exploded, but it went off when he was just six feet away.
"There was a guy hosing it and then there was this big flash and
then you saw severed fire-fighting hoses lying around spewing water
and that was it."

At first they let the fire fighters do most of the fighting. Incredible feats of courage and strength were numerous—men running
into flames to save other men; a 130-pound lieutenant lifting a 250-
pound, fully armed bomb by himself and heaving it into the sea.

There were also horrible scenes of death and mutilation. The
entire aft deck and quarters below it became infernos of vaporizing
steel. "When the pros got tired, they asked for volunteers."

Sawatzky was given an oxygen mask and sent down into rear
Hangar Bay 3, right below the flaming flight deck. It was so dark
and smoky he couldn't see. "You just followed the hose until you
found the man on the end of it and relieved him. I said, 'Where do
you want me to point it?' He said, 'Wherever it's hottest.' I was
scared, but we didn't have the fear they had up on the flight deck."

Afterwards, Sawatzky worked in the makeshift morgue. "That
left a lasting impression on me. . . . I think it was later in the day,
or the next morning. Our squadron lost so many people [44] that
they wanted representatives to make identifications based on a ring,
or some other part. . . . To have someone bring over a container
about the size of a tennis bag and say 'Here's two more'. . . . It's
just something you'll never forget. . . . Some people were actually
boiled in the fire-fighting water."

The *Forrestal* was forced to limp home to the United States.
The final death toll totaled 134, another 62 crewmen were injured.
Twenty-one planes were destroyed, 43 damaged. "It shouldn't have

happened," Sawatzky said years later. But the *Forrestal*'s crew didn't know how to handle its missiles in combat—a problem that those who were arguing to start up a fighter weapons school would finally address. It was a problem that Sawatzky himself would help to solve.

☆ PART II ☆

Looking For Answers

☆ CHAPTER 8 ☆

In 1967, the Navy, as part of a top secret project, received an enemy MiG-21 via a circuitous route devised by the Defense Intelligence Agency. Although the predominant feeling among Navy policy-makers was that dogfighting was a thing of the past, there were still those who wanted to see firsthand what they were up against, test it, and devise ways to shoot it down. Our generally poor showing against the MiG worried and embarrassed them.

The '21 had first fallen into the hands of the Air Force. But at that time, the Air Force was suffering under ACM restrictions. Although they had a fighter weapons school at Nellis Air Force Base near Las Vegas, pilots couldn't fly their planes as hard as they wanted. The generals in charge were concerned about accidents in the Phantom, which they felt hadn't been built for ACM. So when pilots got in the MiG and flew it, they didn't fly it hard. The Air Force pilots flying Phantoms against the MiG didn't fly hard either. The practice fights were coming out about even: Air Force would win some, the '21 would win some.

The Navy sent Marland W. Townsend, then head of the F-4 RAG at Miramar, to evaluate the newly acquired asset. "Doc" Townsend was a fighter pilot's fighter pilot. A Georgia Tech and Princeton-trained engineer, as well as a Korean War vet, Townsend, a career officer, had flown and mastered almost every plane in the Navy. He was sent to a top secret desert spot where the MiG was kept and allowed to fly against it.

"I beat [the Air Force pilots flying the MiG] at about a turn or turn-and-a-half because they simply would not go vertical with it. They would pull the nose up a little bit, start turning, and, Christ, by the time we pointed towards each other and made our initial pass, I would simply go vertical, do a roll over the top, see where he was going, and come down and I'd be in the saddle. . . . It was a piece of cake." He wondered, "What's so secret about this? . . . Easiest plane I've ever fought in my life." He began to think, "Maybe we're not in so much trouble after all."

VX-4, the Navy's Air Development Squadron at Point Mugu, California, north of Los Angeles, whose task, among others, was to develop new fighter tactics, was the Navy agency handling the joint Air Force-Navy work with the MiG. Tom Cassidy, a fleet pilot who had joined the VX-4 staff, was project officer. Cassidy, who would later become an admiral, had been instrumental in getting Navy access.

"I didn't know Tom and he hadn't been a test pilot," recalls Townsend, "and, you know, well I was surprised that it hadn't gone to somebody from Patuxent River [the Navy Air Test Center in Maryland]. Well, Tom had been watching [Townsend beat the Air Force pilots in the MiG] . . . and Tom's got balls, that's all there is to it. Tom took that damn thing up. We went roaring at each other and Tom went straight up the same time I did and that rascal just stayed up there and we eventually had to come point our noses back down. I could not get behind him. And ultimately, he got behind me, and I thought, 'This is a different breed of cat.' "

With Cassidy in the '21, it was a deadly weapon.

"We split out again and took a tear at each other. This time I'd intended to turn much faster and at a much slower speed. But Tom did the same thing. He countered it, turned out, and we really went hard at it again. He could fly that airplane, and it would fly better slowly than the Phantom did. . . . It was all over the sky, just like the Phantom . . . but it was controllable, just like the Phantom. . . . The Air Force guys—and I am not picking on them—but they were unwilling to put it in deep buffet. Well, hell, Tom would fly it in deep buffet the whole time. He was happy as hell doing it. We finally decided the only way to handle this airplane was to fly a much higher energy operation, just stay fast."

On a Sunday morning, the third day, they met for a final fight.

"One-on-one. Coming straight at each other on a radar intercept. Picked him up, just tucked the nose down a little bit and held my turn at 450 knots all the way around."

It was a high G turn, straining the Phantom to its limits. At slower speeds, the 21 could turn inside him. But at this high speed, the MiG strained and lost energy.

"I went vertical and he didn't have enough energy to go up with me. He dropped his nose. I rolled over the top of him and dropped behind—and stayed behind. . . .

"Well, I'm telling you, that turned out to be a morning he'd never forget because I ran him out of fuel. He was not going to let me stay back there. He was sure he could get rid of me. We were supposed to have a floor [probably 5000 feet instituted to save the precious acquisition] but we were down in those mountains there."

Neither was going to give up, even if it meant crashing the plane.

"I was just sitting back there . . . 'Fox 2, Tom . . . Fox 2.' "

Fox 2 is code for Sidewinder being launched.

The lesson that came out of those early fights in the remote desert, recalls Townsend, "was that the MiG is pretty formidable if it's flown properly, and we were going to have to fly our airplanes a lot better than we were flying 'em if we're going to do well against them."

Cassidy's project was codenamed "Have Doughnut." The "doughnut" was the canopy sight used to aim at the enemy.

"Doughnut was the thing that started getting people's attention," says Townsend. But the information they were going to be getting would be too secret and too specialized to be disseminated in the RAG. They would need a special school.

☆ CHAPTER 9 ☆

John Nash was getting impatient. He had been reassigned as a tactics instructor at VF-121, and his scheduled backseater for the day, Bob Kern, a friend from his two cruises in Vietnam, hadn't arrived. He wanted to get on with it.

They were scheduled to fly a one-versus-one dissimilar hop against an F-4 student, twenty-one-year-old Robert Arsenault, who had been having problems of late. A dissimilar hop was the RAG's official terminology for an adversary training flight in which the two planes were dissimilar. Instead of Phantom against Phantom, as most of the earlier tactics hops had been set up, Nash and Kern would be flying against Asenault's F-4 in a TA-4 Skyhawk (the T stood for "Training") modified from the basic A-4 by the addition of a rear seat.

Dissimilar hops had been introduced to the tactics syllabus in the RAG's burgeoning effort to make tactical instruction more realistic. In Vietnam, Phantoms didn't fight Phantoms, except in illegal, after-mission training fights, or rare mishaps. The TA-4 was small, maneuverable. They were more like a MiG-17 and more like what the student fleet pilots would likely encounter in a real dogfight.

It was near their scheduled departure time of 1445 (2:45 P.M.). Nash had already conducted the preliminary briefing: "The initial part," he said later in a statement, "was concerned with armament capabilities of both the F-4 and the . . . simulated MiG-17. . . . I explained to Ensign Arsenault the flying qualities and capabilities of the A-4 versus the F-4. I told him that he could consider the hop a success if he could just keep the A-4 out of a lethal firing cone [an area behind the F-4 where the A-4's simulated guns would score]."

Arsenault's chances of simulating a missile shot against *him* were "very poor," he told the student.

Basically, the delta-winged TA-4 was quicker and more maneuverable than the larger Phantom, which had more sustainable speed. It could reverse direction in a smaller radius—much like the MiG-17. That meant that if Nash was chasing him and Arsenault turned in the normal manner—pulling four or five Gs in a wide, arcing turn—Nash could turn inside of him and call a tail shot.

The point of the instruction today was to make Arsenault complete a maneuver that would prevent such "joining": a nose-high, rudder reversal; in effect, a near "hammerhead" turn. The maneuver would slice the big Phantom back around on a dime, so to speak, eliminating the wide arc, putting it back in its previous flight path for a possible shot at the bogey's face, or at least a close pass back by the bogey and more reversals until he finally gained the advantage.

The pass had to be close, because if there was more than minimum "lateral separation," as they labeled the distance between the passing airplanes, the bogey, with its better turning ability, would still have a chance to jump in behind the Phantom as it went by and shoot it. Otherwise, the F-4's speed would pull it away from danger by the time the bogey had turned.

Arsenault, who by now had nearly 60 hours in the Phantom and had been doing very well until this phase of his training, had consistently failed to perform the rudder reversals with other instructors, who had correspondingly given him "downs." "He was a good student," recalls Nash. "He'd been given extra lectures and extra flights . . . but he continued to do the same thing—make slow, arcing turns. It was just a matter of getting aggressive. If he didn't do it right today, they'd give him a disposition board. He'd probably lose his wings." But as Nash pointed out, "He could conceivably graduate, join a ship overseas and be in combat two days later. . . . We were pretty demanding in those days . . . probably over-demanding. But there was a war going on."

Arsenault knew the stakes. "He was a young bachelor type. . . . He may have been distressed. . . . I found out later that he said he was going to get [his previous instructor to] . . . ram him, you know."

Nash had briefed him: When you come out of that reversal, ". . . point that airplane right at me . . . and keep it pointed at me." [At three or four miles distance, you could do that as you were speeding back, correcting for any collision as you got close.] "You want him to get aggressive. That's what it took."

Lt. Nick Dries, a 28-year-old RIO instructor from St. Cloud, Minnesota, would be riding in Arsenault's back seat. If Arsenault had any questions—needed any fast answers—all he had to do was ask Dries. Dries had two and a half years combat experience in Vietnam.

Nash finally decided to leave without Kern. He didn't need a backseater on this hop anyway. As it turned out, it was lucky for Kern.

☆ ☆ ☆

Nash had been assigned to the RAG (the replacement air group responsible for training pilots to fly F-Y) after leaving VF-213. Only the best got the RAG, the Navy's fighter jet training squadron at Miramar, or VX-4, the Navy's shadowy Air Development Squadron at Point Mugu. Most of the pilots he flew with had been sent back to the training command in Texas to help with basic flight instruction. His first job at the RAG had been ferrying replacement Phantoms back out to the fleet, because of the heavy combat losses suffered each month.

From the day he arrived at the RAG, Nash wanted to get into the tactics section. "They were kind of an elite group." He couldn't just sign up, however. "I asked to get in and they said, 'Who are you? You gotta pay your dues.'"

Tactics had been in a state of evolution since Nash had gone through as a student in 1963. At that time, a would-be F-4 fleet pilot was lucky to get two ACM hops in the intercept-dominated syllabus. One pilot who went through it later described it, "They were a blur, and the big thing was not to crash into each other." Few knew what they were doing, and those who did got little out of it.

In 1965, Scotty Lamoreaux, the head of 121, and Merle Gorder, the skipper of the F-8 RAG (VF-124) at Miramar and a champion of ACM who would later be instrumental in the setting up of Top Gun, got together and instituted the first official "dissimilar" hops. Instead of having F-4s fight each other, F-8s, which resembled MiG-21s in performance, were sent against the students in F-4s. But hops were infrequent, and the F-8 pilots, concerned with their reputations, were more bent on punishing than teaching. After all, it was their fighter plane that was being phased out to make way for the Phantom.

Under Doc Townsend the tactics course had begun to expand. Along with Joe Brantuas, an intense instructor from Queens who would go on to become one of the first F-14 squadron skippers, there was Sam Flynn, who, with help from J. C. Smith, had written the first F-4 tactical manual back when the plane had been introduced to the fleet; Sam Leeds, a quiet, cerebral innovator about whom Mel Holmes would later say, "He could always make you feel dumb, but he kept you interested, pushing"; and big Dan Macintyre, a former enlisted sailor like Brantuas, an F-8 pilot, Blue Angel, and the resident MiG killer. (Macintyre was credited with an official "probable" in a fight over Kep, October 6, 1965.)

These instructors, and the others with them in the tactics section (the first, as a group, who were all Vietnam combat veterans) were beginning to change the intercept dominated F-4 tactics course. With Townsend's help, they had commandeered the TA-4s from VA-126, the instrument training squadron. They'd increased the number of ACM hops from four to seven, which gave some continuity to the experience. And they had begun to give definition to the new fighting tactic formation which would be the basis of what Top Gun would soon teach.

The tactic was called "loose-deuce." While before in intercept, the Phantoms would enter battle one behind the other, with a separation of perhaps three miles, in loose-deuce two planes flew abeam, or in "combat spread," as they called it, about a mile or a mile and a half directly across from each other. The position enabled each aircraft to watch the other's rear. Instead of trying just for a head-on shot, they were both "loose," and could go up, out, or any other way, depending on what the bogeys did, either one of them becoming the "free" or "engaged" fighter. A problem with intercept was that in order for the missiles to guide, the bogeys had to stay on a constant course without much deviation. The loose-deuce tactics recognized that the bogeys probably wouldn't, and it gave the Phantoms new versatility in the fight. If they lost the head-on shot, one Phantom would tangle with the bogey while the other Phantom protected him.

One day several months after Nash arrived, he ran into Macintyre over the water. "It had become obvious that you had to beat somebody in tactics to get in," Nash recalled. Macintyre was his chance. "I was by myself. . . . We [Macintyre and I] spotted each other and just had at it. It wasn't very hard . . . a couple of turns, and I waxed his rear end."

Macintyre tells it differently (as is often the case in such jousts, seldom witnessed by anyone but the participants. Today, however everything is monitored by computer so the days of the feuding draw are mostly over.) Macintyre says of the first time he and Nash fought, "I wasn't really that impressed with John." But Nash was persistent Macintyre added, and did beat him, "maybe once." Both pilots are hazy on the details. It was a long time ago. But Nash was soon admitted into the elite tactics fraternity as an adversary pilot.

Macintyre had been part of the last six-member team to win a FAGU gunnery championship. "At FAGU," recalls Doc Townsend, "we could teach one or two carefully selected fleet pilots the fine points of air combat in depth. He would return to his squadron and spread the doctrine."

Macintyre and his teammates had scored highest against FA-GU's maneuvering drone. But with the school's demise, all that was left for a Navy pilot in the way of sustained ACM training—apart from illegal hassling—was exchange duty at the Air Force's Fighter Weapon's School at Nellis.

Almost everybody in tactics had been through the three-week Nellis course. After Macintyre's return, building on an idea of Leeds', Macintyre had suggested to Townsend they create a "detachment" that would concentrate solely on dogfight training.

"We discussed this with the Commander Fleet Air Miramar, Capt. P. E. Gallatin," remembers Townsend. "As I recall, he was most supportive, but there were limited assets and none available with which to commence such a program. It is my opinion that a number of officers [above Gallatin] did not yet share our enthusiasm for this plan.''

Regardless of Gallatin's superiors, ultimately the chief of naval operations and his deputy for air warfare set air policy. And they, working from the Pentagon, had not yet seen the need for a Fighter Weapons School. In their minds, the air war was basically an attack (bombing) war, and Townsend's main duty, according to their directives, was to provide fleet pilots—and airplanes—ready for *all* phases of aerial warfare.

☆ ☆ ☆

Nash and Arsenault, with Dries in Arsenault's backseat, took off separately, and were vectored by "Ruthless Ruth," the military controller, to commercially restricted airspace 20,000 feet above the Pacific, midway between the coast and San Clemente Island, about 75 miles out. In those days, that was "Indian Country." You couldn't enter it without getting jumped.

The nose-high reversal was part of an overall strategy being developed against the MiG-17. The '17 had to keep its speed up to utilize its turning advantage. But every time it turned, it lost speed, "bled energy," as they said. The Phantom had an afterburner, which would help it to escape after its turns. Most '17s did not. So the Phantom, extending speedily with every turn in order to keep out of the MiG's weapon range, was going to try to make the '17 turn a lot, which would eventually render it slow and vulnerable—meat on the table, as the pilots put it.

The arena for this strategy could be likened to a giant fish bowl. Both planes would sprint to the bowl's edges; the Phantom would try to keep the sprints in the vertical plane, which was the best utilization of its afterburner advantage. As long as the F-4 started the fight out of the MiG's firing cone, kept its vertical turns tight— as the rudder reversal would make them—and its lateral separation in the return passbys minimal, its overall speed and performance advantage would keep it "offensive." The '17 just couldn't catch it unless the F-4 pilot made a mistake.

But Nash also taught flexibility. Adapt to your adversary. After his initial passby and runout, the F-4 pilot was supposed to pull his nose up steeply, dropping a wing in back to see what the bogey was planning. "If he turns left," said Nash "you turn left. If he turns right, you do the same. [This puts both of you going around in the same circle, which means he has longer to catch you.] If he makes a wide sweeping turn, you don't have to turn so sharply. But if he makes a tight turn [as most better-turning adversaries will] then you're going to have to turn tightly too."

Hence, the rudder reversal.

"You're basically yawing the airplane up into the steep vertical," said Nash, "to about 120 degrees of bank." [The tail's swinging out, allowing you to see behind it. The nose is going higher.] You're rapidly losing speed, going into buffet. At about 225 knots there's a marked difference in the response-pressure on your rudder pedal. Suddenly, thirty pounds of pressure moves the rudder much easier. "That's your cue," Nash continued, "it's time to start slicing the airplane back around." Optimally, you'd like the bogey to be coming around 90 degrees from your heading at this point. That's the farthest he'll be from you before he starts closing again.

"If the F-4 was an airplane that wouldn't stall in this condition," Nash said ". . . I would just pull [the stick] right at him [the enemy] . . . but you're going to depart doing that . . ., [end up rolling back over the top and to the inside and losing control.] [So] you control-balance it into the slice, using rudder and stick together. You've got left aileron [a moveable flap on the wing] for left bank . . . and then left rudder [the flap on the tail] starts to overbank you. So you wind up putting in forward stick to stop the climb . . . and then start feeding in right aileron and backstick to keep the airplane from rolling over. . . . Now the left rudder is inducing roll . . . so you start to relax the back stick pressure . . . easing out the left aileron . . . going to some right aileron just to try and maintain control. . . . You're pretty well cross-controlling at this time."

It was more of an art than a science, he said.

He'd play one control against the other, finding the hair-fine balance. "It's the edge of the envelope. . . . Some guys get really terrified, think they'll turn into a pumpkin or something." Nash used to purposely depart the Phantom with students in the back seat, take it right up there, and then let it go ahead and nose-slice over or slide down backwards, losing control. He wanted to show them that it was recoverable; that they'd survive even if it did go over the edge. The Phantom was a very good airplane in that regard.

Arsenault and Nash's first pass was nearly head on. Nash immediately made a hard turn after him. "He [Arsenault] had the RIO in the back seat . . . [who] would tell him what to do. And when he saw me coming around with ninety [degrees] to go," said Nash, "then he started turning back." But it was just another arc. Nash cut across it, positioned himself a mile astern and radioed "Atoll."

Nash one. Arsenault zero. In a real fight, the student and his RIO would be dead.

"Let's do it again," Nash said disgustedly. "You gotta get your nose up . . . way up. . . . Get more rudder into it. . . . "

Arsenault wasn't balancing stick and rudder enough.

Arsenault and his RIO charged again. This time, Arsenault pulled harder and got a better turn; it wasn't a hard reversal, but at least it was tighter. But his lateral separation wasn't far enough. Nash shot him again.

Arsenault and his RIO made two more passes and Arsenault was shot two more times. Needless to say, he was in trouble.

"I broke off the engagement," Nash wrote in his report, "and asked for a ninety-degree beam set up [one plane comes at the other at a 90° angle] by Ruthless Ruth." As the two planes zoomed off to their starting points, "I [Nash] discussed the fact over the air that he [Arsenault] had been too gentle with his turns and that he was allowing me the missile tracking time required for a successful shot. [Arsenault] acknowledged the comments with a 'Roger.' "

Arsenault and Nash streaked by each other head-on. "He had a lot of speed this time," said Nash, "I turned behind him, but I was a couple miles back."

Suddenly Arsenault was doing better.

They raced downhill, with Nash chasing him. "I can remember asking 'What's your speed?' He said '550,' or something. I said, 'Okay, start the nose up. He did it, but it was kind of another easy turn." From the back, Dries said, "Here we go again." It looked like another arcer to both of them. "But then the nose snapped up and Arsenault put the thing into the vertical where it belonged."

[He had sliced it backwards doing a perfect reversal.] "First time anybody'd seen him do it," Nash recalled.

Zooming back up, his separation was good enough to keep Nash from jumping him in time. Nash would have to chase him again—just as the strategy called for.

Nash raced after him. He figured that the sudden adeptness was just a fluke and that he'd get the young pilot when he arced at the top. He moved slightly inside what he projected to be Arsenault's returning flight path. He'd lead-turn him with a rudder reversal as he went by.

But Arsenault made another good reversal, and this time, instead of just aiming for a close passby, he put the F-4's nose on Nash's nose—just as he'd been briefed. He was finally doing everything the way he was supposed to.

"I wrote it off as a good move and pulled the airplane a little bit to the right," said Nash (counter to where he was going a split-second before). Nash was going to try and get outside of the passby. That would give him room to hopefully turn on Arsenault in time.

"But he countered that too," Nash recalled, by correcting and aiming his nose once again at Nash. They were coming straight at each other, the A-4 in about a 50-degree climb, the F-4 teetering on what would have been a 15-degree dive. "We're probably half a mile apart at this time," Nash said, "3000 feet or so."

Nash was impressed. "But then I got the sensation he was cutting me off. . . . I pulled a little more to the outside." The A-4 was nose high, "perhaps sixty degrees," close to standing on its tail. Turning was much harder. All Nash could do was slow-roll it.

"I kind of . . . rolled it to the right and reversed my bank," Nash said. "I looked out the left side and he [Arsenault] corrected again." They were now only about 1800 feet apart. Mere seconds. "No doubt about it," Nash recalled. "He was going to be real close."

Nash kept trying to roll to the right. "I am doing about 160 knots . . . decreasing speed rapidly. I peek over the canopy rail . . . he's got me boresighted. . . . I tried to go farther. . . . You're thinking, what's the dumb shit doing? . . . . He's going to take my paint off. . . . "

The approaching Phantom wasn't talking. "It all happened so fast. . . . He may have been all smiles," Nash recalled, "you know . . . finally gotten the picture . . . finally gotten aggressive. . . . The fact that I was decelerating and he was accelerating may have tricked him. Who knows?"

Encapsulated in the back seat, Dries had a blind spot up front. "He probably didn't know I was there," Nash said.

With the angry F-4 rapidly growing in his vision, "I just put in right rudder and rolled the airplane belly-up to him. . . . I said, boy, this is going to hurt. . . . I was out of ideas. . . . He was wings level, coming right at me."

The two planes collided at about 28,000 feet. All Nash remembers about the impact is a "brilliant yellow-orange flash in the cockpit" and "getting stuffed up under the instrument glare shield," the A-4's dashboard, so to speak. "He put his canopy through my tailpipe and his left wing up through my back seat" (where Bob Kern would have been sitting). According to a Navy message, a "massive fireball" was seen 20 miles away.

Arsenault and Dries died instantly.

Nash's first inclination after the crash was to reach back for the stick. But then he thought, "I've got to get out of here." He pulled the ejection handle normally between his legs. The harness he was still strapped into "slammed me back against the seat and I felt the canopy go."

It seemed to him that he tumbled for hours. His oxygen mask got caught over his eyes and for a time he thought he was blind. He fell, spinning, convinced he'd ejected too low. But his chute finally opened. There was "a tremendous shock." He bit a sizable chunk out of his tongue.

He looked down and found himself "just a couple of hundred feet above my airplane. . . . It's tail missing." [It was falling to the water.] "I looked over to the left . . . and here's this big black ball of smoke where the Phantom had been. . . . It looked like a nuclear blast. . . . There's nothing there but tiny little pieces of . . . looks like tin foil, aluminum foil coming down."

Two open chutes from the other Phantom drifted eerily. They were empty. Positioned above the seats, they had been ejected by the impact and opened automatically at a predetermined height.

It took Nash 13 minutes to reach the water. After hitting the water, "I immediately got in my raft."

A helicopter from the carrier *Ticonderoga* arrived in 15 minutes. Once inside, he began to get the shakes. "Everything started to bother me," Nash recalled.

Nash moved away from the open door. "By this time I think you realize you're alive and you don't want to take chances . . . do something dumb." [Until then it had all been automatic. No fear. No concern.] "It was all, you know, just like we'd been trained . . . the ejection, coming down in the chute, the whole works. It was all second nature to me." [But now] ". . . you really start thinking about whether you're going to live or not."

The rescue helicopter took Nash to the *Ticonderoga*. He was in a daze for a few hours. The physicians drew blood "to see if I'd been drinking, I suppose," and gave him dry clothes. "I sat around there. . . . I really don't know what's going on." The next thing he knew he was calling his wife from a Miramar phone and then explaining what had happened to Doc Townsend.

"I felt . . . bad, but, God, I did everything I could to keep him from hitting me."

Dries' and Arsenault's remains were never recovered. Nash went to the memorial service, then stopped by Dries' house afterward. When he was a student at Miramar he went to 17 or 18 memorial services in 18 months. "The thing is, you never see a body . . . never any hair, teeth or eyeballs. . . . One day the guy's there and one day he's not. . . . It's not like going over to a casket, taking a look at some friend . . . There's nothing there.

"I guess we become cynical about death. . . . All the people in Vietnam you bombed, you never saw the remains or the bomb damage or stuff like that . . . the people that you hurt. If you did, you'd probably quit doing it. . . . You just get detached. . . . You know it's going to happen, but you always feel it's going to happen to somebody else."

An investigation found Nash free of any responsibility, though such an accident could have had devastating effects on dogfight training. But Capt. S. W. Vejtasa, Commander, Air Fleet Miramar, wrote in his endorsement of the findings "The aircraft accident described in this investigation . . . is of course most regrettable. In considering this particular air combat maneuver, thoughtful consideration was given relative to its value in the training syllabus because of the high potential danger it presents. The training of replacement pilots in air-to-air tactics is a necessity, albeit the high risk of mishap, and such training must continue."

Vejtasa was not one of the Navy's policymakers. But his comments on the need for dogfighting training were reflective of a growing change in attitude among higher ranking naval officers. The realities of the war were causing a shift in strategy.

☆ CHAPTER 10 ☆

For Mel Holmes, the war had ended just a month and a half before the *Pueblo* crisis.

Holmes quit the Navy after his second cruise, primarily for family reasons, though he now regretted his decision. He missed the adrenaline rush, the action, and the camaraderie—despite the terrific money that he would be making with Northwest Orient.

The war had appeared to be winding down when he left at the end of 1967. The Navy had offered him a commission in the regular Navy, but he'd done his two combat cruises. The fighting (the fun flying) would be over, and he'd have to serve stateside. Worst of all, he would have had to leave the "Dogs"—the VF-143, commonly referred to as "The Pukin' Dogs." It was a squadron he'd never forget: CO Doc Townsend; his long-time friend Tom Roger. Bob Hickey. Duke Vermileyea. Terry Born. All the other hard chargers.

"A lot of squadrons had trouble. People did not want to go into combat," said Holmes. "But we had guys banging on the schedule officer's desk to get more missions. Not a coward in the group."

There were also the guys who didn't come home: Christensen, Frawley, and Bill Lawrence. His own RIO, Jim Bailey. Others. Either dead or POWs. Leaving them had been one of the hardest things he'd ever done.

While Holmes' training in the Phantom at 121 back in 1964 had focused on missile intercept, rather than air combat maneuvers, in VF-143, he had a succession of skippers who were true fighter pilots. Holmes recalled "They gave me the latitude to do what I wanted. . . . We flew the plane to its limits. . . . You couldn't find many skippers who would allow that. . . ."

Doc Townsend was the executive officer, then skipper on the second cruise. "Mel was young," Townsend said "but he had all the right instincts. He would hang in there no matter what happened. . . . He was always there when I needed him."

Townsend made Holmes his wingman. After a mission, he and Holmes would fight, or, more often, "tail chase," which is the fighter version of follow the leader. "Jesus Christ that was exasperating," says Mel. They'd end up with a lot less fuel than they were required for recovery. But Townsend would tell him, "I don't worry about you. You're going to get back on board. The main thing is to get you trained to do what I expect you to do."

"I'd come back with a thousand pounds of fuel, eight hundred pounds of fuel," Mel said. "Bingo," or minimum fuel, was around 2300 pounds.

The missions that Townsend and Holmes flew gave Holmes extraordinary training, as well.

"I think the most harrowing time was on my second cruise," said Holmes. (Doc and he decided to go MiG trolling after a strike on Kep. They went north by themselves.) "All of a sudden [the North Vietnamese] unloaded on us with a sky full of SAMs. Hell, must have been twenty of them coming at us at the same time. . . . All you had were all those sounds coming in out of your ECM gear and you just fought your way out of the damn thing. . . . "

Holmes learned to push the Phantom until the wings shook. "You knew you were at maximum performance," Holmes recalled, "if you pulled it beyond that then you'd start bleeding performance, and if you didn't pull it up to there, you weren't getting quite the performance you could."

So Holmes would hold the Phantom's performance there, right at the edge. "You're always in danger, always at the point of losing your life. But I never thought I'd buy it. Guys don't do that."

In his first few months, the Air Group lost four planes and three pilots while working north. All the downed planes had been from attack (bomber) squadrons, including LTJG Dieter Dengler, whose tale of capture, torture, and sensational escape was printed in *Life* magazine.

In March, the Dogs lost their first crew: Bill Frawley and Bill Christensen, great friends of Holmes, who were last seen flying into a fog bank at 500 feet.

Jim Bailey, a 6'6", 220-pound Mississippi farm boy, had been Holmes' RIO. More than once, Bailey had saved him in shore leave fistfights. Since then, Bailey had become a POW, as had CMDR Bill Lawrence, the CO, with whom Bailey had been flying when their F-4 was shot down.

Holmes' six-year reserve obligation had been up during the first turnaround, and he and Judy had discussed his getting out. But the Navy told him he could stay with the Dogs if he signed up for another cruise. That clinched it.

But the second cruise hadn't been as much fun as the first. The mood of the country had changed. Where before, the Dogs had been treated like heroes, by the second cruise, his mother back home in Oregon was receiving threatening phone calls. On board the *Constellation*, his new carrier, "the old fire and ball-busting spirit seemed to be missing," he wrote home. "We have two people down with colds and one or two who never want to fly anymore."

On the one hand, while flying two, sometimes three, missions a day, during one of the worst casualty periods of the war for naval aviation, Holmes had become an expert pilot. But on the other hand he had become frustrated. He still hadn't seen a MiG, and was beginning to think he never would. And he was fed up with the politics of war.

"It was really very taxing in that many times we thought we had the North Vietnamese down where they could not function properly, but [our] government would let them go. That was the most exasperating part. In September we bombed everything—every railroad, bridge. They couldn't move anything. . . . We had them on their knees. Then we got this moratorium—the idea that they had to keep the peace feelers going all the time . . . that was the worst part . . . . We'd bomb them . . . to where we finally could win this damn thing, and they wouldn't let us go ahead and win it."

But as Holmes discovered, sitting at home out of the action was more frustrating yet. When he saw the headlines during the *Pueblo* crisis—"North Korea Seizes U. S. Intelligence Ship; President Calls

Up Reserves" —he knew things were going to heat up all over again. In the end he decided that he couldn't stay out; he had to get back in. He picked up the phone and called Doc Townsend.

☆ ☆ ☆

Dan Pedersen, operations officer for VF-92 on the *Enterprise*, was experiencing the same frustration Holmes had been experiencing on the *Constellation*.

"We went over the beach or near Haiphong every day for two weeks," remembers Pedersen, a lieutenant commander at this time. "The first week was typical. We took a lot of SAMs, heard some MiGs and saw a hell of a lot of flak. But by the end of the two weeks . . . they were out of SAMs and . . . almost out of Triple-A . . . the MiGs weren't playing. Then we stood down for three weeks and when we went back all hell broke loose again. They'd resupplied."

Pedersen came to call it "MacNamara's War." Many of them did. "I really don't like to talk about myself there. . . . I came back from that cruise and we had lost seventeen guys [from the Air Wing] . . . thirteen of them in the last two months of the cruise. . . . If you'd have collectively looked at the air wing crews in those days, there wasn't any happiness. It was dogshit hard work and we were losing every day. . . . I lost two close friends in a week. . . . Damn, it was miserable. I don't mind if you lose a guy once in a while. That's part of the game. But when you lose them for stupid unjustifiable reasons, totally preventable, and you knew it was preventable. . . . If you choose to get involved, go in smart and fast and win in the shortest amount of time."

Pedersen had not been prepared for the politics of the war. From North Island in 1957 where he'd begun logging thousands of hours in Skyrays, Demons, and Furies, through a tour as a Phantom instructor at 121 and the early war years with VF-213, his career had been a steady climb up the ladder in terms of satisfaction and recognition. Even two years shore duty helping the Navy design and build a computerized fleet defense system to aid ships in air battles had been "a good experience." His fitness reports were excellent. As J. C. Smith would later observe, "Dan was admiral material, no doubt about it." Dan had the right mix of ability, bearing, and leadership. His big hands-on-hips, John Wayne type of motivation got the job done.

"Some of the grandstand bullshit that went on there . . . some of the pseudo heroes . . . I'll tell you why I'm so sensitive. . . . I went out as part of a rescue team late one day [and] . . . a good pal of mine, a Vigilante [2-seater A-5 reconnaissance plane] driver and his backseater, went in on a photo run with an escort near Vinh, took a high-speed hit, and down they went. The chase pilot, one of the senior people in the Air Wing, a commander, a 'Washington fighter pilot,' had been escort. And of course this guy's voice comes up . . . several octaves higher than normal yelling like a kid telling us about the parachute and where the crew was. The reply was, 'Okay, hang on. Help is on the way. We'll relieve you and you can go on the tanker for fuel.'

"We went in there and flew right to the spot where he said that he was, and I looked around for the escort plane. The North Vietnamese weren't shooting actively. It is not the kind of place you want to hang around, but it wasn't bad. But this guy is yelling over the radio the whole time, and we asked him for his location. I said, 'I'm over the spot if I heard you correctly. We're here. In fact I see smoke on the ground.' And he said, 'Yeah, that's where the airplane is.' And he said, 'Now do you see any sign of chutes? Signals?' I said, 'Where are you?' The guy wouldn't answer. I kept asking, 'Where are you? Come on, let's get together so we can find them and get a helo in here before the ground troops get here.' He said, 'Oh, I'm out over water.' Guy lost his damn nerve and went out about sixty miles to safety and left those two guys on the ground, and they spent from 1967 to 1972 in a prison camp."

The restrictions on the running of the war doubled Pedersen's anger. Everything from target selection to the angle of dive to the type of bomb to be used was dictated by the White House. " 'Whiz Kids' . . . what expertise did they have?" Pedersen asked. Targets that were killing his friends were off limits. "If you put people in harm's way you should let them win." Good commanders, he felt, would attempt change and even "deviate" from the rules, regardless of the risk to their careers. "But a shitpot full didn't."

94

Four of his best friends decided to get out of the Navy. They joined the airlines.

"It was totally a political war, totally manipulated. I was so pissed . . . so frustrated . . . I would have gotten out [too] if it hadn't been for my love of flying," Pedersen recalled.

In 1968 Pedersen was assigned to be an instructor at VF-121. His other duty was as Ops Officer, the number three-man in the squadron. It was a choice assignment. The RAG tactics section concentrated on ACM. "It'd be a chance for some more good flying," Pedersen recalled. [A chance] "to breathe again. . . . Anytime you can go back to Fightertown . . . it tells you you're still in the pipeline for promotion and command. And that is really what most everybody is looking for."

☆ CHAPTER 11 ☆

On the morning of May 7, 1968, five F-4s from the carrier *Enterprise* engaged two MiG-21s from North Vietnam. According to documents, the F-4s were only able to shoot two Sparrows at the MiGs, neither of which hit its target. One of the Phantoms, crewed by VF-92 members, W. M. Christensen and W. A. Kramer, was shot down by the outnumbered MiGs (though Christensen and Kramer ejected and were recovered).

The engagement occurred at the start of what was to become known as the "*America* Debacle," a series of dogfights in spring–summer involving F-4s. Two Phantoms would be shot down and over thirty Sparrows fired with only a single MiG kill. Information about the engagements is sparse, but the following can be pieced together.

On May 9, 1968, two days after the VF-92 encounter, two more *Enterprise* Phantoms engaged three MiG-21s. Altogether they fired four Sparrows at them, and claimed one "probable" and one "possible" kill, neither kill was officially counted.

A little over a month later, on June 14, 1968, two *America* F-4s, call-sign "Root Beer," shot four Sparrows at two MiG-17s without a hit. Fifty hours later, two *America* F-4s ran into two more MiG-21s, and shot four Sparrows, again without a hit. Again, one of the Phantoms was shot down. CMDR W. E. Wilber and his RIO LTJG B. F. Rupinski, both of VF-102, ejected. Wilber became a POW and Rupinski was listed as "KIA" (killed in action).

In all, fourteen Sparrows had been fired at a cost of over $150,000 apiece in a little over one month. In addition, two $4 million Navy airplanes had been destroyed, not to mention the loss of the aircrew. Yet the Navy had not a single kill to show for it.

Three more times that month, F-4s from *America* and *Enterprise* ran into MiGs; they shot a total of thirteen more Sparrows and didn't get a hit.

While the F-8s continued to do reasonably well in battle, primarily with the tail-shot Sidewinder, it wasn't until July 10, 1968, that Roy Cash, Jr., and Joseph Edward Kain, Jr., VF-33 crewmembers from *America*, finally got a MiG in an F-4. They got it with a Sidewinder. The kill only upped the Phantom kill ratio to ten MiGs for five U. S. Navy planes, an overall F-4 kill ratio of a flat 2 to 1. Clearly, the Navy's frontline air combat weapon—plane, crew, and missile—was in trouble. In previous wars, the Navy's kill ratio had been five to eight times higher.

The low point came on August 17, 1968. In a dogfight with two MiG-21s, an F-4 from the *Constellation* mistakenly hit its own wingman with a Sidewinder, causing a fire. Its crew had to eject, and they became POWs.

In the words of LCDR Jeffrey P. Simpson, writing about the engagements in the winter 1983 edition of *The Hook*, a magazine devoted to carrier aviation, "It was apparent that something was desperately wrong."

☆ ☆ ☆

Jim Ruliffson's F-4 circled high above the Navy's El Centro desert test range, 100 miles northeast of San Diego. Beneath him stretched the crater-like Salton Sea, the Chocolate Mountains, with their bombing ranges, and stubborn big-horned sheep.

His squadron, VF-21 was getting ready to return to Yankee Station. He was awaiting his former flight leader, Duke Hernandez—"Cobra I" —who had a new nugget wingman and was making a practice run at the range on the east side of the lake. They had scheduled a fight—one more hassle in the many they'd fought as teacher-pupil.

Ruliffson had been named the skipper's wingman for the upcoming cruise to Vietnam, but he'd still never beaten Duke, never put his mentor away.

Hernandez, who enjoyed a head-turning reputation at Miramar and Oceana, the East Coast fighter base, had taught Ruliffson virtually all that he knew about fighting. Some fighter pilots didn't like to divulge their tricks, but Hernandez had taken pride in demonstrating what he knew. Ruliffson had learned so fast that Hernandez had seldom been able to beat him with the same trick twice. Use the sun, he'd taught. In those few critical seconds when the bogey is blinded, you can gain an advantage. When in the scissors maneuver and the two pilots are swirling around each other, one trying to spit the other out in front, put your adversary on a precise spot on your canopy and hold him there. Don't deviate. Use your canopy like a protractor. Even the slightest variation will throw the pilot out of the enemy's plane of turn, let him get away, possibly spit *you* out in front. But hold it tight and the six o'clock shot is yours. He'll never shake you.

And then there was seat-of-the-pants knowledge—like "feeling" the buffet in a turn.

Because of poor lift, the Phantom lost speed while turning. Therefore, the pilot had to raise the nose and increase the angle of attack (the angle at which the plane met the air). This induced violent buffet. But the violence alone couldn't tell you when you were at the optimum angle—that precise balance where you were pulling the maximum G with the least loss of speed. It was the *frequency* of the shake that told you that. "Repetitive bumps at . . . five or ten a second. . . . It took me a long time to learn that distinction," Ruliffson recalled.

Jack Ensch was in Ruliffson's back seat. Below them, Hernandez roared off the target, arming his missiles, turning his Phantom into a fighter. At the same instant, he "rocked hard" to the side so that he and his RIO, Steve Van Horn, could see what was behind them. "I'd been vulnerable for maybe fifteen or twenty seconds [during the bombing run] and I wanted to make sure there was nobody back there," recalled Hernandez.

They saw Ruliffson and Ensch roaring down to attack.

Hernandez pulled hard into his attackers. They flashed by each other, Ruliffson giving Hernandez's rookie wingman, who was protecting his leader, a feint that "spit him up towards San Bernardino." "My wingman was new," Hernandez recalled. "There was really no way he could hang on. . . . It was really a one-on-one with Jim and me and that's the way it was going to be fought."

Everything was even now. It was a matter of gaining advantage. Hernandez gave his plane another hard turn. "I usually gave it my absolute best at the start," Hernandez stated. "If you come out with a lot of angles on him then you know you can have him quickly. . . . Conversely, if you meet him head-on again, you know he's good because he's just matched your very best."

Ruliffson met him head-on again. "But that was Jim. I knew he could match me. . . . I put on another best turn and he did the same thing . . . "On the third turn, Ruliffson started nibbling an angle on him, Hernandez stated. "In a Phantom, you're measuring a 180 turn in eight or nine seconds at those altitudes, so if your turn is half a second off, the other guy has gained ten percent on you, and ten percent is about 15 degrees. . . . [Ruliffson] was just inspired. . . . He was smelling the advantage and he was just inspired. . . ."

Hernandez couldn't shake Ruliffson. "He was just unbeatable," remembers Hernandez, "and after every turn he'd gain a little more. I tried everything. Vertical maneuvers, zero-airspeed reversals, turns so hard that I was almost blacked out—every trick I knew, but he'd seen them all. . . . and just kept nibbling away."

The turns got harder and harder. The fight ended up in a rolling scissors, the two of them swirling around each other. Rapidly losing speed and altitude, Hernandez tried to sling-shot him out in front, but Ruliffson held him steady on his cockpit, gaining on him every time they zoomed across each other.

"The lights had finally turned on for me," says Ruliffson. "He knew exactly where I was, but there was nothing he could do about it."

Hernandez says, "Finally we were both out of energy and altitude. . . . He had me cold. . . ."

Hernandez acknowledged and broke it off, heading home. Ruliffson joined up on him. "I will always remember that Jim joined up so tightly that he was lifting my wing with his airflow. But I wouldn't look over because I knew he had his mask off and all I was going to see was a bunch of teeth over there."

The next day they scheduled another fight and Duke, who would later become an admiral, beat the hell out of him.

☆ ☆ ☆

Captain Frank "Whip" Ault was one of the few carrier skippers who'd put his gripes about the air failures in writing and sent them to Washington. With his 30-year-career in the Navy nearly over, he didn't have to worry about jeopardizing his career. And having been an attack pilot himself in World War II, he understood the complex workings of missiles, radar, and the weapons platform.

By early summer 1968, the planners of the naval air war in Washington were being criticized. The kill ratio—just a little over 2 to 1 in the Navy (only slightly better than the Air Force) was coming to the attention of the top admirals. It was the worst ratio in the history of U. S. naval warfare.

True, the F-8s were doing better on their own—about 8 to 1 recently—but even that was far below what the Navy cream had been used to. In addition, when one figured that the Phantoms, which were replacing the F-8 as the Navy's front-line fighter, carried *two* crewmen and cost $4 million apiece—compared to a MiG-21's $1 million, or the more numerous '17's $750,000—the exchange rate was abominable.

Supposedly "inferior" North Vietnamese pilots were, for all practical purposes, beating the Navy pilots. The Air Force had an equally low ratio, but at least they had a bonafide four-kill hero in Robin Olds. No pilot in the Navy had more than one Vietnamese MiG to his credit. A lot of it was luck. Most of the Navy's best pilots hadn't even seen a MiG, and after serving the two combat cruises that they were allowed, they were now coming home—just when the MiGs were starting to challenge in greater numbers.

In 1966, MiGs accounted for only 3 percent of U. S. air losses to North Vietnamese defenses. (Triple A was doing the most damage, most recently coupled with SAMs.) But that figure had steadily risen to 8 percent in 1967; and now, in the first three months of 1968, the MiG pilots had accounted for 22 percent of U. S. air losses, a figure that John Morrocco, in *Thunder From Above,* a recent study of the air war in Vietnam, noted "threatened to refute U. S. claims to superiority in the skies above North Vietnam."

"I had been skipper of the *Coral Sea* in 1966–67," said Ault. "We spent considerable time in the Gulf of Tonkin and I had submitted several recommendations for weapons system improvements," including one that the Sparrow become more maneuverable, which was later adopted. "When I got back to Washington for duty in early '68, I was approached by my boss, Rear Admiral [Bob] Townsend [Commander of Naval Air Systems Command] and Vice Admiral [Tom] Connolly [Deputy Chief of Naval Operations [Air]] about some of these recommendations. . . . I . . . went further [and said] that I thought there were many more things wrong with the [weapons] systems. . . . After a couple of months of talking, they gave me an assignment."

The assignment was "to find out why we weren't shooting down more MiGs with missiles." Townsend and Connolly gave him "carte blanche [to] pick anybody I wanted and conduct the study in any manner I saw fit," Ault recalled.

Thick-necked and bald-headed, Ault had earned his nickname, Whip, as an executive officer of VA-55 on the *Essex* during the Korean War. "I told the pilots, 'I can out-drink you, out-fight you, and out-fly you' and there's nothing more obnoxious than a guy who can back up what he says." Ault was notorious for being a man who spoke his mind—a trait that got him into trouble when he was interviewing for the job of executive officer on *Enterprise*, the Navy's first nuclear-powered carrier. His interview was with Admiral Hyman Rickover, "father" of the country's first nuclear fleet and legendary for being hard to deal with.

Ault had known Rickover on a first-name basis in the early 1950s when they both had lectured on nuclear power. But Rickover made him wait four hours in his outer office before calling him in for the interview. "That was deliberate. . . . He wanted you pissed when you came in, and boy, in my case, he got it. . . . I was mad. He said, 'Ault, what makes you think you can even pass the course out at [the nuclear school]?' I said, 'Well Admiral, you have two of my contemporaries in your program [both skippers of nuclear subs]. I stood two hundred and forty-five numbers higher than one of them and fifteen numbers higher than the other. I'm smarter than those guys. . . .'

"He said, 'What do you think is the difference between the job of executive officer of the *Enterprise* and executive officer on a conventional carrier?' I said, 'Not a damn bit. The exec does all the work and the captain gets all the credit.' He jumped up—the Rickover technique included great exhibitions of feigned total outrage—put a finger toward my eye and said, 'You mean to tell me you're sitting on top of eight nuclear reactors and you're telling me the job is the same as the executive officer on any carrier? What would you do if the chief engineer came up and says he has a runaway number seven reactor?' I said, 'I would want to know two things, Admiral. Could he control it, and while he was doing his thing, should I stay in my cabin or stand out on the pier?' "

Rickover was outraged. And when, in response to a question, Ault answered that he thought a jet engine was more complex than a nuclear power plant and that oil plants could do a better job of powering ships than nuclear, Rickover "called my boss [then Vice Admiral Chic Hayward] and told him I was the most irreverent Naval officer he'd ever interviewed."

Townsend and Connolly hoped that same irreverence would help him cut to the heart of the air-to-air problem and bring back solutions.

☆ ☆ ☆

Merle Gorder had gone back to Yankee Station in the Gulf of Tonkin off North Vietnam after his tour as Commanding Officer of the F-8 RAG at Miramar. A captain, he was "more or less Operations Officer of all the carriers out there—the *Coral Sea*, the *Ranger*, any number of them." In two earlier cruises, he'd commanded an F-8 Crusader squadron (VF-191) on the *Bon Homme Richard*, and been Air Operations Officer for the U.S.S. *Hancock*.

He knew the fighter situation well.

He traced the problem even further back than the disbanding of the FAGU.

Following World War II, the Navy had a "wealth of fighter knowledge" with which to impart the fighter tradition. But few Navy pilots got to dogfight the MiGs over the Yalu during the Korean War. Most of the MiG fighting was done by the Air Force, so the Navy came out of the Korean War without that same tradition.

The Kennedy Administration's cost-cutting helped to further deteriorate the Navy's training situation. Gorder said, "McNamara knew the price of everything and the value of nothing."

Once the Vietnam War started, "We all knew we needed more training. There were many mishaps . . . people spinning out and killing themselves because they didn't know what they were doing. You had to fight the airplane to understand it. We all knew we needed more training."

But none of them—those people like Gordor—had the power to affect a change in the training schedule.

Gorder had been reassigned as part of Admiral Tom Moorer's office, the Chief of Naval Operations (CNO). Gorder was attached to Deputy CNO, Vice Admiral Connolly, with responsibility for aviation training, including the RAGs. When Connolly, at the direction of Moorer, ordered Ault to solve the fighter problem, Connolly's Aide detailed Gorder to help. With that simple assignment, the first seeds of what was to become Top Gun were planted.

The Navy Fighter Weapons School (NFWS), as it was to be officially called, was "an idea whose time had come," say all those involved. "I knew exactly what I was going to propose," remembers Gorder. "It just had to be documented."

☆ ☆ ☆

The first thing Ault did was review all previous studies of the war's air-to-air combat. "There were safes full of information: the Air Force's "Sparrow Shoot" and "Combat Sage" and carrier battle reports, "Project Red Baron." Later, the opening paragraph in his finished report would state, "Almost 600 air-to-air missiles have been fired by Navy and Air Force pilots in about 360 hostile engagements in Southeast Asia between 17 June 1965 and 17 September 1968." Only about one in ten "had a probability of achieving a kill"—which was well "below expected or desired levels."

But all of the previous studies had been limited in scope. They had not dealt with the total picture. Ault's approach, he decided, would be to examine the entire weapons system—plane, radar, missile, aircrew performance—from "womb to tomb," he later called it. He tapped four others to join Gorder on the team: Burl Hayes, a civilian from the China Lake Weapons Center; W. W. West, another civilian from the Navy's Corona Weapons Lab; CDR B. H. Gilpin, Missile Center, Point Mugu; and a third civilian, O. C. Robbins, from the Naval Air Systems Command.

Each of the experts was to concentrate on a key question: Was industry delivering a "high-quality product" to the Navy? Were components of the product being properly managed and handled by shore units enroute to the Navy? Were the carriers storing, maintaining, and handling all elements of the weapons system properly? Were the Navy's aviation overhaul and repair activities producing satisfactory products?

Gorder was to document what they found out.

They fanned out, visiting Naval air stations like Miramar and Oceana and testing grounds such as China Lake and Point Mugu. They went to seven weapons stations, including Seal Beach and Concord, and visited many commands and industrial plants, among them, Raytheon, Westinghouse, McDonnell–Douglas, and Rocketdyne—over 27 sites in all, interviewing and collecting data. Ault and Gorder concentrated on the Yankee Station carriers, talking to the aircrews and digging through after-action reports.

"When you get to one of these studies you look for what I call the 'Aha!'," says Ault, now president of his own consulting company in Washington. Early on he thought he had one such "Aha." The Sparrow had been conceived largely as a one-time-only missile for use on an intercept mission in which it would be fired at an enemy high-level bomber. It was not really supposed to return to base.

But it *was* returning to base, every fifty to one hundred times before it was taken down, checked, and reserviced. "We thought that was it, especially when they found out that the Air Force was down-loading its [Sparrows] after [only] ten flights and running them through the test equipment. However, when we looked at the performance . . . the Air Force and Navy were within a thousandth of a decimal point in kills with the Sparrow." Obviously, carrying the

A Top Gun detachment circa 1970. J. C. Smith, fifth from right, back row, had succeeded Dan Pedersen as Officer in Charge. Steve Smith, another member of the original Top Gun instructors, is second from left, back row, in sunglasses. Lou Page, wing commander, is at left of Steve Smith, and RAG commander Dick Schulte, wearing a 121 baseball cap, is standing at far right.   (U.S. Navy photo)

An F-4 Phantom being prepared for takeoff.   (U.S. Navy photo)

Dan Pedersen and backseater J. C. Smith in the cockpit of a modified A-4 Skyhawk, plane most frequently used in adversary training flights at Top Gun. (U.S. Navy photo)

Darrell Gary (left) and Jim Laing prior to a strike into North Vietnam from the U.S.S. Kitty Hawk. (U.S. Navy photo)

John Nash (left) with RIO Bob Kern aboard the U.S.S. Kitty Hawk in 1967. (Courtesy of John M. Nash)

An F-4 flying over Vietnam.   (U.S. Navy photo)

F-4s and other planes on the deck of an American aircraft carrier off the coast of North Vietnam.   (U.S. Navy photo)

Jim "Hawkeye" Laing in the spring of 1968 on the U.S.S. Kitty Hawk. (U.S. Navy photo)

Pilot Jim Ruliffson climbing into the cockpit of his F-4. (U.S. Navy photo)

Mel Holmes (right) and J. C. Smith with Brig. General Robin Olds (carrying flight helmet) at Miramar in March 1970, about to begin a dogfight demonstration. (U.S. Navy photo)

A formation of F-4s, flanked by two of the secret MIGs used by the VX-4 squadron. (U.S. Navy photo)

A Phantom with its hook extended, about to make a carrier landing. (Robert L. Lawson/ Tailhook Photo Service)

An A-4 chasing an F-4 in a dogfight training maneuver. (Robert L. Lawson/ Tailhook Photo Service)

Jerry Sawatzky
(U.S. Navy photo)

Randy Cunningham (right) and Bill "Willie"
Driscoll, America's first aces of the Vietnam
War.   (U.S. Navy photo)

Two Phantoms escorting a Russian "Bear" bomber.
(U.S. Navy photo)

An A-4 and an F-4 dogfighting from Miramar.
(Robert L. Lawson/Tailhook Photo Service)

A Phantom launching one of its Sparrow missiles.
(U.S. Navy photo)

A Phantom, playing the role of an "attack" plane, delivers its bombs over North Vietnam. (U.S. Navy photo)

An F-4 about to be launched. (U.S. Navy photo)

missile beyond one flight wasn't the problem—or at least the only problem.

Shortly after Ault had started work, he was summoned back to Washington: "In the first twenty days that I was assigned to the job [June and July 1968], the Navy fired something like two dozen Sparrows and hit nothing. I found myself standing on the carpet in front of Admiral Moorer [the CNO himself]."

Ault knew Moorer well. He'd served under him on the *Shangri-La* in 1960-61 when Ault had commanded carrier Air Wing 10. "During a NATO exercise, he and I had to deal with the 'Hero' phenomena" —dangerous electro-magnetic radiation near ordnance. Whip antennas on the bow of the carrier were generating electromagnetic energy around some of the catapults that was enough to fire a Sidewinder. "I took him down there one dark night and showed him the blue fire dancing around the airplanes. . . . He groused about it but he turned them off."

Moorer started grilling Ault on the failure of the Sparrows. "I thought I told you to solve this problem, Ault. You've been working on it for three weeks," Ault remembers him saying. "I guess that was another turning point in my career," said Ault, "because without even thinking I said, 'Admiral, you and your contemporaries have taken about twenty years to screw this up and I've only been working on it twenty days. I think I deserve a little more time.' "

He had fired a direct salvo at the CNO and those around him, blaming Naval policy for the air wings' problems. Moorer, Ault recalled, eyed him for a few seconds, "trying to decide how to deal with such impudence. Finally, he must have decided it wasn't worth disciplining me over and sent me on my way."

Eventually, when his report was delivered on January 1, 1969, it identified 242 problem areas that needed improvement—"a virtual jungle of problems: some readily and easily solvable; others requiring more funds, more time, greater effort and sustained perseverance and follow-through," the report stated.

The problems ranged from not specifying the highest quality product in the original order, to multiple machine and aircrew problems during an actual fight.

The missiles, Ault pointed out, were more like complex airplanes than simple bombs. But they were being treated like bombs. The Sparrow, for instance, had, in addition to its warhead, a complicated radar receiver, lots of electronic circuitry, moving wings, and a motor. "I had lunch with some guys in the Navy Training Command in Jacksonville," Ault recalled. "This old chief ordnanceman asked me, 'Captain, can I speak frankly?' I said, 'Give it to me.' He said, 'Well, I'll tell you, sir, you treat them fuckers like bombs and they're gonna act like bombs. We're not maintaining them right.' "

The missiles would sit on racks without checks or preventative maintenance and be flown for a hundred missions without a test or overhaul, sometimes disassembling from vibration, or accumulating moisture, which would short the circuits. When they were finally sent back for servicing, they were often reworked with unqualified, cheaper, defective parts.

"We were tweaking circuits," Ault stated, "but what was happening [was] when parts ran out they'd go to the equivalent of [a generic electronics store] and say, 'Okay, we need some five microfarad capacitors here and a few resistors. They'd just buy 'em off the shelf, whatever they had. And maybe the response characteristics of that capacitor would be entirely different from the original."

If they had the right part, they often didn't have the expertise. Escorting a Raytheon vice president through a Yankee Station carrier work area, Ault and the VP watched an F-4 squadron maintenance crewman "lay out twelve feet of schematics across the hangar deck trying to figure out what was wrong with the Phantom radar on which he was working. He hardly got it all laid out when a forklift full of bombs ran right across the middle of it. . . . I said to the VP, 'The trouble with you guys is you put on your white smocks back there in Massachusetts and don't understand what happens when your system gets into the hands of the great American sailor. . . . This isn't your five micron lab atmosphere. . . . Probably the circuit that kid wants is under that big greasy tire track right there."

In the air, the problems multiplied:

First, at least 25 percent of all Sparrows fired didn't go anywhere but down because the rocket motor wouldn't ignite. "The problem," recalled Ault, "was that we had converted a rail-launched missile to a gravity-drop missile and all the complex initial guidance things that happened to that missile as it was sliding down the rail now had to happen as it got to the end of the lanyard."

Second, the Phantom cockpit was designed for distant intercepts of bombers. Missile switches and radar reads were low in the cockpit, forcing the crew in a close dogfight to take their eyes off the bogey. "We summarized by saying, what you're requiring these people to do is fight a heads-up fight with a heads-down system. You had to look in the cockpit when fighting the F-4. . . . You had to listen for the growl of the Sidewinder in your headset. You had a guy in the back seat who had to say, 'I am locked up on that thing, Boss [before firing the Sparrow].' Then you gotta have some agreement between the front and the back that, yep, that's the guy."

Third, it took a full 5.2 seconds for the Sparrow to be launched from lockup, 1.4 seconds from trigger-squeeze to missile-away. "They had a dead time in the system of something like three seconds for [radar setting] and yet the average time they had to fire was 2.2 seconds," said Ault. A MiG just wasn't going to hold still for that length of time.

Fourth, the radar could not be counted on to hold a lock in a hard-turning dogfight. "It was extremely difficult to keep a target illuminated in the boresight mode due to the narrow beam width of the radar antenna," said Gorder's report. Ault added, "It was a damn good system—the radar and the computer, the best of its time—but it had been designed for fighting relatively non-maneuvering bombers." Some likened its new task to keeping a flashlight beam on a frightened fly in a dark room.

Fifth, Sidewinders were having trouble making the Gs and were breaking apart in flight.

The list went on and on.

Worst, as Ault and Gorder already knew—most of the F-4 pilots and RIOs had little or no dogfighting training, and knew nothing of their missile's performance envelopes. "Numerous missiles fired in

107

combat have missed," said Gorder's report, "because they were fired out of envelope at low altitude against a relatively small maneuvering target by a U. S. fighter aircraft with a missile control system mechanized for a high altitude, non-maneuvering bomber."

Pilots were guessing at parameters and guessing badly. The maximum and minimum parameters in which a Sparrow could be fired effectively changed constantly during a swirling dogfight. They were different at lower altitudes than higher altitudes, and different depending on whether you were behind, in front of, or pointed at the side of the bogey.

For instance, in a dogfight at 5000 feet, you had to be within one-half mile to two miles for a good tailshot with the Sparrow. You also had to be within a certain "lethal cone" projected from the target's tail. The cone was a fluctuating, irregularly shaped pattern emanating from the bogey's front, back or side. It was a mile to three miles if you were abeam of him and was two to four miles for a good head shot. Your missile had to be within the parameters of the invisible cone in order to work properly. In some cases, the latitude between minimum and maximum ranges was only 500 feet.

Few pilots or RIOs even knew the parameters, let alone were instinctively and instantly able to gauge them in the G-stressed combat arena. It was something you had to study and practice.

Ignorance about missile performance was so widespread, said Ault, that "we had a case or two, you know, in practice out there in the Philippines, where we did shoot our own airplanes out of the sky. Therefore, it had to have happened a few times in combat [in fact, it did]. In the melee up there, you simply don't know who you are shooting at."

At least one Sidewinder had exploded on launch, killing the pilot.

"The point is . . . we sent our people out there not trained for dogfighting. We sent the aircraft out there not equipped for dogfighting. And, finally, from a standpoint of the readiness of the equipment, we sent systems out there and occasionally (I probably should use the word 'frequently') we got into a nose-to-nose combat situation where neither the guy flying the airplane nor the airplane itself had ever before fired a missile."

In August, as part of his start-up, Ault invited most of the stateside fighter pilots he respected to Point Mugu for a kick-off conference on what was wrong and what they could do about it. "It was a pretty serious indictment of the state of naval aviation," recalls Ronald "Mugs" McKeown, a VX-4 project officer at the conference. "It was nice to have this Sparrow and be able to shoot from thirteen miles out, except that we had to visually identify the enemy. So we trumped our own ace. By the time we could see him visually, we're inside the minimum range of the missile. . . . We had a lot of those dilemmas. . . . No guns on the F-4. Little money to practice . . . or teach tactics. . . ."

Jim Foster, who was also at the conference and would head VX-4 during the crucial months ahead, remembers, "Just too damned many of our friends were getting lost in battle." They all agreed that "a little graduate course in tactics" was what was needed. "Basic training," says Ault. "We got to send airplanes and pilots out there that have fired [the missiles] . . . and had a piece of everything that the guy flying a [fighter] should have mastered before he found himself in combat out there."

Gorder put it in writing: "Since the Fleet Air Gunnery Unit [FAGU] was decommissioned in 1960, there has been a great loss of expertise and continuity in the air-to-air weapons system capability within Navy fighter squadrons. There is a need to establish a fighter weapons school to reverse this trend and to eliminate aircrew and ground personnel error in weapons system and air-to-air missile performance."

The proposed school would "be required to train selected pilots [the best] and supervisory personnel of all fleet and marine fighter squadrons . . . twenty aircrews in the F-4 per year and ten pilots in the F-8 per year." Those aircrews or single pilots, as had been the case with FAGU, would then go back to their fleet squadrons and become their air combat maneuver teachers. The school would be organized under a specially picked "officer-in-charge." He would select instructors in all phases under him.

The Ault report made other major recommendations. Both the Sparrow and Sidewinder should be redesigned to become true dogfight missiles; a "heads-up" aiming display should be repositioned on the upper portions of the cockpit so pilots wouldn't have to look away from the fight. In order to better train pilots, Ault suggested that a revolutionary new device be built: an Air Combat Maneuvering Range (ACMR). The ACMR, using computers, would track practice dogfights, would eliminate guesswork and unsupported kill claims, and would aid in teaching tactics, weapons performance, and air combat safety.

Moreover, the Navy needed a new plane for dogfight maneuvers. Eventually, this would become the F-14 Tomcat. It would be faster and more maneuverable than the Phantom, have guns as well as better missiles, and better radar.

Most of the major recommendations would take time. But the Navy Fighter Weapons School was something that could be initiated immediately.

As Ault and Gorder headed out to Vietnam, the recommendation for the new school was already being forwarded.

☆ PART III ☆

Top Gun

☆ CHAPTER 12 ☆

Dan Pedersen, as Mike Guenther remembers, had the appearance of a movie-star fighter pilot. "He always wore a red turtleneck under his flight suit, a baseball cap, and Rayban fighter pilot glasses. . . . We'd fly at dawn and the first brief was like 4:30 A.M. . . . He'd come in and wake up one of the [dozing] students and say, 'See that guy over there?'—pointing at me, big gapped teeth out front—'We're gonna kick his ass today.' "

With his big-frame swagger and polished bearing, Pedersen had the flair that the officer-in-charge (ONC) needed, according to Phil Craven, who was then the head of Air Wing 12, under which the new Navy Fighter Weapon School was to be formed as a department within VF-121.

Although a lieutenant commander, Pedersen was fairly new in the RAG, having arrived only a few months before. But already he'd taken over the number three spot of operations officer in the huge squadron and was next in line to take over the tactics section.

"I had flown a little bit with him," says Craven, "and knew his talent. He not only had the motor skills and was a good aviator, but he also projected himself as a good aviator, as a man who knew what he was talking about. . . . He was very thorough in preparing himself and making sure that the instructors prepared themselves. That's the sort of thing we were looking for."

Most importantly, the head of the new school was going to have to be able to ride herd on the best of the best. Each of the instructors to be picked for Top Gun would be enormously talented, each with his own ideas, as well as a strong ego.

The school was going to need both an organizer and a motivator. It needed someone who could galvanize these usually hard-to-handle individuals toward a single higher purpose: teaching other pilots, whom they'd normally take pride in beating and humiliating, to be as good as, or even better than, themselves.

The head of Top Gun would need a unique personality, one as strong as the instructors he was going to lead, but with enough charisma, purpose, and tact to enforce his decisions with subtlety. No one was going to bully these guys. They'd try to cold-cock him at the bar, or, if they weren't big enough to do that, they'd try to humble him in the air. He'd have to be able to win their genuine respect.

"The thing I liked about Dan was that he'd go to bat for his officers," recalls Darrell Gary. "I had a medical problem. It was going to interfere with my flying. Dan asked the admiral to back off." The admiral did just that.

Mike Matetich, Pedersen's wingman in the early 1970s, likened him to Knute Rockne. He was "a big proponent of being a team player. . . . He always told me, 'We'll share our joys and we'll share our troubles.' "

Matetich remembers an instance of how far Pedersen would go to back his men when the FBI sent a message to their ship asking if there was a "Commander Matetich" aboard. Matetich was a junior officer. But to help the squadron get some much needed furniture, he had signed a requisition with the higher rank. "Dan came in and asked me what it was all about. When I told him, he said, 'Okay, let me handle it.' He took heat from the admiral and everyone else, but I didn't get a thing."

Pedersen was a "facilitator," says Jim Laing, "a get-things-done" type of leader. He was "forceful" and "creative," says Gil Sliney. "He'd say, 'Okay, guys, this is what has to be done and this is the way we're going to do it. . . .'" Matetich adds. "He could get the troops to do anything."

But friends closer in age reported a more human dimension to Pedersen—that he worried about the success of the school, that at least once he came back shaking his head over his lack of forcefulness in a speech that he made to the admirals, and that sometimes he got so angry at a mistake made by a RAG student that he'd swear to "kill the son-of-a-bitch." But then he'd compose himself, go back, and show the utmost patience to the student.

He was a "politician," remembers Holmes, who recalls Pedersen making decisions unpopular within Top Gun to win favors from outside units whose help the elite group needed. Nash found Pedersen sometimes distant and aloof. "It was hard to get to know the real Dan."

The youthful, dimpled exuberance of Pedersen's ensign days had given way to a driving maturity of purpose: to excel as an officer and aviator. Years later, during a stint as captain of an aircraft carrier, he had a pamphlet entitled "Secrets of the Super Performers" that he liked to give to young officers. It said, "The leader does not say, 'Get going!'. . . . He says 'Let's go!' and leads the way. . . . The leader assumes that his followers are working with, not for him. . . . He helps those under him grow. . . . He has faith in his people. . . ." Other traits the pamphlet extolled included an open mind, self-esteem, accountability, goal orientation, positive response to pressure, and an ability to take risks.

Actually, tactics head Sam Leeds had been first in line for the new job. As creator of the earlier and smaller tactics detachments, he had insisted on improving tactics to evolve the Fighter Weapons School idea. But his RAG tour was due to end soon, and he was scheduled to leave for a new post on the East Coast; he eventually would become a skipper of the first F-14 squadron.

"I could have been selfish and taken it [the job] and left in the middle," Leeds remembers. "But this was going to be a long-term program. It wouldn't have been right to whoever followed."

Thus Pedersen, slated to succeed Leeds as tactics head, was next in line.

"At first he [Pedersen] didn't want to do it," says Leeds. "I don't remember the details, other than the school was an unknown entity and we didn't know how it was going to turn out."

Pedersen remembers, "He called me over and said 'We're going to start a dedicated [meaning it would be backed] tactics operation. Do you want it?' We sat down with the Ault data and I thought, 'If this is such a good deal, why aren't you [Leeds] going to do it?' "

The elitism appealed to Pedersen, but he realized the potential problems. Resources would be limited. Although the Ault study justified the school, there were still powerful officers opposed to it. Not only would the school require planes that they thought should be used for other purposes and would increase the risk of accidents, but also, as George Hearing, an analyst for CNO at the time, recalled: "ACM is a contact sport. It can hurt. It can be very humiliating. There were plenty of F-4 guys—you know, senior guys—who were afraid of it."

Having the Navy's safety center on his back was not what Pedersen needed. He knew that he'd have to do double duty; that is, run the new school *and* tactics. They'd all have to do double duty. But he liked pressure; in fact, he thrived on it.

Pedersen, with Leeds in tow, went in to see RAG skipper Hank Halliland. "I asked him, 'How much time do I have?' He said, 'As fast as you can put it together.'"

Two of the people Pedersen immediately picked to be instructors at the new school were Mel Holmes and Jim Ruliffson.

Ruliffson was proud to be invited to what Pedersen and Leeds had described as a graduate level school for dogfighting. Having stepped directly into tactics at 121 two months before at Leeds' behest, following a tour in Vietnam, he had really taken to it. While he had been worried when he first joined (he wasn't sure how good he would be as an instructor), he had begun to feel himself the professional equal of pilots like Holmes.

Ruliffson's natural abilities and instincts had helped him as an instructor. He found that he liked explaining how things were done. He knew the Phantom inside and out, and he could articulate that knowledge in a way in which others could learn. He could also demonstrate what he was talking about in the air. In the two months he'd been in tactics, he'd already made a reputation for himself.

It would be Ruliffson's job to teach the Top Gun students how to maximize the use of their missiles. "We all knew nobody knew a hell of a lot about them. It was one of the first times the Navy admitted it was deficient. . . . Somebody had to teach it, so I did."

Mel Holmes would write the syllabus section on aerodynamics and tactics. Since returning to the Navy the previous February, he'd been flying tactics hops daily (sometimes three or four times a day) testing the limits of the plane.

"As an instructor, you're always experimenting to see how far you can take it. Sometimes you make excursions beyond the envelope to see what the plane will do. . . . I've departed the airplane many times. . . . Oh, never really a full-fledged stall, but a partial . . . what was called a 'post-stall gyration,' just before it went into a spin."

Holmes now had such a command over the Phantom that he would routinely use departures—departures that would later kill other pilots—as a technique to turn quicker.

It was while fighting that Holmes made many of his discoveries about techniques and maneuvers.

"I was up fighting one day, trying to turn to the left but [the other plane] was getting the angle on me. Because I [had been using] this accelerated stall and post-stall gyration to flip to the right, I thought, well damn it . . . I'll just try it to the other side. So I crossed the controls and fed 'em in opposite of what I'd been doing before and the airplane this time actually post-stalled and gyrated to the left, where I wanted it to go in the first place."

Roaring to the right, his Phantom suddenly "swapped ends," as he called it. He recovered it almost head-on to his surprised adversary.

In anyone else's hands, such a departure would be an out-of-control emergency. To Holmes, it was just part of his bag of tricks.

As Ruliffson remembers, "Until we got this license to really concentrate on tactics we didn't know how good of an airplane we had. . . . You had to explore the edges day in and day out and come back and talk about it to your peers. You'd say, 'Well, how about this? How about we try that?' One guy might find out things that someone else didn't have the ability to do.

"I guess the best example would be Mel. I thought I was a dynamite Phantom driver," recalled Ruliffson, "but Mel was one guy who always beat me one-on-one. . . . He could make that airplane do things that other people couldn't. He couldn't teach it because nobody else could do it. . . . What he was doing was actually departing the airplane, taking it outside of its actual flight envelope and controlling the recovery from that excursion to come back in where he wanted to. He was very close to spinning the airplane and you don't want to spin swept-wing jets as daily practice. But he did . . . the airplane would turn better in an incipient spin than it would just in actual flight. . . ."

It was a fun time for Holmes. He was solidifying his reputation. Coming into tactics, he'd picked up a new call sign. Up until then, his call sign had usually been "Big O," for the "O" on the front of his college baseball cap. But after getting a little intoxicated at a change-of-command ceremony, he and Bill Frawley had gone golfing. He hooked a shot near a den of rattlesnakes. Frawley saw him swinging away and yelled, "What's the matter?" Holmes yelled back down, "Nothing. Just a few rattlers." He was taking them out with the club.

The name "Rattler" stuck.

Pedersen needed an assistant, as well, someone who could get things done, and someone who wouldn't take no for an answer. Without their own funds, the school was going to have to scavenge to get the things they needed.

He tapped Steve Smith as the one to forage for equipment.

"It only took me a few weeks around Steve to realize he could do just about anything," Pedersen recalled. "He was one of those high-energy guys . . . ran around with a list in his pocket and usually got 90 percent accomplished each day."

Smith, Jim Laing and Darrell Gary were among a handful of RIOs chosen from the *Kitty Hawk* and *Enterprise* to serve as RAG instructors at the new school.

Although still a junior officer, Smith—because of his aggressive personality and experiences in the war—was now a consummate pro. A "crazy," as he liked to refer to it.

His seniors described him as dedicated. His own description was "programmed."

On an early detachment to Yuma, a Marine base where pilots in 121 practiced bombing, rocketry, navigation and tactics, he was thrust into the role of acting officer-in-charge. Detachments were like small carrier squadron deployments, this one made up of 100 men and 10 airplanes. There was lots of potential for trouble, and those in charge came down with the flu. When Smith was able to lead the detachment in a successful completion of the syllabus, it bolstered his growing reputation.

Pedersen's first request to Smith was to find a place for the instructors to work.

"He said, 'Oh, by the way, we need a place to work.' I said, What do you mean a place to work? He said, 'A place to hold the school, like a building.' "

The RAG was already bulging at the seams. As the largest squadron in the Navy, it was a virtual factory in high gear, pumping out replacement pilots and NFOs at an unprecedented pace. There wasn't so much as a *room* available, let alone a building.

"He [Pedersen] said, 'Have you seen those old trailers they have around the base? The big trailers fixed on foundations?' I said 'Yeah.' He said, 'Well, there's some over by base Ops and if one of them was to show up over here, well, that sure would be neat.' "

"Now you don't just walk up to base Ops and say, 'Can I have your trailer over there? Is it okay if I just take that?' It's not going to happen. But if you drive up at 10 A.M. Saturday morning when there's a construction company with a mobile crane working nearby, and you ask them if it's okay if they will set it on your truck for you, they'll say 'Sure, no problem.' And then you can get them to take it off at the other end and you set it up on blocks and you've got your building."

Pedersen said, "We didn't want anything fancy—just a little privacy, a place to work, teach, brief, and debrief."

The little metal trailer was barely 50 feet long, 16 feet wide, and 12 feet high. It looked like the temporary offices of a construction company at the site. But it had doors and windows. They put it on the tarmac, placed an old metal trash can out front, and painted it dull gray with bright red trim—[It was] "the most obnoxious color we could find," recalled Smith, because "anything stolen you aren't going to paint with red trim. Right?"

Monday morning they were open for business. But they still needed furniture.

"I found out later that we could have gotten anything we wanted from salvage. But I've only been in the Navy four years at this point. What do I know?"

Smith started visiting other squadron areas "acquiring a small amount of furniture on a matching basis. We got a table in one ready room, a chair in another. If they wanted to see my paperwork, it was in the safe. Everything classified. I'd be happy to show you, but I don't know the combination."

In fact, the safe was "acquired" the same way.

"I found an empty one that was locked," Smith recalled. "We brought a forklift over, ran it up to the hangar, and took it out." Later he called the official base channel. "I said we had a safe, number such-and-such in our custody, and would they come out and change the combination."

"They came out but they wanted to know where the custody card was. I said, 'Well, shit, I don't know where that is. I guess that's another thing the commander forgot to tell me about. He could have saved me so much work. He just said do it.'... I said, 'Can't you guys just make one up for me? I'm just a junior lieutenant. . . .' "

So they made up an official custody card, did all the paperwork for him, and gave him a safe that he'd stolen.

As Pedersen said of Smith, "Just wind him up and let him go. . . ."

Smith, at age 27, was capable of a variety of demeanors, depending on the situation. If a senior officer gave him a hard time, he'd get tough, acting as if "I knew exactly what I wanted and it'd be his ass if I didn't get it." If a civilian or junior officer interfered, he'd take the opposite tack, telling them he was just a junior officer following orders. "Whatever was needed to get the job done," Smith declared.

☆ ☆ ☆

In December of 1967, John Nash had been asked to help the Navy deploy the new F-111 fighter-bomber in a secret program code-named "Harvest Reaper." While top Navy brass didn't like the plane, which was being forced on them by Secretary of Defense Robert McNamara, as far as the rest of the Navy was concerned the airplane was coming aboard in the near future, and a cadre of pilots had to be trained to fly it.

Already having used up his two allotted combat cruises, this was a way for Nash to get back in the fighting. Unfortunately, during a routine landing, a malfunction of the fuel transfer system pooled most of the plane's gas in its aft section and weighed down the tail. The plane bucked out of control 100 feet above the runway. When it started to rear over on its back, Nash had no choice but to call eject. He realized he and his co-pilot, who would come out together in a capsule, would probably be shot into the runway, but a crash was imminent.

Luckily, the force of the ejection charge righted the plane, and both men were shot straight up, and the capsule's chute opened just before it hit ground. As a result, Nash broke several vertebrae in his back and ended up strapped to a board in the hospital. The crash automatically eliminated him from the F-111 program, and he was ordered grounded for almost a year, which was the mandatory period for such an injury.

In November 1968, just as the Navy Fighter Weapons School was getting off the ground, Nash, who had faked recovery, was flying again, but in a bombing squadron at Nellis' Fighter Weapons School. Wanting to get back into fighters, he pulled some strings with friends back in Washington and returned to Miramar.

With the bombing experience at Nellis, Nash was assigned to take over 121's air-to-ground syllabus. Pedersen brought him in to do the same in the new Fighter Weapons School.

Nash was skeptical about the fledgling school. "My question was, 'How are we going to teach these guys everything in thirty days?' We didn't have any airplane assets . . . we were depending on [VF] 126 [the instrument RAG, which had A-4 Skyhawks, which the school would use as MiG-simulators] to provide bogeys. . . . I was certainly skeptical of what the response in the squadrons was going to be."

The virtually unknown school not only had to ask squadron commanders to send their best pilots to a trailer in Miramar for four weeks to attend the new school, but they also had to request that the pilots bring their own planes.

"Nobody had ever heard of us," Nash recalled. "What was the incentive?"

Although he liked bombing, Nash was also upset that he wasn't teaching ACM at the school. "The guys who were instructing it weren't any better than I was, maybe not as good. But I was the only guy that could explain air-to-ground theory."

But he was also scheduled to fly adversary, which gave him a chance to vent his frustration. "My main concern was that we turn out good students," Nash said. "We all knew that we might be flying combat with any one of the students in a very short time." Therefore, he had accepted the role that Pedersen had assigned to him. He also had to accept a new call sign: "Smash!"

☆ CHAPTER 13 ☆

Pedersen and the other instructors split the trailer into two sections. One section was a large room for classes; the other section was for offices. Pedersen and Smith became its only permanent residents. The classroom had a chalk board, a movie screen, tables, and several rows of student chairs. As Pedersen remembers, the furnishings were spartan at best. "Everything was at least 20 years old and was cast off from other squadrons."

The one convenience was a portable coffee maker. They still didn't have a typewriter, but at least they were near the flight line.

In those first few weeks, they all read the Ault findings, pouring over them into the night. "You wanted to make sure you understood what the task of the school was supposed to be," says Pedersen.

One of their first major meetings concerned implementation of the findings. They came up with three basic thrusts for the school, which they thought would make an immediate impact on pilot training.

"The majority of us agreed that we had to start flying the airplane better and differently than we previously had in training," says Pedersen.

In the hands of aggressive fighter pilots, the Phantom had proved to be more than a pretty good machine. It had great power and thrust; it could out climb anything the enemy had, which was an ability that could be used to maneuver for a shot or (if necessary) escape. At high speeds, those exceeding 450 to 500 knots, it could even probably turn horizontally with the MiGs.

But most Phantom pilots were either ignorant or afraid of these capabilities. They'd been told the plane was primarily an interceptor, that it hadn't been built for what pilots like Holmes and Nash were routinely doing with it.

McDonnell Douglas' representatives were already complaining that the increased dogfighting at the RAG would cause premature stress. Such training was too dangerous, they said. People were going to die!

In fact, there *had* been an increase in minor breakdowns and tears. Nash and Holmes (among others) had lost slats and bent wings. But there had been no serious damage; the Phantom, they'd discovered, was a bruiser.

They finally decided to write down and formally codify what they'd been doing in the plane in order to determine the how's and why's and aerodynamics behind their techniques. In that way they could explain what they were saying in the classroom, as well as in their aerial demonstrations. That would pave the way for ACM as policy, they hoped, thereby silencing any critics.

Right now, their techniques were a secret art. A pilot might talk about them in the bar or be dazzled by them in a chance fight. But few really understood them. Most were just part of each good pilot's bag of tricks. If they were taught, they were taught only to those students or wingmen lucky enough to get instructors or flight leaders who knew them, and were willing and able to demonstrate them.

"We'd all experimented," says Pedersen, "but it hadn't become doctrine."

Now they'd make it doctrine. They'd interview the aces, the engineers, and the hot fighter "jocks" in every service. Their syllabus would become the bible for transforming the Phantom into a full-fledged fighter plane, thus refuting the naysaying "demon drivers" who'd been trained on intercept. Out of the new generation of pilots (i.e., the more malleable ones), they'd create pilots capable of fighting the MiG.

But flying the plane to its limits and defining, and explaining the Phantom's abilities aerodynamically was only part of the preparation necessary to win in North Vietnam. They also had to get the book on the enemy; they had to gather more intelligence on the MiG and the MiG pilots until they knew both as well as they knew themselves.

"A true professional finds out his enemy's weaknesses and exploits them," says Pedersen.

But such information wasn't available on the MiG. Even the RAG's training emphasized Phantom against Phantom. They needed more intelligence on the MiG. They needed planes with MiG-like qualities to train against.

Finally, they needed to take the Phantom's strengths and the enemy's weaknesses and create new tactics that would ensure victory. This was the bottom line. "In a real dogfight," as their successors (future Top Gun instructors) would become fond of saying, "there are no points for second place." This last task would entail not only new ACM tactics, but also new radar tactics.

"How do you dogfight on your back at 180 knots with the radar pointed at the ground?" posed Pedersen. In that position, the radar picks up ground clutter. "How do you use radar in close that was designed to be used essentially straight and level against a distant bomber?"

Pedersen's answer was to bring in the best scope people he then had at the RAG, including Jim Laing and later Darrell Gary, and have them write the syllabus. Although Laing and Gary were the youngest RIO instructors at the RAG, they had the most combat experience of the group.

In particular, the pilots needed to improve early bogey sighting and identification techniques, and ensure that their planes were ready to dogfight—to be "offensive," as they called it—as soon as they entered the arena. The instructors needed to heighten pilot-RIO teamwork or, "crew coordination," as Pedersen called it.

"It is not simple. . . ." said Pedersen. "The guy in the backseat is running the radar and he's got to talk . . . what we call 'talk your eyes into the bogey.' Once you see him, then the pilot never takes his eyes off . . . then you maneuver physically to bring your weapons to bear."

Two heads (and two sets of eyes) were better than one; they generally all agreed. And four, they reasoned, were better than two, as in a two-plane loose-deuce formation.

These were the advantages they wanted to develop. But it would require work.

☆ ☆ ☆

The coordination between crew members particularly needed work. In 1965, when J. C. Smith and Lou Page had gotten the first confirmed MiG kills of the war, the Navy was originally going to award Silver Stars only to the pilots in the engagement. Though Smith had found the bogeys and directed the intercept, he was to get a lesser ranking Distinguished Flying Cross. The decision reflected the second-class stature of backseaters at the time.

J. C. balked, "I told my CO 'You can take these wings and shove 'em up your ass. I won't fly another mission.' . . . It was ridiculous. . . . I wasn't going to accept it [the lesser award]. It would set a precedent . . . . "

The Secretary of the Navy happened to be on the *Midway* at the time, and there was a quick reversal of the decision. The Navy didn't need one of its first bonafide air heroes resigning. Smith received a Silver Star as well. But the policy continued. Now J. C., who had been reassigned to the RAG, would be instrumental in breaking down the distinction between pilots and RIOs.

As a RIO, he was brazenly confident. Gary remembers him calling a "Judy"—claiming contact with a practice bogey they were looking for and thereby relinquishing the help of a ground controller—miles before the bogey could have been in range.

"But we didn't know that. We were just JOs [junior officers] and figured it was some of his magic," Gary recalls.

Laing remembers "He [Smith] came in and said he could fly better than any of the pilots."

According to Darrell Gary, J. C. Smith had said " 'Pilots got their heads up their ass. You gotta tell 'em which way to go, when to turn.' It rubbed off on the other RIOs. He made you feel good about yourself and your capabilities."

Mel Holmes called Smith one of a kind, a jester, and a magician. He was an incessant talker in flight who sometimes drove pilots crazy, according to Pedersen, but he was also an "Iceman" when things got rough. "I've seen him stay calm in a spin," recalled Pedersen, "telling a kid what to do when there were only seconds left."

Smith received most of the problem students at the school. "If he couldn't help them, nobody could," remembered Pedersen. "Have you any idea what kind of guts it takes to get in the back seat with an inexperienced pilot who's about to be washed out?"

☆ ☆ ☆

One of Smith's first contributions was helping to collect information on the enemy. Traveling in civilian clothes on commercial airliners, he and Pedersen flew to Washington to begin their search at Naval Intelligence at the Pentagon.

One connection led to another as they explained why they needed the information. "It wasn't like going up and talking to CNO. CNO's a piece of cake to talk to. The President would have been a piece of cake to talk to. [But] we needed to talk to somebody that knew more than the President or CNO. . . ."

Smith and Pedersen finally hit the jackpot in the bowels of the CIA. They found boxes of first-hand, heavily guarded information about MiGs, such as specific speeds in maneuvers, ratios, turn rates, and armament.

At first they weren't allowed to take notes, so they'd emerge from sessions with the material and rush to record from memory transcribed conversations that sometimes lasted as long as three hours.

It wasn't long before they were making periodic flights back to Miramar with suitcases full of material, worrying (from a security standpoint) about a plane crash and about their notes being scattered on a public hillside and being lost to the pilots at the school who needed them.

The other instructors at the school were gathering information too. Holmes spent hours talking to fighter pilots in officer club bars and ready rooms, as did Ruliffson. They read everything that they could find in the base libraries, and they visited other commands. Steve Smith unsuccessfully attempted to get action reports of MiG battles from the fleet.

The School's stolen safe was soon bulging with material. The research, however, was time consuming; although they needed the information, the time that they had spent accumulating it had decreased their flight time, thus further cramping their double-duty work schedules. In addition, without proper clearances (which would take time to get) they were being denied access to certain restricted files.

One day it occurred to them that they needed a security-cleared intelligence officer.

Intelligence officers were hard to find at Miramar, especially those in air intelligence. "Air" denoted recent experience with fleet squadrons off North Vietnam, which the school wanted. Finally, someone suggested Chuck Hildebrand. Hildebrand was unhappy with his job as communications officer of a Miramar-based, photo-reconnaissance squadron. Still, when Steve Smith called, Hildebrand expressed bewilderment over what the Fighter Weapons School was.

Smith, who'd spent considerable time checking on Hildebrand, had been told by those who knew the young Wausau, Wisconsin, native that he was both versatile and imaginative. He told Hildebrand what little he could about the school. Hildebrand was interested, but asked, "How can you get me orders? I'm already assigned here?"

Smith, in fact, didn't know. In the Navy, junior officers seldom (if ever) saw quick reassignment, except in combat. "I wasn't high enough to know the priorities we were getting. . . . I didn't know that somebody senior to anybody on the entire base at Miramar; somebody in the Pentagon could get that man permanent change of station, bang, just like that."

Bluffing, he told Hildebrand, " 'I'm assured it will happen if it's what you want and it's what we want' and I'm sitting there thinking, 'This guy's really buying this shit.' "

Smith decided to meet Hildebrand. The two hit it off better than he'd expected. A former economics major in college, Hildebrand, like Smith, had worked in banks before joining the Navy at the height of the draft. Like Smith, he'd wanted the adventure and applied to fly, but poor eyesight had channeled him into intelligence. He'd spent two cruises as VF-51's air intelligence officer (AI) aboard the *Bon Homme Richard*. The VF-51 squadron was made up of F-8s and had its share of MiG killers.

Smith remembered Hildebrand had told him "Well, you know, I'm TAD [on temporarily assigned duty] here, and have to be replaced. . . . It'll take time." Smith asked him, "Can you check in as soon as you get your orders? Will that simplify it for you? Can you be here the next day?" Hildebrand told him "Sure." Smith, of course, had his fingers crossed, not knowing whether or not he was going to be able to get Hildebrand transfered. Nonetheless, Smith told Hildebrand, "Fine, I'll be back in touch with you and let you know how it looks this afternoon."

Smith knew that pilfering a building was one thing, but nabbing an air intelligence officer with a top secret clearance was another.

Early on, Pedersen had given Smith a contact to use if necessary. The contact was Pete Kellaway, the number two man on CAG Phil Craven's staff. All the squadrons at Miramar reported to Craven, and unknown to Smith, Craven had deputy chief naval officer aide Merle Gorder in Washington supporting him.

Smith phoned Kellaway and explained the problem. Kellaway put Smith on hold while he went to talk to Craven. When he came back, he said, "We'll take care of it."

About an hour later he got a phone call from Hildebrand.

"How'd you do it?" Hildebrand asked.

"What do you mean?"

"You told me to check in right after I got my orders, right?"

"Right."

"I got 'em."

Suddenly, in the pause that hid his surprise, Smith realized the clout that was behind the Fighter Weapons School. "All I have to do is pick up the phone and anyone giving me shit disappears," he thought to himself. "This is going to be fun. You can steal but you can't go to jail. . . ."

☆ ☆ ☆

Hildebrand reported to the school's trailer in February 1969. Technically, he was assigned to 121, but actually he was full-time at the school.

"I suppose I was a little intimidated by this group," Hildebrand remembers. "They tended to treat you differently. . . . They were always willing to work on your weak points and try to find some way to bug you, which is what they should be doing as aviators—always looking to exploit weak points. . . ."

Hildebrand began taking the trips to Washington and Nellis, and he finally got the after-action reports on recent MiG engagements. These were the debriefs taken from fleet crews right after their fights. With them, as well as with other things he got from vaults in Washington and elsewhere, he was able to prepare the school's first "threat lectures," which were briefs he gave to the instructors about who and what they were up against.

"We had a section that dealt with Soviet air tactics, tried to compare and contrast their methods of fighting in the air with ours, which was very different. Their style was very structured. They basically controlled the situation back at headquarters . . . the tactics were set and dictated to the pilots by what they could see from a radar picture. They told their pilots what they should do, what directions and headings they should take."

Soviet tactics had changed little since World War II. They built short-range air superiority fighters to protect their homeland. The North Vietnamese used the Soviet equipment and had Soviet advisors, some of whom flew their planes, "so their tactics were basically structured along Soviet lines." The North Vietnamese pilots trained in China, Russia, or in Soviet satellite countries.

Hildebrand found out that the enemy trained approximately the same length of time as U. S. Navy pilots. "They [the Soviets] would practice a particular type of routine over and over again. . . . If we could disrupt that routine we could disrupt their ability to cope," Hildebrand said.

The enemy pilots had gotten better as the war had progressed. Before, they would only shoot and run, but by mid-1967, they were challenging more by flying close to the ground, where terrain would prevent incoming U. S. plane radars from seeing them. Then they'd "pop up" behind the American flights, going for tail shots and "working on a 30-degree cone off our tail," according to intelligence reports.

The school compiled dossiers on individual enemy pilots. "We had pictures of some of them," remembers Darrell Gary.

The North Vietnamese had formed their Air Force in 1955 after they defeated the French and left Indochina. But the North Vietnamese Air Force was slow to develop. The first operational unit wasn't formed until American airpower threatened them in 1964. The enemy air force was comprised mostly of farmers and ground soldiers picked for special abilities.

In May 1966, Nguyen Van Bay, who'd joined the North Vietnamese Air Force's 2nd Company at age 28, became the first ace of the war. He was credited with seven victories, including two F-4s (probably Air Force), a Navy F-8, and an Air Force F-105 Thunderchief.

North Vietnamese magazines celebrated their pilots. An article in *Vietnam* (No. 109, 1966) included the following quote: "I could see the U. S. pilot in his cockpit. He looked scared. His light grey headgear turned left and right as if he was calling for help. But his companions had long forsaken him. He made evasive maneuvers to dodge my fire. . . . I clenched my teeth and blazed away with my cannon into the cockpit of the enemy plane. It exploded and plummeted to the ground, leaving a trail of black smoke."

By 1969, North Vietnam claimed several more aces, among them Captain Nguyen Van Coc, also of the 2nd Company, who had six victories. *Vietnam* (Nos. 136-146, 1969), said of Coc: "He hits the enemy with the speed of lightning, [and] together with his comrades . . . adds splendor to their flag, which bears the inscription: 'Attack and win!' "

The most infamous and (as later events would prove) perhaps the most obscure North Vietnamese pilot was Colonel Nguyen Toon, also known as "Tomb." Some believe Toon was actually Van Bay. Others believe he never existed and was made up by America or North Vietnam for their own purposes.

But pilots remember hearing about Toon back in the early part of the war. Holmes, for instance, believes that Toon was the MiG pilot who shot down an American helicopter in the Mu Gia Pass, which was an important supply route from Laos.

He was a "legend when I got there in '69," says Rich Haver, deputy director of Naval Intelligence in 1985, who was also a young airborne enemy listener back in those days. "A hot dog—quiet when he took off. He just used [radio] clicks . . . then he'd talk it up when he came back."

Holmes believes that Toon was trained in North Korea. Haver believes Toon was trained in China. Toon, like most of the good enemy pilots, flew both the MiG-17 and the MiG-21.

The '17—code-named "Fresco" by NATO—was the best plane at turning. Its 37-foot, 11,000-pound body was about half the length of the Phantom, and one-third its weight. It had two 23mm and 37mm nose cannons accompanied by rockets and/or heat-seeking Atolls. It wasn't very fast (not even supersonic), and it had poor rearward visibility. But its light weight and superior wing loading made it extremely maneuverable. It was an aerial "hot rod," as some called it. Its small size made it hard to see, except when it was up close and already had the advantage. Conversely, the Phantom was easier to see at a distance and emitted black smoke, except when it was in minimum afterburner. Because of its black smoke, the Phantom could be seen 20 miles away.

The MiG-21—code named "Fishbed" —was faster than the Fresco. It could exceed 1,380 miles per hour in optimum conditions. It was approximately 50-feet long and weighed 17,000 pounds; therefore the single-seat, delta-winged jet was larger than the 17, but couldn't turn as well. Consequently, it mostly used hit-and-run tactics.

Similar to the F-8, the MiG 21 carried Atolls and sometimes cannons. It had poor rearward visibility, but its small, pointed frontal area made it hard to see and it didn't smoke.

According to Hildebrand, the '21 pilots "were basically trying to set up the six o'clock shot . . . they did a lot of tight maneuvers, things of that nature. . . . And so we tried to give [our pilots] some idea of what their capabilities were so they could basically develop their tactics to exploit them.

"If you can break up their repeated patterns," Hildebrand counciled the school instructors, "it will confuse them." The school concentrated on the less rigid, but more successful tactics of the North Vietnamese aces. "We felt that if we could beat their best," said Pedersen, "we could beat any of them."

But Pedersen and the others became increasingly dissatisfied with second-hand reports and technical intelligence. They were professionals teaching other pilots who would eventually find themselves in "must-win" situations. Accordingly, they wanted the real thing.

☆ CHAPTER 14 ☆

In February 1969, *Aviation Week and Space Technology*, the aerospace news magazine, ran a brief in its "Industry Observer" column that quickly became the hottest topic of conversation in the Miramar trailer, especially when its doors were closed and its occupants were assured of secrecy.

The item from the February 17 issue reported that a Soviet MiG-21 fighter "was secretly brought to the U. S. last spring and flight tested by USAF pilots to learn first-hand its capabilities and design characteristics. The aircraft, which engaged in simulated combat against U. S. fighters, was highly regarded by the pilots who flew it. The evaluation was part of a broad effort by USAF to detail the threat of Soviet air power in planning new aircraft, such as the F-15 fighter."

Because Cassidy and Doc Townsend had been flying a MiG-21, the school had already known of its existence, as well of the Air Force's possession of some MiG-17s. But the instructors were incredulous about seeing the information in *Aviation Week and Space Technology*. The existence of the MiGs was so secret that they had been told that if any of them leaked the information, that person would "disappear."

Eventually, *Aviation Week* ran a large photo of an Air Force MiG-21 with a U. S. insignia on its fuselage, along with speculation about where it might have come from. (By the 1980s it was common knowledge among insiders that the Air Force from its base at Nellis, Nevada, had an entire unit of MiGs that it practiced against.)

☆ ☆ ☆

Foster S. "Tooter" Teague was due to report to the Naval War College 3000 miles away at Newport, R. I. The big, gregarious former Texas A&M tackle was watching the movers pack his furnishings when he got a call from Dick Miller, aviation command detailer. Miller said, "Hey, we are not going to move you to the East Coast. You're going to VX-4. . . ."

Teague sensed catastrophe. "Dick. As we speak, the people are carrying boxes to the truck. . . . I got my orders in hand. . . . I sold my house!"

Teague didn't want to go to Point Mugu. He'd just been through two combat cruises and had courageously escaped almost certain death in a savage carrier fire while trapped with 13 others deep in the ship's hull. "I wanted to go wear sweaters like the rest of the guys," remarked Teague.

Miller telephoned Teague back. "Look," said Miller, "this is the way it comes down. You can have your choice of living anywhere you want on the West Coast. But you're going to VX-4. These are special orders. That's all I can tell you. . . . It's out of my hands."

As a career naval officer, Teague had no choice. He went to Point Mugu.

At Point Mugu security was tight. When Teague arrived, he had no idea that they had a MiG. They only told him they were going to send him into the desert for 200 days. "I said, 'Guys, I just came back from back-to-back cruises. It's been too long. My wife ain't going to put up with this.' "

Born in Bossier City, Louisiana, Teague was a typical war novel fighter pilot. He was two-fisted, action-oriented, and a charmer and a gambler. He'd played football for Paul "Bear" Bryant, and he had Bryant's same persuasive personality.

"The son-of-a-bitch [Teague] could sell anything," recalled Jim Foster, who was soon to be Teague's boss at VX-4. Foster, a former F-8 commander attached to naval headquarters at Norfolk, Virginia, was helping both VX-4 with its special projects and the Navy Fighter Weapons School get started. He wanted Teague to use his special talents to help the Navy get MiGs from the Air Force.

"Normally it would be an Air Force thing to exploit the MiG," said Foster, "but Tooter and his guys had a written test plan. . . . They said, 'If I had it, this is what I'd do with it.' It was typed, drawn and bound. . . . At the first meeting, we laid down the plan. Hell, the Air Force was just getting started. . . ."

Foster, whose last job before arriving at Norfolk had been air boss (traffic manager on all the launches and recoveries) on the *Bon Homme Richard*, had been among the flight leaders in the early part of the war who had seen the F-4 problem coming. "If we'd just had to fight MiGs in the F-8, there wouldn't have been a problem," Foster recalled. "But we had to fight in the F-4 too. . . . That caused a bunch of us to really get interested. And, of course, one of the big things was to try and get some MiGs."

Foster had been instrumental in the acquisition of the MiG. In April 1969, he relieved Nello Pierozzi, a former Blue Angel, as skipper of VX-4, and shortly thereafter he was on his way into the desert for his first look at the "assets."

Taken to the hidden location, Foster was admitted into a huge, lighted hangar. "I was absolutely amazed," says Foster. Not so much at the airplanes, which he knew a lot about, but at the secret site.

"The airplanes were fascinating. . . . But the kids had briefed me very well. Tom [Cassidy] had spent a lot of time with me. I had to review all of his reports [when he had been in Norfolk], so I was pretty much up to speed."

Foster's first flight was in a MiG-17, which was a gleaming silver plane in which "everything was written in Russian. The only thing that was a problem for me was taxiing," Foster said, "and [Tom] had told me it would be. It was just unnatural. . . ."

The MiGs had less sophisticated control systems than the Phantom. The controls were operated with compressed air, while the Phantom used hydraulic fluid. To steer the Phantom on the ground, the pilot pushed on the rudder pedals. This didn't work in the '17. Foster had to thumb a little "paddle" valve on the stick to maneuver for takeoff.

"You screw up a little bit . . . wander around a little bit," said Foster. "You stop. Now what the hell do I do? Of course, you got a chase guy sitting right behind you in an [F-4] talking to you. . . . I finally found the runway, which is quite an interesting process. Didn't know where it was. Couldn't see it."

Finally, Foster was ready to take off. One of the officers climbed up on his wing and gave him last-minute instructions. He lifted off nicely.

"I was kind of worried about keeping lined up on the runway with this crazy air paddle . . . but it just lifted into the air like a T-33 . . . felt like one too, you know, the old, lumbering 'Shooting Star.' And flew like it. It had a stick extender that tickled the hell out of me . . . up a little above and between your legs. Fairly comfortable. But if you really wanted to pull on it, push a button and the stick telescopes up. . . . They would put their feet up on the instrument panel and just pull the hell out of it."

The whole approach to steering in the MiGs was less advanced than the Phantoms. Rods and pushrods operated the rudder and flaps. "I don't think we'd build an airplane like they do because the safety factor isn't there. Shitty construction. . . . But the finesse in their airplanes was years ahead of ours. . . . Here's a MiG-21 [which he also flew] that flies at Mach 2 and it has rivets [wind-resisting bolts] sticking out on its outer skin. Using air, instead of heavier hydraulic fluid, greatly reduced its weight."

He was amazed at how easy the 21 flew. "I hit the burner and I didn't feel any thrust. . . . You only got a couple hundred pounds of thrust out of the damn thing. . . . Stoke the burners on the F-4 and you're pouring fuel like a firehose with two guys holding. [Next to the MiGs,] the Phantom was like a 'goddamn barn door in the air.' You survived because of its two fuel-guzzling engines."

While Foster flew the MiGs, he was primarily there to supervise. VX-4's mission was to test the MiGs and discover ways to exploit them in combat situations, as Cassidy had already been doing under "Doughnut." Cassidy had made a film of the '21, which he was allowed to show to selected people in the fleet. However, Foster felt the MiGs were going to have to get more exposure if they were going to do American pilots any good. "My contribution in this whole business was primarily one of salesmanship," said Foster. He "sold" what they came up with to Washington. Most of the actual experimentation under "Drill" (the code name for the new project) was conducted by a small group of Navy and Air Force pilots under Teague and VX-4's resident test pilot, Ronald "Mugs" McKeown.

McKeown was another rising Navy star who, like Teague, had been raised and had played football in the Southwest; namely, Ysleta in El Paso, Texas. A Naval Academy graduate, he'd played fullback on the 1961 Navy team that had featured All-American Joe Bellino and had gone to the Orange Bowl.

Following two combat cruises as an F-8 pilot, McKeown had been assigned to Edwards AFB for astronaut school. "It was the follow-up Apollo Program where they were going to shoot a shot a month to the moon," said McKeown. (He was only one of two selected from the Navy, but they ran out of money.) "Then I was going to go into the X-15 program and they cancelled that too. . . . I said 'God just doesn't want me to go into outer space, I guess.' So then they said, 'Well, do you want to go to Pax River or VX-4?' I said, 'Well, I guess I'd like to go to Pax River and do some testing.' And then Nello Pierozzi came in and talked to me and told me about the programs they had at VX-4."

At VX-4, McKeown was made Air-to-Air Project officer, Sparrow Project officer, and manager for the rewrite of the F-4 tactical manual.

☆ ☆ ☆

Over the next few months, Teague, McKeown, and the others compiled hundreds of hours in the MiGs. "It was an amazing airplane," says Teague of the '17. "We flew it 255 times with no downs." It was simple and cheap, nothing like the expensive machines America had.

But "if a nut had backed off a gauge, the pilot would be eating a thousand pounds of something. . . . To lower the [landing] gear on that little beast you had to lift the toggle switch, turn a pump on, wait till the pressure builds up, put the gear handle down, and then the landing gear locked. You had to turn the pump off and recover it with the toggle switch. In our airplanes you just flipped a little button."

But pilots are supposed to be well trained, according to Teague, so he thought the '17's frugal simplicity was beautiful. "They had a little bitty pump, not as big as a grapefruit, and it ran the flaps and gear for taking off and landing. . . . And you could get a re-light [of the engine] at 42,000 feet because you had a little compressed air cylinder on the front of the engine, not quite as big as a volleyball. It was full of pressurized air. . . . Flame out at 40,000 feet, pull this toggle switch, and it literally pulled the valve open. I mean there were no electronics there . . . nothing complicated . . . just flooded your engine with oxygen and you'd get a re-light. . . ."

In the air, the '17 turned better than any airplane Teague had ever flown. He would tell opposing pilots that he was about to fight, "Okay, I'm going to start you at my six and you won't win this fight. . . . You roll in and you call when you're tracking and that's when the fight starts. . . . It was a standard joke. . . . The plane flies perfectly well at 100 knots, you know. So you could do a little trick and he'd be out in front of you so quick he couldn't believe it. . . ."

But the constant experimentation also began to reveal weaknesses in the MiGs. Because of its elementary control system, the MiG-17 would lock up at high speeds.

"We found out very quickly," remembered Teague, "that the MiG ['17] goes out of control at 450 knots. . . . He [the 17] locks up at about 425 and he goes absolutely left wing down . . . his wing warps. . . . So if he goes 500 knots he's out of control. He's in a left wing roll and can't do anything about it. So just do 500 knots and it becomes only a question of eyes. Keeping the guy in sight and keeping fast. . . ."

Fighting the '17 in a Phantom, according to McKeown, "was like being a giant with a long rifle trapped in a phone booth with a midget using a knife. That's really the way you found yourself. . . . You wouldn't let him [the enemy] get in where he could cut your guts out. You had to push him hard . . . drive him around the sky. But the big secret was to preserve your separation—approximately a mile and a half—so that you were always out of his weapons range and within your own."

They found out the MiGs couldn't roll with the Phantom, which led the school to devise a special defense: If a MiG was on your tail, the Phantom pilot would feint a roll to one side, and then jerk the plane back to the other side. As the MiG tried to follow, the Phantom, with its better roll rate and greater power, would increase the separation between the two planes, extending with each roll, until it was far away enough to turn and come back into the fight.

"It was counter to a lot of classic fighter doctrine," says McKeown. "The F-4 had such thrust advantage that in thirty seconds or so you'd be out of [the enemy's] gun solution."

For those situations in which barrel rolling didn't work, McKeown devised a maneuver called the "bug out." This involved wrenching the Phantom away at an angle perpendicular to the MiG's line of flight (and hopefully his belly) and giving it full throttle. If that failed, McKeown would deliberately "depart" the plane (take it outside its flight envelope) as a last resort maneuver.

"If you want to slow [the plane] down for some reason, you want this guy to overshoot . . . you want to go from 450 knots to 90 knots as fast as you can . . . don't pussy foot it . . . Depart it."

He'd jam the stick forward, whip it back, then jam it forward again, "which would get you through about one, one and a half, negative Gs. Then pull it [the stick] as hard as you could and reverse rudder. At that point you could generate enough yaw rate and the airplane would float."

At that point the other plane's momentum would carry him [the enemy] past McKeown, and he would be overshot—out in front of the Phantom like a sitting duck.

"Nothing slows you faster than that. . . . You want to throw such a move on him that the minute he sees it, he's gone. . . . But you've still got a problem, you're not out of the woods yet. . . . You've got to get your energy back . . . accelerate. . . ."

Another technique taught by the school was turning. In order to turn with the MiGs, the school instructors advocated "lag pursuit" —staying to the rear and outside of the opposing MiG. Instead of trying to turn inside the MiG's turn (which they couldn't do), the pilot would slide to the outside. Phantom pilots would fly faster and use their larger turn rate to stay behind the MiG and push his smaller radius. The pilot could actually turn with the MiG and gain speed until he had enough to target a missile on him and get a shot.

"Lag pursuit," as a result, became a big buzz word.

"In any endeavor," recalls Foster, "there is a place where you cross the bar; where you find the confidence that now you are a pro;

that you can do that which is expected of you. . . . It happens with carrier pilots. When you first brief them in practice on the field, they're tentative. They may be the hottest jocks in the world, but there is something inside them that says, 'You're playing in an area where, buddy, you can bust your ass.'. . . But as you go along and finally get them on the boat a few times, maybe just five or six . . . you can tell. . . . the bravado goes. . . . It's still there but it's not being flaunted any more. . . . He is now able to go forth in the world and do his duty."

Foster had a group of pros to work with, and he and Dan Pedersen at the Fighter Weapons School were soon to combine forces.

☆ CHAPTER 15 ☆

At Miramar the pressure on Dan Pedersen and the Fighter Weapons School instructors mounted as the opening of the school approached. Though working relentlessly, they had still not finished the syllabus. Part of their problem was splitting their time between teaching students in 121 and putting together the school. Everyone had at least two hops a day with 121 students, "and in the meantime," remembers Steve Smith, "they've got 16 hours of writing to do. It took a lot of research and thinking through. Then they had to wait for a two-fingered typist to return drafts. Stuff like that. . . . And I'm going back and forth saying, 'Keep writing.'. . . You don't have an index. References. Bibliography. . . . You don't have pictures or art for the cover, or each chapter. . . ."

The course had to be professional: "Graduate level," says Pedersen. "That was the key word."

Smith said, "We just kept taking it apart to see what we didn't have and what we needed. John [Nash] comes in with two or three chapters on air-to-ground. . . . And the next thing, Mel discovers that he doesn't have just two phases on tactics—he's got *four*. . . . You hear it in the bar and it's an evening's talk. But put it down on paper and it becomes four separate courses."

Yet, they still didn't have the first class registered.

"Dan resolved who the students would be with the CAG," said Smith. Two squadrons—one from the East Coast and one from the West Coast—would provide two crews and airplanes each, and they were going to be here on March 9, or whatever day it was [it was actually March 3]. . . . I'm supposed to coordinate it. . . . Very quickly I've got two commanders on hold each saying, 'Fuck you.'

They don't like this. They don't want their guys coming. They are saying, 'Who are you? What are you?' "

"The rest of the Navy didn't know we existed," remembers Pedersen. "These skippers and their pilots and RIOs are saying 'who the hell do you think you are? We're gonna stop our operations and just come out there . . . ?' "

Smith tried restating the purpose of the school in order to negotiate. When he hung up with the West Coast commander, he called the squadron's executive officer, whom he knew, and briefed him, "so that when the skipper says, 'Get the Ops officer in here, I want to know about this goddamn school,' " he'd be familiar with it. In the end, however, Navy brass had to order the commander to send his two squadrons to the school. Having friends in high places saved the school once again.

The East Coast commander, too, gave Smith a difficult time. Smith couldn't persuade the commander about the importance of the school over the telephone. Smith called the squadron CAG and asked for the operations officer. "I asked their Ops officer if he was aware of what was going on on the West Coast—Fighter Weapons School and all that. I laid the whole bag of shit on him. . . . I wanted to let him know that he should brief his air wing commander on it. Lots of stuff coming down. Graduate level school. If they were lucky enough to get chosen, they'd get to do this; but probably because they're East Coast pukes and didn't have any [war experience] we wouldn't take 'em. You really needed war experience. It was a real badge."

The ploy worked. "By the time the Ops officer said 'You two crews take airplanes and go to San Diego,' he had a major morale problem on his hands. I mean they were going to kill to get to go. And they weren't going to cancel. . . . Once you've got them thinking this is special, you've got to beat them back with a stick."

☆ ☆ ☆

Jerry Sawatzky joined the Fighter Weapons School as an instructor in early 1969. After returning to duty following the fire on the *Forrestal*, he was assigned as a flight leader to 121 at Miramar. His job as flight leader was to shepherd a class of students through their training, to make their schedules; and to be a coach, guide, and mentor to them. But he wasn't getting in much ACM. The low point came when he got beaten in a practice fight by a flight surgeon. In the little spare time he had, Sawatzky began to fly with the tactics instructors of the future Fighter Weapons School to hone his skills. He began by listening to the briefs and getting a feel for what was going on.

On his own time, he got checked out in the TA-4, then started riding in the backseat on adversary flights, "getting familiar with handling radios and not just watching the guy in front," he called it.

He also watched the F-4s.

Eventually, they let Sawatzky fly in the front seat, and soon he was flying bogey to the tactics instructors when they wanted to try out a new maneuver. Vern Jumper remembers Sawatzky showing him a move he'd never seen in the TA-4.

"He [Sawatzky] was checking me out as an adversary. . . . I hadn't been used to moving the [T]A-4 around like that because it was an instrument plane. . . . We got up there and he showed me some outside rolls to [keep] nose-to-tail [separation]. . . . Let's say [the bogey's] pulling hard to the left and you're closing at about 400 knots and you see you're going to overshoot. You barrel roll to the right and go outside in a real high, nose-high, high-G barrel roll. [This] eats up your airspeed and opens up the nose-to-tail distance real quickly. . . . Then you turn back into him [the enemy]. Really neat maneuver. . . . I thought, 'God, that's impressive.' "

Sawatzky then graduated to the F-4, which was a much more difficult plane to fly. One day, in a hard-fought dogfight, he beat John Nash.

They met head-on at about 15,000 feet, "and then we just got after it," Sawatzky recalled. It was a high-G fight and got very fast, very slow, straight up, straight down. . . . I remember John calling me one time—I was steeply nose-down and my wings were rocking quite badly and we were at 6,000 feet, maybe a little lower [rapidly closing with the ground]. I remember him telling me 'Watch it!' and I told him something like, 'It's all right, I got it . . . .' We finally started to get low on gas and knocked it off. I think it came out a draw. . . . I was just happy to do well. . . ."

As a result, "Ski," as Sawatzky was called, was asked to join the school's staff. By early 1969, he, along with the rest of the instructors, was awaiting the impending arrival of its first class.

☆ ☆ ☆

The syllabus was finally taking shape. The staff had outlined a four-week course: three weeks of air-to-air maneuvers, and one week of "air-to-mud," a bombing segment, which Holmes and Ruliffson, among others, opposed but could do little about.

Early in the preparations, Ruliffson realized he needed to know more about how the Sparrow missile worked. Raytheon engineers had come to Miramar to lecture on the homing missile but, according to Ruliffson never were to be able to make the transition from how the missile worked electronically to how the pilots needed to use them tactically. It was up to Ruliffson to make sure Navy pilots understood the weapon. He finally asked the company to conduct a special class at its Bedford, Massachusetts, plant "so we could go as deep into the missile as we felt we needed to," Ruliffson recalled.

Ruliffson came back to Miramar with as thorough a knowledge of the radar-directed weapon as any engineer and with enough material for a course two hours longer than what he taught to RAG students. Basically, he wanted to teach the Top Gun crews how the missile worked and therefore "how they could successfully deploy it."

From Ruliffson's point of view, the Navy had given them a plane without a gun and then had told its pilots the missile would do all the work for them. . . . "They were just expecting it to work like magic."

Ruliffson illustrated his points with, among others, a reference to the "Doppler Effect." An approaching train's whistle, for example, rises in pitch as it nears an observer and drops as it passes. The rising and lowering is due to the change in the number (or frequency) of sound waves striking the eardrum.

In the same way, radar waves from the Phantom reflect off a MiG. Relative position and location are crucial. In order to get a

Sparrow "lock" —meaning strong enough signals to track—the pilot has to make sure that the MiG is within the missile's radar envelope. The envelope was narrow, analogous to a flashlight beam, although much more irregularly configured. If the MiG did a quick, hard turn out of the envelope, the Sparrow went "stupid," similar (although at much faster speeds) to World War II searchlights losing enemy bombers in a night raid. The bomber, if evading, could escape in the darkness.

In addition, pilots must flick on the proper switches, which are purposely complicated to guard against accidents, in order to activate the missile and radar. To allow the proper tracking time, they had to fire when the target was least likely or able to initiate a lock-breaking maneuver, such as when it was head-on or when they were directly behind it.

Training hops were designed for the course to test the crew's ability to do all these things in a quick and efficient manner.

The idea, explains Ruliffson, "was only to take shots that you knew were going to be good. Never waste a missile. A lot of people say shoot one off to scare the guy. We never advocated that. The course centered around how to get in the envelope the quickest, which resulted in the quickest kill, which is safer. You're not predictable when you're not engaging long."

Mel Holmes had written chapters on everything from advanced flying techniques in the Phantom to getting the kill. "We expanded quite a bit on what we taught in the RAG." The heart of his message was "go for the six," or "go for the angle." "On your first turn," says Holmes, "you should know what the other pilot is doing, and if he's bad, kill him."

Holmes began with the F-4 manual, which each new RAG student received, and he then expanded it, giving more details on things they might run into. Holmes recalled, "I went into all kinds of elaborate defensive maneuvers that hadn't been covered in the RAG but which [with practice] could be done in the Phantom" (e.g., a high, negative-G maneuver that was more utilitarian than liked).

Negative Gs are unnatural and uncomfortable. If a plane is upright and suddenly noses over, the pilot instantly rises and experi-

146

ences negative Gs. The blood rises. If the pilot effects the maneuver with any speed, he's smashed to the top of the cockpit. The upward-rising blood can burst blood vessels. It causes what is called "red out," a flood of red color in one's eyesight followed by a loss of consciousness.

The "natural" way to make such turns is to flip the airplane over and then go down. The Gs then press the pilot to the seat. It's the way he normally takes Gs.

But taking advantage of the MiG-17's bad roll rate, Holmes taught that if the MiG is on your tail, pulling an angle on you to take a shot (meaning he's moving out from behind you to get his nose on a spot in front of you to fire at), "just shove that damn stick forward [pointing the nose down] and hold it forward. . . . One potato, two potato. . . . Up to five or six seconds. . . . Your eyes are getting red, but you've got to hold it."

Because the MiG can pull more positive Gs than the Phantom can pull negative, "we hope he'll roll his airplane to follow."

When he does that, the Phantom pilot yanks the stick back, thus taking advantage of the seconds needed for the MiG's roll and escapes.

Traveling to Tyndall Air Force Base in Florida in late 1968 or early 1969, Holmes got into a shouting match with John Boyd, an Air Force aerodynamist whose studies on "energy maneuverability" had become classic and whose works Holmes was incorporating into the syllabus.

"Energy maneuverability" was a catch phrase for the precise speeds and altitudes at which the Phantom performed at its optimum. It was through energy maneuverability that the instructors gave mathematical credence to their finding that flying the Phantom over 450 knots would assure that it could turn with a MiG-17.

"This was when a lot of fighter conferences were going on," remembers Holmes. "We were getting the shit kicked out of us [in the war]—all the U. S. fighters were. TAC [the Air Force Tactical Air Command, which directed the Air Force's fighters] wouldn't recognize it, but ADC [Air Defense Command] did. It was responsible for defending Korea and they knew they were in deep trouble."

Boyd, who as a colonel would later help conceive the F-16, was telling a conference that the F-4 was mathematically incapable of fighting a MiG, when Holmes, at the prodding of Sawatzky, finally broke in: "I said, 'Colonel . . . you don't take [into account] the people in the airplane, the weapons system, the capability of the [enemy pilot]. . . . You can't tell anything until the first turn. That's how you're gonna tell how good this guy in the other airplane is. You can't tell me I can't take an F-4 and fight a MiG-17—that [the] MiG-17's gonna beat me every time."

"He said . . . you don't fight MiG's in an F-4 . . . we'll lose wars that way. . . ."

"We got into a verbal argument. . . . The guy, I think, did brilliant work. . . . I [Holmes] told him that you've got to put the human aspect [into fighting] or you're defeating your purpose. . . . You can put a guy in the best airplane in the world and put him against a guy with better capability but in a worse airplane, and the guy with the better capability is going to win."

Such strategy clashes helped hone the course.

The course's introduction contained a bibliography of classified and unclassified publications. The classified publications eventually included: "Aircraft Handbook [*characteristics and performance*], Eurasian Communist Countries, 2 February 1968"; reports on "Project Have Doughnut" and "Project Have Drill"; the *F-4 Tactical Manual* with "secret supplement," and volumes I, II, and III of *Energy Maneuverability.*

The unclassified publications were mostly books and articles by famous aces and aviation writers: Galland's *The First and the Last,* Pappy Boyington's *Baa Baa Black Sheep,* "No Guts—No Glory" from the USAF Fighter Weapons Newsletter, March 1955; *The Blond Knight of Germany, The Air Marshalls, Zero, In the Company of Eagles, God Is My Co-Pilot,* and many more.

Another crucial document was "Southeast Asia MiG Kill Analysis." "We talked about engagements where [pilots] did something wrong," says Ruliffson, "then we talked about engagements where they did something right.

"A gross example of what not to do," he remembers, "was an actual case of firing off all your missiles 14 miles in trail while still in search. The [Sparrow] didn't work in search. It's out of its envelope by about 1400 percent. . . . Others hit the wrong button. . . ."

The "good" MiG briefs were few; they involved F-8 kills. "There weren't many good F-4 kills," Ruliffson recalled, "except for J. C. Smith's."

The heart of the school curriculum was flying, which culminated in the teaching of loose deuce tactics, which was the best application, as far as the instructors were concerned, of just about every good principle of ACM. It involved two fighters in loose combat spread— a mile to two miles abeam—with each covering the other, and each with the ability to lead a coordinated, gang-up strike.

Loose deuce was aggressive and versatile. Either fighter, regardless of whether it was the leader or the wingman, was free to attack, depending on who saw the bogey first and who was in the best position for the attack. The attacker would then become the "engaged" fighter; his job was mainly to press the attack, to force the MiG into making a mistake or at least to goad him into a "predictable" flight path. Meanwhile the other plane would climb above the battle as the "free" fighter in order to take advantage of what the engaged fighter set up.

In effect, they'd sandwich the bogey. The free fighter would probably take the first shot, but either one could take the initiative, depending upon what the situation provided. While watching and maneuvering for the set-up shot, the free fighter would also defend the engaged fighter.

"It was like an intricate dance," says Pedersen. Timing was critical. Communication was critical. "One guy would be up here and the other would be pressing. When the MiG makes a mistake, the guy up here tells [the engaged pilot], 'I'm coming in.' [The engaged pilot] breaks off. . . ." The two planes, in that situation, would switch places. Loose deuce was essentially a bully tactic that pitted two against one. Teamwork was crucial with two planes working in mutual support. "The guy with the best sight of what's going on can grab the lead," says Ruliffson. It also helped to capitalize on the RIO advantage—four sets of eyes were better than two.

A RIO could even take charge in a fight. This was revolutionary doctrine. The Air Force, which flew a rigid, four-plane formation called "fluid four," wouldn't even let a wingman (second, guarding pilots in a two-plane pair) take charge. It was considered disrespectful.

"We saw gross instances of this," says Ruliffson. "One [Air Force] colonel had fired all his missiles. . . . The MiG had slid in front of his number four plane. [The pilot] said, 'Hey, boss. I got him right in my sights. What do I do?' [The colonel] said, 'Let's go home.' Hence, he preferred to lose an opportunity to shoot down a MiG because he, as the leader, could not take the shot."

A deep rift developed between the Navy and Air Force because of the two differing doctrines, which the syllabus alluded to under the heading "Why Does the Navy Fly Loose Deuce?" One answer was that the Navy didn't have as many planes, tankers, or bombs as the Air Force. The syllabus emphasized that the deciding factor was "Loose Deuce had proven effective in combat. Fluid Four has not proven effective in combat."

The syllabus pointed to the Arab-Israeli War of 1967 in support of its statement. The Arabs had used fluid four, while the Israelis, using loose deuce, had virtually eliminated the Arab air force (although the formation was only one of many factors which figured into the victory).

☆ ☆ ☆

The chapters to be included in the syllabus were finally taking shape. According to Steve Smith, they were compiling a book "the size of Pacific Bell's." Smith found himself running copy back and forth for proofreading. Finally, they had chapters one through nineteen, but they didn't have any pictures or illustrations

Smith located a draftsman and had everyone submit illustration ideas. The main art came from the F-4 flight manual—McDonnell-Douglas' "Spook," or cartoon phantom: a little bad guy in a big black hat and oversized tennis shoes, with his black coat covering his face, and only his eyes visible.

They took the background art out and put the spook on the cover. He appeared throughout the final book—riding the Phantom like a horse, chasing bogeys, throwing fat fused bombs at Asians, standing in the shadows, and challenging: "Let's get on with it!"

Smith put his initials on the Spook's tennis shoes, replicas of high-top Converses.

"I passed it through whoever was checking it, saying the initials stood for 'SuperSpook.' But they stood for Steve Smith."

Getting the syllabus bound and printed was almost as difficult as getting it written. "At one point we were going to take up a collection to get the $1200 or whatever," recalled Smith. But the Navy finally came through, and one sweltering day in early 1969, Smith, Sawatzky, and others began assembling the tome.

"We had something like three hundred pages laid out over every surface in the trailer. . . . It was summer. Someone came into the hot trailer and absent-mindedly turned on a fan. [It was something] right out of a Chevy Chase movie. We were both clear across the room and saw it coming." Hundreds of pages of the unbound books scattered throughout the trailer like confetti, and they had to start over.

As the course lectures were perfected, the instructors brought in students from the RAG as an audience to try them out.

"They ran the first lessons by us," Gil Sliney, one of Pedersen's student RIOs, remembers. "Drive that MiG to your strength. . . . [The Phantom] is effective above 420 knots, below 30,000 feet. Fifteen thousand is optimum. . . . Sidewinder envelopes got bad with a lot of Gs. . . . I thought it was incredible . . . best stuff I'd ever heard."

But though the relatively inexperienced students loved the course, the instructors were still concerned about what the experienced fleet pilots would think.

☆ ☆ ☆

Only one thing remained before the school was opened for business. The instructors needed a nickname.

The name "Top Gun" had been in use in the Navy a long time. It had been the name of an annual Navy air weapons meet. Pedersen's future ship, the aircraft carrier *Ranger*, had long been known as "Top Gun of the Fleet," and F-8 pilots frequently called themselves "Top Guns," as did the F-8 Fighter Weapons School, which was chartered separately by the Ault report but was soon to fade and disappear.

The name connoted images of the Old West—the fastest and toughest gunslinger around. Everyone immediately loved it, and even today Pedersen doesn't think "you could come up with anything better."

Holmes and Steve Smith came up with a patch for Top Gun students and instructors: a MiG with a "pipper" on it. The pipper was the round visual gunsight in front of the pilot on the Phantom canopy. However, the school discovered that using the MiG was prohibited because it designated a certain country or group as the Navy's sole adversary. As a result, remembers Holmes, "we put slats and things on it to make it look a little different."

The name and patch were in a way farfetched (as some pointed out) because the Phantom didn't even carry any guns, it was the spirit that counted. Top Gun. Dead-eye best.

☆ CHAPTER 16 ☆

With the war needs easing restrictions on dogfighting, fighter pilots at Miramar were having a field day in the times before the school opened.

Saturday morning was often the busiest—the result of challenges and insults hurled at the previous night's happy hour. Other RAG instructors fought the Top Gun instructors relentlessly.

Holmes remembers one fight with an F-8 instructor after each had sent his students home.

"I said, all right, you want to keep it visually, or you want to go out on radar contact. . . . He said ten-mile separation and we'll do it through the controllers. . . . So we went out, picked him up on radar as he turned, so we knew right where he was at. . . . I've never seen a guy so eager and so ready to beat somebody and make so many damned stupid mistakes so fast. It wasn't a turn and a half and I had him shot. He was so eager, he turned so hard, started giving us his belly. I just popped up over the top, and he slid out in front and within about ninety degrees, I had him," Holmes remembered.

"I said over the radio, 'You can't lead-turn us anymore. We're not intercept pilots anymore. You're gonna have to fight us.' I could hear him saying, 'Okay! Okay!'

"We separated again a short distance. I think we were running out of fuel. We came back head on. The second time it was a pretty good fight. But I guess I was out to embarrass him. We went down. . . . When the Phantom goes to 4,000 pounds of fuel and gets really light that son-of-a-gun is a hell of a machine, a good machine. It can turn well at that particular weight [and] with the engine they had in the F-8 . . . I think it can outturn the F-8. So I just turned the hell out of him and ended up about 20 feet underneath his tail. No matter what he did I just stayed with him . . . just about 20 feet under his tail. . . . I had black jet exhaust smoke on my tail when we got back. . . . "

Nick Cris, who years later would head Miramar's adversary squadron, was a student going through the RAG at that time. "The F-8 kicked shit out of the F-4 for years," he remembers. "But by the time I got there that was starting to change. From about 1969 on, it was exactly the opposite. The F-4 destroyed the F-8. The reason was they learned how to use their airplane. . . . The F-8 was a high-altitude fighter, MiG-21 class. Basically, if you went up to 30,000 feet to fight them they'd eat your lunch. So you stayed down at 15,000. . . . The difference is aerodynamics. Basically, the F-8 is much sleeker than the F-4 [maneuvers better in thin air]. The F-4 is a brute . . . bigger motors. Thrust is relative to altitude. Those motors do a much better job at low altitude."

Cris says instructors were held in awe in those days, much more than they are today. "There was a different frame of mind then," Cris recalled. "First, you [the student] knew you were going to war. They had a big sign over the door [to Hangar 1]. It said, 'Are you ready for combat today?' Everybody who got orders to 121 knew they were going to Vietnam. Then you looked at the [instructors] and knew they'd been there. You knew you had to learn from that guy everything you could, because your life depended on it. You knew it, and they knew it. . . . They were constantly fighting each other to establish the pecking order."

On Cris' very first RAG flight, he was treated to a Holmes–Sawatzky battle.

"I was a brand new student. . . . It was my FAM flight [first familiarization flight]. But the weather was too bad for me to take off and land, so rather than scrub the hop, Mel, who was supposed to be the pilot in my back seat [telling Chris what to do] said, 'Okay, you get in the back and I'll take it to Yuma where we can land and switch places. . . .' He took Jerry Sawatzky and another guy in the same situation and the [four] of us took off together.

"I don't know if they planned it this way or not, but basically they went into a one-versus-one and ended in a vertical scissors going up. . . . [They went] to zero air speed . . . and close enough [as they walked around each other] that I'll bet you that if either had opened up the canopy and taken out a .38, he could have shot the other. . . .

"Then we both started backing down . . . very scary . . . especially on your FAM one. . . . We're just backing down through space. . . . Sawatzky loses an engine—they don't work very good going backwards, don't get a whole lot of air. So his nose drops and he starts falling. Then WE start falling—neither one is controlling the airplane, but neither one is going to stop the fight. . . . There was a phrase then, 'It's better to die than look bad.' That was a way of life in those days. You'd ride it into the ground before you'd lose."

With such aggressive tactics, there were bound to be accidents. Sawatzky watched an F-8 below him run out of airspeed while trying to zoom away from another F-8. The higher crusader fell back and plowed into the pursuer. At the time Sawatzky, fighting Holmes, was almost out of airspeed himself and had to back down through the debris.

"There was a big orange flash. . . . All these pieces were flying everywhere, and his [the F8 pilot's] engine went by me on the left. . . . It looked like a tie clasp that the engine companies give out . . . 'cause it came nose first and you saw the little bullet-shaped nozzle. . . . The rest of the airplane had been shredded away."

Nash says they developed a kind of sadistic humor. "Mel and I were out fighting a guy named Bob Nickleson . . . Nick, we called him. He was in an A-4 and got it real nose high and fell through, got into an inverted spin. So we were calling altitude because you're supposed to eject at 10,000 feet. We're calling the altitude at 20,000 18,000 [and] ol' Mel's up there yelling, 'Ride it, Nick. Ride it.' Here's a guy in a vertical spin that is extremely uncomfortable [not to mention dangerous]. You get about minus three Gs. You just hope you can get out at 10,000. . . . But we were just sitting up there watching. 'Ride it, Nick. Ride it . . . ' "

Nash, whose marriage was deteriorating, craved the jousting. "I couldn't stand to go home. . . . You'd get an airplane, either by yourself or with somebody else, and go looking for F-8s or other

Phantoms. . . . He didn't know you, you didn't know him. You didn't know what was going to happen . . . that was the essence of ACM. Unpredictability. You can talk about some of the maneuvers, write them in a syllabus, but it was always different, depending on who and what you were fighting."

From the moment a pilot took off, he had to be on guard. "It was so embarrassing to have some guy get behind you, shoot you, and then fly up on your wing," remembers Cris. Another trick was "hot-nosing." From a hidden approach underneath, a plane would "pull up right in front of you. Scariest thing in the world. [You're] just flying along minding your own business and bam! An F-4 or F-8 just plants one right in front of your airplane."

Eventually, most of the Top Gun instructors decided not to fight each other in similar airplanes. "It just boiled down to an ego thing," says Holmes. "Who's the best? We knew somebody was going to get hurt."

The flying at Miramar was intense. For Mel Holmes, his job was everything to him. Holmes was from a small town in Oregon, and he had risen through the Navy pilot ranks until he was now considered one of the "best of the best"—an instructor at Top Gun, teaching the best the Navy had to be even better. Everything else paled in comparison.

Sawatzky, too, found the pace grueling, as well. He had two or three hops a day, which often resulted in total exhaustion. Like Holmes, Sawatzky found his marriage in trouble. In fact, of the seven married instructors who started the school, only two—Ruliffson and J. C. Smith—would finish their careers still married to the same woman. The flying, the ACM; and the demands of ego, time, effort all "played havoc with the families," recalls Pedersen, who himself was eventually divorced.

Yet the flying was also full of thrills and accomplishment. It had to do with proving oneself under the most stressful conditions and with having what later would become known as "the right stuff."

Measuring up was something the pilots had to do day after day and over and over again. It meant staying cool in the most fearful moments. Mel Holmes had such a moment during a "routine" dogfight with Jerry Sawatzky one day.

The two, in the course of the fight, found themselves in what some call "the death spiral." To Holmes and Sawatzky, it was simply a nose-low, vertical scissors—two fighters viciously swirling downward, each trying to get at the other's six.

"Last-ditch maneuvering," said Holmes, "I used it frequently against the A-4. You're either in a standoff, or he's gaining on you."

Sawatzky was gaining on him. Holmes, his Phantom nose down and ahead of Sawatzky, was looking back over his shoulder and didn't see the fog bank ahead. What he did see was Sawatzky abruptly stop the pursuit and veer level.

Leveling off was just the mistake Holmes was looking for. He'd jam the rudder, rolling the Phantom over until his canopy was precisely 180 degrees across from Sawatzky's, and then he'd tug into a basic downward Split S, coming back up on Sawatzky's tail. Fox two. He'd have him.

The maneuver wasn't for the novice. In fact, as usual, Holmes was flying right at the edge of the envelope. Because he was flying slow for the Phantom, even a hairline of deviation would send the plane reeling. But he was flying on automatic, the brute machine an extension of his body, his flying senses so finely tuned to the critical thresholds that he felt as if he and the plane were one.

His Phantom was nearly out of critical flying energy. Even with the aid of the roll and the precision economy of his execution, it would still take 4000 more downward feet for the plane to gain enough speed and Gs to turn nose up and come back to bear on Sawatzky.

He kicked in the rudder, rolling into Sawatzky, putting Sawatzky right at the top of his plane. "About that time," Holmes recalled, "I looked at the goddamn altitude. 'Jesus Christ. We're at 2500 feet!' " He now knew why Sawatzky had backed off. He also knew he was in serious trouble. There was no way he and his backseater were going to be able to make that turn with so little sky left.

As the Phantom roared into the fog, cutting off the sunlight, the thought occurred to him that maybe he'd "bought the farm."

Inverted like a diver about to come down in a head-first, backward swan dive, he suddenly had to change course. If he continued to pull through in his curling Split-S maneuver—an approximate 140 degree arc—he'd smash into the water. He needed about 2000 more feet than he had to complete the turn.

His only choice was to bring the wings level while they were still inverted and accelerate forward, even though that would speed him still faster toward the water. When he'd gotten rid of the G-force and picked up enough maneuvering energy, roll over and pull up.

"It took superb courage to do what you had to do," said Sawatzky, who'd already decided Holmes was going to crash and was changing frequencies on his radio in order to call Search and Rescue. "When you consider how nose down he was and the turn he had to make, only his skill and feel for the airplane could bring him up. It's awfully hard to use your head in a situation like that. Every instinct tells you to keep pulling on the airplane."

Pulling back on the stick is the normal way to make the plane go up. "But if you do, you can't accelerate. . . . You've got to unload [the G-force] and get the burble off the wings and let that ram air flow through the engines to develop thrust."

Unable to see in the fog, Holmes was now relying solely on instruments and his own instincts. He jammed the stick forward to neutral "zero G" and simultaneously hit his rudder and ailerons, thus rolling the wings level with the horizon. The Phantom, still inverted, shot forward towards the water, picking up speed he needed to complete the maneuver.

"Time was very, very critical," says Sawatzky. "He didn't have much of it left."

Gaining energy, he snap-rolled the Phantom upright. Instantly, he had only 60 degrees to go to pull the plane level, instead of the previous 140. Now he jerked the stick back and felt the plane turn upward.

Holmes recalled, "You've got this little angle of attack gauge which tells you the optimum performance. . . . I went to it and just pulled to the optimum without stalling out. The RIO in the back seat said we went below sea level on his altimeter, but I have no idea how low we got because I was so damn concentrated."

In all likelihood, the Phantom's exhaust probably churned the water.

Above the fog, Sawatzky was ashen. "I can still remember how bad I felt. Mel was a very good friend. . . . He's one in a million . . . just one in a lifetime."

But Sawatzky's mood suddenly brightened. Below him, Holmes' Phantom popped out of the clouds. A big smile burst across Sawatzky's face. "When I saw him . . . I thought, 'You son-of-a-gun Mel . . .' "

All Holmes said was something to the effect that the fight was still on.

"You don't dwell on what happened," said Holmes. "You get rid of it . . . [and try to forget] just what a dumb shit you were to let yourself get into that situation. It's the attitude that you're invincible. You made it. Forget it. . . . Every pilot has instances where he could have bought the farm and didn't. If you haven't come that close, then you're not flying that airplane the way you should."

Holmes didn't concede the victory and Sawatzky didn't claim it. "If I hadn't come out," says Holmes wryly, "he could have chalked it up, [but] he backed off, remember. . . . But everybody loses sometimes. There's not a soul out there that never got beat. That's a fallacy. Because there are times when you get yourself into a pickle. . . . But you learned from it. It was a constant learning thing. . . . You'd almost think there never was a fight that you didn't learn something new."

☆ CHAPTER 17 ☆

The Dirty Dozen had just finished showing at one of Miramar's perimeter theaters when the first F-4 Navy Fighter Weapons School class convened on March 3, 1969. The movie was appropriate to the scene unfolding in the little trailer: a battle-hardened instructor, Dan Pedersen, challenging a group of combat standouts hastily assembled from the best the Navy could muster. These recruits, however, were hardly misfits. The eight pilots and RIOs assembled before the instructors were dedicated career officers, and some of them were academy graduates.

Among them were pilot LT Ron Stoops; RIO LT Jim Nelson; Michigan-born LT Jerry Beaulier, an aggressive pilot who would make the biggest impression on his instructors; the smooth and capable LT Cliff Martin, also a pilot; John "Pudge" Padgett, whose current claim to fame was that he'd punched out on his FAM flight. The other RIOs included LT Jack Hawver, who would later complete the NFO course at test pilot school; red-haired Bob Cloyes; and Ed Scudder. All the recruits were regulars as opposed to reservists. The Navy wanted their Top Gun experience to stay in the Navy.

"You know the *Top Gun* movie?" asks Pedersen, "the portrayal of the animosity between the guys? It just never would have been tolerated. I'd have sent the guys home instantly for that."

But that didn't mean the men weren't cocky. The four crews came from VF-142 and VF-143, sister squadrons on the *Constellation*, which had recently returned from an almost eight-month combat deployment in Vietnam.

Doc Townsend likes to tell the story of Beaulier, who as a RAG student fed up with F-8 talk about "being the last of the gunfighters and so on," scaled the huge VF-126 hangar at Miramar at night and stole their glass-encased authentic Crusader sword. "Jerry was really something," recalled Townsend. "He just showed up with it and we took it to happy hour and showed it to them along with films of their six's. They wanted to fight."

In fact, the F-8ers did start a fight, says Beaulier. Swinging at Townsend, who had rubbed it in by taking the sword up in his Phantom to Mach 2, which the Crusaders could not match, and then attaching a certificate of same to the relic before handing it back.

But when it came to flying, all the pilots were serious and conscientious aviators, screened by the school exactly for those qualities. Each pilot knew from his own experience that there was a problem in the war with regard to dogfighting and that what they had been picked to attend so hastily was special and might help them better their fighter piloting skills.

"You didn't have to put a lot of talk on them," says Pedersen. "They were pretty excited already."

Nevertheless, remembers Nelson, Pedersen, "gave a rousing 'Welcome aboard' . . . almost a joyous type thing. 'Let's learn this together. Let's go out and see how we can turn things around' . . . I was very impressed."

Pedersen didn't dwell on how shaky things were yet at the school. Pedersen was still desperate for adversary airplanes. And while the instructors had the first week's schedule planned, they still were not sure how the course was going to end. "We had the book done," remembers Steve Smith, "but we were still working on the lectures."

"It was going to be a learning experience for us as well as them," remembers Steve Smith. Mel Holmes felt a mixture of apprehension and excitement. "We were going to be the bogeys against them and they weren't beginners . . . but there was the sense that we were starting something new . . . we were going to try and change the philosophies of the squadrons. . . ."

The class first was shown slides and graphs on the Vietnam kill ratios; they were then led through the Ault report. "We hadn't been doing well [in Vietnam]," says Nelson. "It wasn't very encouraging."

At this point, the ultimate goal of the school was underscored: "to build a nucleus of eminently qualified and highly trained fighter crews" which would return to their respective squadrons and serve as teachers.

"It isn't enough to be a good aviator," Pedersen told them, "you're going to have to be able to impart that knowledge."

To a man, they admired the lieutenant commander in front of them. With his hands on hips and his face set with purpose, Pedersen evoked a sense of awe and inspiration.

"He said, 'Hey, we're going to teach you guys to be graduate-level fighter pilots,' " says Beaulier. "That was it. I mean he was really good. He was good to fly against. . . . You need that kind of guy, somebody really tough to keep everybody on track. . . ."

"We'd met them [the class] on a Sunday," recalls Holmes, "got to know their backgrounds, told them ours, discussed what was going to happen. The first week was nothing but classroom. Then we threw in a few flights just to get them back in the swing. . . ."

Pedersen first wanted to build their confidence and to make them feel comfortable with what the plane could do. He wanted to make flying the plane to its limits second nature, so that they would remain collected during the maneuvers and concentrate on what the opposition was doing.

He liked to take them up and depart the airplane—"straight up . . . to zero airspeed . . . let that big machine start backing down, with smoke and stuff coming out of the intake. . . . You shouldn't do it tactically—we had a rule you couldn't do it—but we did it to prove how the airplane would come out of it. It would pitch over as it got momentum going backwards, go nose down and then start flying in that direction. It's fairly violent. I wouldn't want to do it every day, but what a confidence builder. . . . First [if they hadn't done it before] they're scared to death, but then, when they learn to handle it . . . 'Well, shithot!' "

As Hawver remembers, "It was really impressive pushing the envelope. It was impressive because our commander gave us his planes to do that in. . . . He trusted us. If you lose your airplane, he's in trouble. He's responsible. . . . But everybody had an aggressive, winning-type attitude. We realized we had a problem, our track record hadn't been good . . . [and] when it finally got down to where the rubber met the road, it was guys not knowing how their weapons systems worked . . . we needed it."

Darrell Gary explains that after they got the students through the ground school, they began asking them questions about their future adversary, the MiG pilot. "What's his training? What kind of background does he have? How is he likely to react in a fight? Let's talk about his equipment. Let's talk about his aircraft. Let's talk about his missile capability. . . . They didn't have access to the intelligence we did," Gary remembered, "and we took the information, sifted through it, got the most essential items, and then presented them in a format they could understand."

The students were encouraged to contribute, which they did. "I remember Dan and I going head-to-head in an argument about the complexities of the missile envelope," says Hawver. "The Raytheon guys came in and gave us all these viewgraphs . . . overlays. . . . No way we could remember all that stuff. It was too complicated. We needed some simple rules of thumb. I told him so . . . As RAG students we couldn't have said anything about it, but all of a sudden we're elevated as [Fighter Weapons School] guys. . . . We'd spent a few days going through it, and he didn't like the criticism. Nobody likes criticism. . . . But I guess he thought about it later, because they eventually changed it."

With everybody feeling "pretty good about themselves," says Darrell Gary, "we'd say, 'Okay. You guys think you're good? Let's go out and see how good you really are."

Tom O'Hara, a RIO in the third class, describes what inevitably happened: One of the instructors would, as O'Hara put it, "eat us alive." The instructor did exactly what an experienced MiG pilot would do, and the result showed.

"I was the kid and they were the experienced guys," recalls Beaulier. "I had maybe 500 hours and they had 3000. . . . But you still think you're invincible—if you don't, you're not much of a fighter pilot. You look at them and say, 'Hey, I've got to steal from these guys, take their goddamn experience, and put it in my bag. When I know as much as they do, I'll be twice as smart because I already know what I know.'"

If a student started to get too good, the instructors would take him out and show him a little humility. The first class was eager to learn from the beginning. It was the school itself that was doing the second-guessing.

"I remember we were double-hatted, because we were working very hard to put crews through the tactics phase of the RAG and still trying to build [the Fighter Weapons School] syllabus," says Ruliffson. "And we were very worried that we would be viewed as second rate, you know, not having put something together that was really worth something."

One continuing concern was the quality of the adversary planes available. The school was dependent on the RAG for TA-4 Skyhawks which the RAG used for instrument training. The Skyhawks weren't as agile as the school needed. And sometimes, because of maintenance and other problems, the school wasn't even getting those.

"We brought in some A-6s [as MiG simulators]," remembers Steve Smith. The A-6, a tough little bubble-canopied bomber nicknamed the "Intruder," was making a name for itself in North Vietnam. Marine pilots were brought into the school to fly the plane in advisory training hops. Smith's Marine pilot, while experienced in other planes, had only ten hours in the Intruder.

"It got a little hairy up there," but then Smith started getting to him (the other pilot). "It went better. I mean at first he wasn't even a good adversary. But then he started becoming a *very* good adversary. The net result was that when he came back he had a lot more confidence in his airplane and himself."

And the Fighter Weapons School had another good adversary to help fill the dearth.

As Beaulier remembers, "All we'd ever done was canned intercept ... [and] suddenly we're doing a ton of hassling. Dissimilar ACM. You start off flying against other F-4s and then against A-4s and the F-8s and then whatever the hell else they could get up ... we'd have a lecture in the morning, then go up and try it. . . . It was really good."

Nelson recalls, "When we started we were pretty much fighting horizontally ... let's get into a big wheel and let the other guy kill us. But [then we learned] about the vertical end of the game. . . . You go high to build energy . . . trade speed for altitude . . . that's potential energy [because] when you come down, you retrieve it. You always want to keep your speed up. If you get down to 300-350 knots, you can't go vertical. . . ."

Speed is life, repeated the instructors over and over.

The key exercise for the students—the one from which almost all others stemmed—was "2 v. 1": two Phantoms versus one bogey. It was classic loose deuce strategy—ganging up on your opponent. The way to win, the students were told, is to play your advantages, such as numbers, speed, and power to climb, and not to let your adversary play his.

There were many moves that could stem from 2 v. 1, but, basically, they all boiled down to isolating a single opponent and then hitting him together in sequence.

Pedersen and J. C. Smith liked to talk about "the egg." A dogfight usually took place in an egg-shaped sphere of sky around and inside of which the battling planes swirled. The "engaged" fighter would "drive" or "bait" —a controversial tactic also called "dragging" —somewhere inside the egg. (You basically gave him [the enemy] your six in order to give your partner a shot.) Meanwhile, the "free" fighter would zoom up or out, usually turning over on his back (if he were going extreme vertical), observing momentarily the fight below, and then roaring back down when he saw a chance to come in. It was similar to a tag-team match.

Pedersen said, "Our advantage in my mind, and Sam Leeds's and Mel's and the guys was . . . to work the airplane up and down because the MiGs couldn't get up there with you. It kept us right on top of the fight where you could look down and see 'em. Now when you go up like that . . . you're not looking in the cockpit. You're not looking at the gauges. It's strictly hands, feet, and rudder while you're keeping track of what's outside . . . you get up there at about 160 or 170 knots [and] you should probably start feeding in rudder to end up on your back, laying on your back at about 110, 120 knots. What you're really doing then is you're starting to fall through, okay?

But you're not really falling, you're flying. . . . One guy's down in the egg hassling while you're in the vertical coming over the top to get back in."

Keeping sight of the enemy was crucial. "If you lost him," says Pedersen, "you could bet he'd end up on your six." The up-and-over maneuver demanded precise knowledge of the envelope. "Some of them [the students] would get up there and not get on their backs fast enough. They'd stall . . . get committed nose-high and not feed in enough rudder until it was too late . . . [they'd] come falling back downwards. . . . The airplane would spin and you'd lose it if you didn't handle it right" —which was why they'd demonstrated the maneuver at the beginning of the syllabus in the first place.

"Think of [2 v. 1] like boxing," says Steve Smith, "both hands can't be doing the same thing. In fact, they have to be in opposite places. But they are mutually supporting each other. . . . One hand is in the guy's face. What's the other doing? Momentarily, it's defending. The next thing it's doing is preparing. Then, simultaneously, the one hand comes back and the other one goes in.

"The A-4 isn't going to go up and down. It's going to go around, or it's going to go around and then down . . . in an ever smaller circle." As the plane turned in smaller and smaller circles, it became slower, more vulnerable, while the Phantoms maintained their speed by alternating their attacks.

"So as long as you keep, so to speak, trading places, what you're doing is hitting the speed bag. The speed bag is the A-4 [or MiG]. Each hand keeps going back and forth pounding him. He can never fly in a straight line. He just keeps getting into a smaller and smaller ball [lower and lower]. The ultimate end of any fight doesn't require a weapon to be fired. You can fly the son-of-a-bitch into the ground . . .

"If you do anything else, he's going to point at you and fly across your arc . . . and gain speed. [But] you're slowing him down, tying him up so he doesn't have anywhere to go . . . the whole dogfight is if you slow him down and make him predictable, your partner can shoot him, and vice versa."

The RIO, in such a scheme, is crucial.

"[The RIO] was responsible for prosecuting the attack," says Darrell Gary. "He had to acquire the guy on radar, establish the spatial geometry, communicate that to the pilot and the other aircraft. How many of them are there? What's their formation? How are we going to attack them?"

Laing said, "Part of our success was the ability to train the backseaters to become super proficient in attack geometry so that when they entered the fight their plane was in an offensive position in a very short period of time. . . . Typically your opportunity to kill is going to be just a fleeting moment."

"The school taught the RIO how to take charge and use the radar under stress," says Gary. "There is a world of difference between acquiring a guy when you are flying straight and level and he's out there 30 miles away, and when he's over here 30 degrees off the nose, and you're pulling seven Gs trying to get the nose on him and you're trying to communicate that to the pilot and get a lock on [for a missile shot]."

The need for constant communication between pilot and RIO was critical.

"You're constantly talking to each other," explained Smith. "You got four guys up there. They all have to recognize each other's voices . . . I mean the chatter never stops. There is not a break. They get so good at it that even though they are cutting each other off, they're not cutting each other off. All four are talking the whole time, and they all know what the other guys are saying."

"They told us we gotta talk a lot more," recalled Nelson. "The guy on the radar has to constantly be telling the guy up front [what's happening] because the guy up front has got to keep his eyeballs out of the cockpit looking for the target. . . . It's a constant patter. . . . And you've got a wingman. . . . You're telling your wingman exactly what you're doing. 'You got the first man. I got the second.'. . . 'You go high. I'll go low' . . . exactly what you're doing, exactly how you're setting up the game."

☆ ☆ ☆

While the first class was in session, Dan Pedersen, J. C. Smith, and perhaps some others, went up to Point Mugu one day to see

Jim Foster at VX-4. By now, there was a steady exchange of information between the two units. "There was a common bond," says McKeown, "about, hey, we got a mutual problem here. We got to solve this."

McKeown was coming down to Miramar and briefing 121 students on what he and the others at VX-4 were learning about fighting the Sparrow.

The two units also had a spirited tactics exchange. "We'd have the fight of the week every Friday," recalls McKeown, "and come back saying, hey, we got a thing that works great. Let's go down and show it to the RAG. They'd listen and say no fucking way. These kids can't do that."

At some point, they were shown the *Doughnut* film and then, after Foster pulled strings and got them clearances, they were taken to Nellis, and then to the desert, to be introduced to, and then later allowed to fly, the captured MiGs.

As head of a department whose job it was to teach other fighter pilots how to fight MiGs, Pedersen had been studying the intelligence about them night and day for nearly six months. Suddenly, gleaming under powerful lights, there were the objects of so much of his efforts.

"Dan and the boys came up and we started learning," says Foster. No longer were the Top Gun students dependent on secondhand sources for information on MiGs.

☆ CHAPTER 18 ☆

The fear that comes with flying high performance jet planes at the limit of their envelopes, especially in war, was always there in the minds of Top Gun pilots. "It was something everybody lived with," says Darrell Gary. "It gripped different people in different ways."

He and Laing, now rooming with a third flyer at a beach house in La Jolla, which they christened "the Lafayette Escadrille," were having the time of their lives. They were the youngest instructors at 121, and now they were teaching at Top Gun. They were at the pinnacle of their profession. But it was a profession fraught with danger—a lifestyle that could end in the blink of an eye.

Occasionally, after a fatal training crash, or following a weekend all-nighter, when they were physically and emotionally drained, they'd go down to the beach, stare at the ocean, and reflect.

Training didn't lessen the fear—just its frequency. One time, for example, Gary and a student pilot, and Ruliffson and a student RIO, were in Phantoms fighting two F-8s. Gary's pilot wasn't the most gifted, and they were pointed up at one of the Crusaders. "He was nose-high trying to turn inside the F-8. We were losing airspeed, turnability and controllability.

"I told him, 'Don't pull any harder,' but he decides he's going to get the kill. This guy's got no feel for the airplane at all. If you yank on it, it's going to spin. . . . So I'm saying, 'Al, don't,' and he just reefs on it with all his strength, and the airplane does this big shudder and . . . it departs violently; the air falls off one wing rapidly, the nose flops down, and we're pasted up against the canopy."

They were upside down, spinning, and flopping. "The nose goes from straight up to down and wanders in figure eights just below the horizon," Gary remembered.

If they didn't pull it out by 10,000 feet, they were required to eject—if they could.

"You have to bring the control back to center . . . and release the drag chute which will catch air and snap the tail up," Gary said. The nose will point down at that point, letting the pilot accelerate and fly out.

"So I told him, 'Al, take your hands off the controls. [Then they'd naturally go to center]. . . . Release the drag chute.' . . . But old Al, somehow nothing came to mind . . . 'Al.' I'm firmer now. 'Pull the drag chute.' Eventually, Gary found himself screaming at his student. 'Al! Goddamit! The drag chute!' "

Gary thought that they'd bought it at the time. "I don't think he ever got the drag chute out. He finally took his hands off the controls and put 'em up on the dash or something. . . . We flopped around some more but the nose pointed down."

They started regaining air, getting in a dive.

"Now you want to talk to him easily . . . ease him back into it. The biggest danger right then is just as you begin accelerating, the guy has the adrenalin going and he cranks back on the stick too hard again and you get into another stall and go right back into [another spin]."

They recovered at about 12,000 feet, only to see the F-8 they had been fighting careening by them in its *own* spin. "He must have thought we were on him, reefed back and lost it himself. . . . He finally recovered close to the water. . . . Poor guy. He just set course for Miramar and never came back."

Some mishaps in training didn't have as happy an ending.

Mike Emmitt was an F-8 pilot who was a good friend of Gary's and Laing's, a contemporary who was going through the F-8 RAG at the time they were at Top Gun. He was always at the Lafayette Escadrille's parties, as they were at the parties at the nearby beach house Emmitt shared, which had been christened "the Traveling Medicine Show."

One Friday, Darrell and his date, Sherry (who later became his wife), and Emmitt and his date went across the border to Tijuana for a night on the town. The next morning Emmitt had a Saturday morning training hop—a dogfight against his RAG instructor. In the midst of the fight, Emmitt spun his plane and fell through the sky. He had a chance to eject, but the canopy never opened. In the investigation they found that he'd undone his chute harness.

"Evidently, he'd wanted to see better during the fight," said Gary. "In the F-8, the restraint mechanism didn't allow you to turn around very well so you could see over your shoulder. He'd undone that, and then when he'd spun he couldn't get it back on. . . ."

For a long time afterwards, Gary, Laing, and their wives would have Margaritas at sunset and think of Mike Emmitt. . . .

☆ ☆ ☆

The Top Gun students and faculty managed to have fun, as well. Jim Laing and Darrell Gary, for example, hosted many a party at the Escadrille. The Lafayette Escadrille had been actor Victor Mclaglen's summer home—a perfect "snake ranch," as all the Miramar flyers in those days called their bachelor party houses (invite a girl over and show her your "snake"). "Sometimes I remember having to break into my bedroom and throw people out just so I could get some sleep," says Gary.

They'd found the house through a newspaper ad placed by its owner, an elderly woman named Oly, who was a fixture in La Jolla. The only thing she required was that they pay the $250 per month rent in person. "Then she'd break out the Chivas Regal and [the payee—they rotated] had to drink one with her." They kept it clean and repaired for her, and she'd go to bat for them when condominium neighbors nearby would complain about the parties.

Made of white stucco, the three bedroom house had two baths, and a three-car garage in which they kept their latest assortment of ground transportation.

The first piece of furniture they bought was a $10 used refrigerator in which they installed a keg with an outside spigot. "We always had beer on tap and rarely if ever locked the doors. . . . People would just arrive, particularly on Friday and Saturday nights. . . . I'd come in sometimes and not have a clue to who the people were who were drinking our beer. . . ."

Typically, remembers Gary, they'd go out three or four nights a week. "Down to the Beachcomber or Bully's or the Rhinelander

. . . maybe get lucky . . . Jim and I always seemed to get the early flights. . . . We'd head in about 4:30 A.M., have early briefs, and launch at first light."

They'd fly two or three hops a day, getting off early in the afternoon. "We couldn't wait to get out, go to the beach, then in for a power nap—hour, hour and a half—maybe some dinner and out again."

Wednesday night was happy hour at the Miramar Officers Club. "They'd have strippers and everybody just kinda ran amuck . . . squadrons hanging together, pouring beer on each other and lighting their hair on fire. . . . Everybody was in a hurry to have a good time because generally they were going back on cruise. That's probably what made the times on the beach so special, why everybody had motorcycles and fast cars. . . ."

Gary particularly remembers the Downwinds Bar at this time, "Nothing in it was breakable—no glass. They gave you beer in a plastic cup. They'd pack people in and I guess the fire marshal or whatever only allowed so many at one time. So girls would climb over the walls and guys would help them. . . . After about 30 seconds there was beer everywhere, and you'd be slipping and sliding and fights were generated just by everybody falling into everybody else."

A drunk PSA stewardess—says Gary—once leaned down and bit Laing's rear end. "To get his attention, I guess. Sure got mine. . . . I've seen the band punch out Marines . . . one was being real obnoxious. A guitar player just stepped down and cold-cocked him. There was this really beautiful blonde named Marsha . . . she was one of the groupies that came around . . . kind of outrageous in terms of her behavior. . . . I've seen her physically knock a guy down, sit on his chest, and punch his lights out."

There were fights at the Escadrille, too.

One night, says Gary, "some guys from the beach started getting too friendly with the girls. . . . One of our guys took exception and they went outside. . . .

"This one guy was going to hit [our guy] in the back of the head with a brick, so I grabbed him and flung him up against the chimney, which is on the back side of the house. He hit his head and fell down. The next thing I knew they all descended on me. I saw Ed Dowling, who is five-foot eight . . . jump up in the air and hit some guy in the face. Broke his hand . . . the guy we're trying to save, he goes over the fence and is gone. . . ."

It ended when a basketball player friend arrived and started swinging at the unwanted guests with a bat.

"We had some colorful nights," Gary recalled.

☆ CHAPTER 19 ☆

"Everything we did every day," says Steve Smith, referring to the Top Gun instruction, "was geared to keeping the students at a certain speed and a certain altitude. . . . If they weren't keeping it there, we showed them what happened as a result, which was that they were either out of the fight or about to die.

"I would be flying with one of these guys and I would say, 'Okay, take it straight up. Right now.' [The student would say,] 'Why? I want to go down.' 'No. We're establishing. We're going up.' Pretty soon we'd be going over the top and coming back down. 'Now do you see why we're up here? If we were down there you'd be trying to get back up here now, and he would be above you, and you would be slower. But now you've caused him to become a ball and you're the string. Had you done anything else, it would have been the other way around.' "

Energy maneuverability was a key to the maneuvers that Smith was teaching.

Within the general framework of staying fast, staying below 30,000 feet, and using the vertical, there were various tactics and maneuvers that they told the students would get them quickly to the enemy's six o'clock position for a missile shot.

One tactic was the "High-speed Yo-Yo" —the ball on a string to which Smith referred. When the bogey returned horizontally, the student went up, dropped a wing in the bogey's direction and kept him in sight. When the bogey completed its turn, the student was taught to drop behind it to regain his speed in the dive down to the bogey.

Up and down, up and down, they taught. "You're driving him around in a circle," they said. "The other guy's flying over the circle looking for a predictable flight path so he can come in as quick as he can."

The predictable flight path was the key to shooting down a MiG. This was the short period in the fight when the MiG was steady and vulnerable. Its position then, albeit for only a few seconds, was calculable and fixed.

"Most of our [kill] tactics were dependent upon the ability of two airplanes to coordinate [as a team]," says Laing, referring to the loose deuce formation. "If, for instance, you were attacking a single target, you'd try to fly on either side of him . . . bracket him and have him turn toward one of them. Once he commits [to one side] he's presenting his tailpipe to the other."

But, of course, it wasn't always so simple. There were an infinite number of variables in a fight, such as the capabilities of the airplanes, their speeds, directions, and altitudes, and differences in the competence of individual pilots. In addition to yo-yoing, bracketing, and various other tactics or maneuvers, the school also taught pilots about "baiting" or "dragging." The engaged fighter in the team was to purposely show the bogey its tail in an attempt to goad him to maneuver for a shot. As the bogey did so, he'd be predictable—usually flying in a reasonably straight line for a number of seconds. The free fighter could then swoop down for a shot.

The tactic was controversial. It meant the baiter was predictable and the free fighter unprotected. "You were betting your life on someone else's skill and weapons system," recalls Dave Bjerke, who was in the second class and later became a Top Gun instructor. So the Top Gun instructors instituted a series of safeguards:

- Only drag for a short period of time.
- Always keep out of the bogey's gun range.
- Keep the bogey in sight at all times so you can evade if he shoots a missile.

"Let's say there are two A-4s out there over water," says Bjerke, "and we're coming at them [head-on] in Phantoms. The distance is 30 miles. . . . Maybe they have you on radar and maybe they don't. One thing you can do—a good tactic back in those days—is to take a cut away from them, a 30 degree cut . . . the idea is to swing around them [passing by each other] and come up behind.

"But let's say they see us, and [as we pass] turn into us. [Now they're stalking the Phantoms.] They decide to attack the outside guy. That would be smartest. . . . He becomes the engaged fighter. . . . He says, 'I'm engaged.' [Instead of continuing his turn,] he pushes the stick forward . . . goes to zero G, getting rid of induced drag, and accelerates. . . ."

Now he's dragging, racing forward as fast as he can, luring the two bogeys behind him. They are predictable. The free fighter knows that they are going to be in a relatively straight path and he has a few seconds in which to maneuver behind them for a shot.

"But the [engaged fighter] must keep sight of the bogeys." To do this, he swings his tail out a little bit so he can look back. The Phantom has a blind spot at its six o'clock position. "If he shot an Atoll at you, you wouldn't know it's coming." He'd never shoot guns because he's got to be inside 2000 feet "and the engaged fighter keeps his distance."

So the dragging Phantom keeps "swinging his tail out" with the little rudder action each time the bogey "drifts" back to his six.

In order to definitively test the students' newly learned skills, the instructors decided on a live missile shoot.

"The thing I remember most about the school," says Beaulier, "was it was the first time we'd really shot against a maneuvering target in a simulated engagement."

Previously, all he and his squadron mates—indeed, most fleet pilots—had done in the Navy was shoot at nonmaneuvering drones. The targets were sitting ducks, and they "took absolutely zero skills" to shoot down, says Pedersen. And to save costs, they hadn't even been allowed to hit the drones, just shoot near them. The Navy wanted to reuse the drones.

But now, for the students' final exam, the school was arming their Phantoms with live Sparrows and Sidewinders and sending up a supersonic Teledyne Firebee. Remote-controlled, fashioned like a jet fighter, it looked and performed like a MiG. And they were going to be allowed to actually hit it.

Pedersen said, "I felt very strongly that we had to have a maneuvering target to challenge the envelope, challenge the missile. One of the real reasons we were in trouble over Vietnam was that guys had not really stressed the missile [in practice]. While we had fairly good confidence in the Sidewinder, we had zero confidence in the Sparrow, particularly in its maneuvering [ability]. . . . It had a crazy envelope, not much of a hit ratio. . . .

"So we wanted to prove to the Navy and ourselves exactly what the missile was capable of and what its envelope was . . . and train guys to shoot in that envelope. . . . There isn't any sense finding yourself turning with a Colonel Toon or somebody like that and getting in a shot position and have it miss. . . ."

"This was going to be like the real thing," remembered Steve Smith. "No bullshit about winning it in the ready room or during the debrief."

"I remember Pedersen bracing us—not really bracing—but telling us don't screw it up," says Beaulier. "[Don't] shoot down yourself or your buddy. . . . They were worried about accidents."

This was Pedersen's biggest fear. The school was new, and the students were untried. One accident and they'd probably be shut down.

☆ ☆ ☆

VX-4 helped them to obtain the range and the missiles for the test. Steve Smith was put in charge. "The missiles were live, but not explosive. But forget about warheads, these were five-inch rockets, seven feet long. They came off at Mach 2 plus the speed of the airplane. It doesn't have to blow up."

The students knew that the drone was a "supersonic airplane" and would maneuver against anything they did. They were locked up on radar. The technician controlling the drone would know their altitude, airspeed, heading, "and everything you can name." Smith would be sitting beside him, "looking at a computer readout," and saying, "Okay, I've been watching these guys for four weeks. This is what they like to do . . . If they do this, move the drone like this . . . and so on."

"It could get very embarrassing for [the students] if they don't shoot the son-of-a-bitch down and it winds up behind them. . . ."

"You got to know where the hell your switches are, where your wingman is . . . what the hell you're doing," says Beaulier.

"Here we are up there off the coast of Point Mugu, a hundred miles," says Bjerke. "We're at 15,000 feet, 300 to 400 knots and in our combat spread for section tactics. . . . Seventy miles . . . fifty miles. . . . He's at forty, thirty. . . . Contact [on the radar]. Okay. We set up in our [section] tactics. The guy [controlling it] is sitting back there with his little stick, listening to us . . . 'Tallyho! Four miles!' . . . Swooosh. It comes swooping through and turns. We're after him. It's making a six-G right turn. . . . It's fantastic. . . ."

"They could pitch it up, reverse, zoom it. . . . It was unbelievable," says Beaulier.

More unbelievable were the results. After four weeks of concentrated training, the squadron pilots knew their planes' performance ability and envelopes perfectly. One by one, "they blew the son-of-a-bitch out of the sky," remembers Smith. They were so good that not only did they hit the drone with their first shots, but they also requested and got second and third drones sent up, even shooting missiles into the debris to watch them hit smaller parts.

Smith said, "It was like . . . you know, we've been in these missile shoots three or four times in our careers and it's always been a pain in the ass—to have to get a near miss. It's so canned. . . . But this was spectacular. I mean, they really got into it."

It was a relief deeply felt by all. "I can't tell you how good we felt at the end-of-the-exercise celebration," said Beaulier. They'd made it through the first class and it had been an unqualified success.

Beaulier's reaction was typical. "I came out with increased confidence . . . really pumped up. . . . If you can give a guy a lot of individual air combat maneuvering against dissimilar machines in a noncanned, nonstructured environment, hell, he's going to be a better fighter pilot. We told them so."

But even as they enjoyed that first highlight, an even better final exam was in the making—a fight with the real thing, the captured MiGS in the desert.

☆ ☆ ☆

Not long after the test, a minor catastrophe of sorts occurred. J. C. Smith and one of the Top Gun pilots had a new F-4, still smelling of lacquer and leather, prized beyond words by the RAG, which owned the $4 million plane. Drill's lenders did not want the MiG used in training, so VX-4, which did, was going out on a limb, pulling all kinds of tricks to get the Top Gun instructors to Nellis and into unauthorized training dogfights, including using RAG aircraft designated for other purposes. Sometimes, VX-4 had no official allotments for fuel or maintenance of the kind required for such training. But the RAG, after jostling paperwork and disguising entries, often did.

VX 4's McKeown, wanting to demonstrate his "bugout" maneuver for escaping a pursuing MiG, had borrowed the new airplane for a test flight. J. C. remained in the back seat. Nobody worried about protocol at the secret site.

"Mike Walsh was closing in on him in a '17," recalls Jim Foster, reconstructing the dogfight. "Mugs' idea was, Okay, I'll let him get close enough to look dangerous, then I'm going to look like I'm going one way, but push the stick forward in the other."

It was a move not unlike those from his football days at Navy. Give a feint to the left by putting the wing down in that direction, hope the MiG buys it, then reverse in the opposite direction.

"When you see a guy's wing go down," says Foster, "you immediately put yours down because you want to cut inside him. You do it subconsciously."

If the MiG pilot bought the move, he might be momentarily confused when the Phantom suddenly disappeared in the other direction. "Mugs would go up and over, and [the bogey was] defeated." If not, you just keep running.

"You can bet that RIO is watching like mad out the back with both hands back there pulling so he can see. The trouble is the airplane doesn't fly very good . . . with negative Gs on it [as it would have as McKeown pushed forward on the stick]. It stalled and spun. It was a flat spin . . . no rotation to speak of . . . there's just no lift on the wing."

179

It was a deadly situation. They were at 11,000 feet—not high to begin with. The Phantom fell like a rock, pinning the two crewmembers up against the canopy. There was little they could do.

"They punched out at the very last minute," remembers Foster, "and damn near landed into the fireball." For a few seconds, Tooter Teague, flying wing with them, thought they'd been killed.

"They just departed like a bastard. . . . I flew right through [where they'd been]."

Someone radioed (according to a tape of the incident): "Did anybody get out? Did anybody get out?"

"I thought I saw a couple of chutes," Teague responded and reversed for a pass by the flaming wreck. Moments later he reported, "I have two standing up. . . . Two standing up. . . . Both waving at me."

Teague's words were a relief to everybody.

McKeown had hurt his back, but basically he and Smith were okay.

Foster, however, was in trouble. The plane, which wasn't his, had to be accounted for.

"I called Hank [Halliland, CO of 121]. I said, 'What are we gonna do, Hank?' He says, 'You just bought yourself an airplane, buddy.' I say, 'Okay, transfer the thing.' He says, 'What'll I use for authority?' I say, 'I'll get you the authority.' "

It was the first real emergency for the Top Gun instructors and ACM proponents at Miramar and Point Mugu. In order to get Halliland off the hook, Foster would have to go to his superior in Washington, Rear Admiral Whitey Feightner, who reported directly to the CNO.

Foster was prepared. Earlier, during an annual Tailhook (carrier pilot's organization) reunion in Las Vegas, Foster had rented out several suites with free liquor and entertainment for the important air admirals, and at least one marine general. "When I got 'em all in there I'd corner 'em and convince them to let me take them to my special site and see my MiGs. I'd picked the [admirals] I'd wanted, of course . . . got special permission . . . put 'em all in the back of my old [transport] at Nellis and flew 'em all out there. . . . Here they all are in whites. . . . I had the whole back end full."

Some of the admirals, whites and all, "strapped in," and flew the MiGs. "Scared me a little bit." Teague, he said, flying wing, became so worried that one of them might be pushing a '17 too hard, that he finally yelled at one, "Goddamit, Admiral, put it on the ground!" From that day on, there was a lot more appreciation.

Foster called Feightner and said " 'Look, here's what happened. I screwed up. Cost us a multi-million-dollar plane, but I need a CNO transfer for the plane. . . . You're going to have to, in effect, override that three-star [in the chain of command over Halliland] so I can take responsibility and write the accident report.'. . . It wasn't Hank's problem. It was my problem."

Foster was later called on the carpet, but he got the transfer. The action was proof that the controversial ACM training had friends in high places—at least for the time being. There had been an accident, but those who could have used it against them weren't given the chance.

The night of the accident, remembers Teague, they'd all gone to a bar, "and a bunch of us—me, Mugs, Mike Walsh—all were standing around telling each other what heroes we were and how lucky we were to be alive and laughing. And this GE rep, who knew who I was and that I was writing the program, came up and said, 'Goddamit, some asshole just blew up one of my engines today' [GE made the new Phantom engine on which Mugs had counted to demonstrate his bugout]. . . . McKeown, hurting from his back injury, put him on the floor with a short right. [The rep] skidded down the dance floor just like in a Keystone Cops movie."

"The rep looked up and asked, 'What'd you do that for?' "

"McKeown said, 'I'm the asshole who blew up your engine.' "

☆ ☆ ☆

With the success of the first Top Gun class, the school was off the ground. They'd had to make a few changes. Midway, they'd realized "we needed more time in the day," said Smith. Instead of eight to five, he'd asked everyone to come in from seven to five, "and if you were flying early, you came in at four-thirty or before."

Nobody blanched. John Ed Kerr, a RAG student at the time, remembers arriving for a five A.M. brief "and there'd be two or three of the Top Gun guys asleep in the ready room. I think they'd either just not gone home for the night, or had made it a point to be there before us."

"By the second class," remembers Pedersen, "we were better skill-wise, energy-wise. . . . We had gone through one class ourselves. We'd adjusted. The flying didn't change that much, but we felt more confident."

The second class—eight combat veterans just in from the Gulf—came in cocky and full of self-confidence. "Hottest guys in the world," remembers Smith. "We told them we were going to simulate such and such, and it was, 'Yeah, yeah, watch my smoke.' "

But then the same thing that had happened to the first class, happened to them. "They'd come back flat . . . embarrassed . . . [they'd say] 'How'd you do that?' "

"I don't remember exactly what class it was," says Pedersen, "but we started preaching the unpredictable. 'Don't do what you've been doing—the same thing over and over. Change your habits. Rethink everything.'. . . Then you'd start seeing the changes . . . particularly on about flight four or five . . . you'd start seeing some sensational moves. . . ."

Pedersen himself had to execute a few sensational moves of his own a couple of months before. Charging head-on in a practice intercept for student RIOs, Pedersen and his backseater, Gil Sliney, flying against Mel Holmes and his student, suddenly felt a "thump" in the rear of their Phantom. The thump turned out to be a marmon clamp breaking. The clamp held together titanium tubing that routed scorching air from the left engine to the outside. A fire light suddenly came on. The escaping air was now igniting metal and who knew what else, Pedersen realized.

Pedersen killed the left engine and instinctively took the Phantom up in the remaining afterburner. "You do that for safety reasons. Altitude usually buys time." It was near dusk. They had been low over the Pacific, south of San Clemente Island. He didn't want to go in the ocean after dark. He'd had a friend lost years earlier. "They'd seen him just before nightfall in a raft. They never found him."

At 22,000 feet, a fire warning light in the remaining right engine came on. Holmes flew alongside them to take a closer look, but he couldn't see much through the smoke. Inside the Phantom, the fire was moving backwards, destroying circuits and hydraulics. Pedersen was losing control of the airplane, but still didn't know exactly why.

Miramar was the closest field, so they decided to try for it. Sliney watched the progression of the failing circuits as Pedersen wrestled with the controls, "but the circuit breakers were popping faster than Gil could call them off." Suddenly, after 60 miles of burning flight, an explosion brought chaos.

With the benefit of the after-incident investigation, Pedersen now thinks that the fire reached a basketball-sized oxygen container. It was probably still full. Flying alongside them, all Holmes knew was that fire suddenly enveloped the airplane.

Holmes called over to them, "Dan, you're on fire! You're on fire! You guys gotta get out. Punch out! Punch out!"

Pedersen was already shouting back to Sliney to eject. "Took me a couple of yells to get him to do it. Then I was free to eject."

He pulled the curtain and his ejection seat exploded into the air. Because they were so high up, a small drogue chute was supposed to open to stabilize them until their seats automatically disengaged at between 10,000 and 12,000 feet, when full parachutes opened. (The temperature at high altitudes is so cold that in order to prevent ejected crews from freezing, their main chutes are designed to remain closed at high altitudes, allowing the men to free-fall quickly to the warmer low altitudes.)

Holmes watched Pedersen and Sliney tumble out; below them their Phantom made a "sweeping left-hand turn" and dove toward the water.

Pedersen, still free-falling, reached up for his sunglasses. "The flight surgeon would raise hell with you for wearing them [in an ejection]. If they shattered, it could blind you."

He tucked the glasses away so that he didn't lose them in the water.

"I looked over and saw the coastline of La Jolla," said Pedersen, "The cove. I recognized all of it. I got to thinking, 'Hey, I've been falling for some time. I wonder how Gil's doing?' Over my shoulder,

I saw Gil above me in a fully deployed parachute. About that time, Mel flew by me, very near. I started to think, 'God, I'm really getting low. Why is Gil in a parachute and I'm not?' "

He didn't know how long he'd been falling. But he did know the seat was supposed to have automatically disengaged. Holmes at the time felt Pedersen still had time left. Pedersen, however, felt he was too low, and he decided to manually separate the ejection seat himself. After separating the seat, he watched it float up and away from him, thinking "I am free-falling now. Terminal velocity."

With no drag chute to slow him down, he was now hurtling toward the water. He reached up and grabbed his parachute's D-ring. "I pulled it out about 15 inches but nothing happened." He put both gloved hands on the stainless steel ripcord and pulled as hard as he could. The cable broke in his hands. The chute was still unopened.

Looking down at the rapidly approaching landscape of La Jolla, confusion gripped him. Had the ejection damaged the chute? For a split second he fought to remember what plane he'd jumped from. Then he remembered the Phantom hitting the water, and it came back to him.

"I looked at La Jolla and said, 'Oh, man, you're in trouble. You got to make it.' " His wife, Madeleine, and their young daughter, Dana, flashed through his mind— "everything I had to live for."

"I've got to do it!" he swore to himself. "I can't go this way!"

It is estimated that Pedersen was at about 3,000 feet at this point; the horseshoe-shaped parachute pack was forced above his head by the velocity of the fall.

"I couldn't see it but I knew it was there . . . " Pedersen recalls. Fighting gravity, he moved his hands up the harness straps and started pulling the parachute down. "I just got it down over the top of my helmet, right before my face and eyes—inches away—trying to hold on to it while falling and it popped right in my face."

The accident board estimated he was at 2,400 feet when the parachute finally opened.

Relief flooded Pedersen's mind. But when he looked down, he saw the dark shapes of large fish, their fins cutting the water. For a moment he thought he'd escaped certain death from the air only to be eaten by sharks. But as he got closer, he realized the shapes were dolphins. He was safe.

In June, right after the second Top Gun class graduated, a message went out from COMNAVAIRPAC, head of West Coast training, to its higher headquarters, CINCPACFLT. It requested "that the Naval Fighter Weapons School be officially established at NAS Miramar on 1 July 1969 under the operational and administrative control of Air Wing 12," which directed the RAG.

"Results to date [of the school] indicated this initial program has been highly successful," said the request. "Until assets [its own planes, maintenance, etc.] can be made available to the Fighter Weapons School, the interim measures used to conduct the first two [classes] will continue through Jul, Aug and Sept. . . ."

The request was certainly no assurance of permanence. That would only come when, and if, the school was made into a separate command, which would give it its own money and planes. Top Gun was still just a department within 121 and dependent on the squadron's policies and assets.

But the school had passed its shaky startup period. Two successful, accident-free classes, heralded by the spectacular drone-shoot scores and participant enthusiasm, had impressed the RAG's overseers enough to give the school a little paper credence, its first official endorsement in the chain of command.

Now the instructors could concentrate on what most of them believed to be their primary task: learning how to better kill MiGs.

☆ CHAPTER 20 ☆

Initially, only a few Top Gun instructors got to fly and fight the MiGs stationed out in the desert.

Typically, the instructors would fly to Nellis, usually in pairs, to be briefed by Teague, or Teague's assistants, who would tell them to fly to a "a certain spot" over the desert in their F-4s "and wait for us."

Then the two VX-4 officers would jump in their F-4 or F-8, fly to the MiG site, get in the MiGs, and speed off to meet the Top Gun crew.

An instructor who made the rendezvous describes the experience in this way: "There's a lot of anticipation. I mean, you've known you're gonna go for weeks. . . . Your heart's pumping away, and you get up there on the range and they're coming . . . ten miles, five miles . . . there it is. Just like in the movies . . . this little silver airplane."

Unlike the Phantom, the MiGs didn't trail smoke. They were hard to see. "Three and a half miles was about the maximum for a visible I.D."

For some, although they were combat veterans, it was the first time they'd been close to the real thing.

"You fly right up alongside of it and look at it. The first impression you get is, God, they are not very good at making airplanes. . . . It's got bumps and rivets showing . . . it looks like shoddy workmanship. But then you square off to fight it. . . . There are good pilots in it. . . ."

By now the Drill pilots had put the MiGs through every conceivable test. With the newcomers in trail, they rolled it, showing how the Phantom could roll better, and put it in a dive, demonstrating the '17's lack of maneuverability at high speed.

"If you can get him nose down," they explained, "and he's low enough, he'll hit the ground."

But the Top Gun instructors also saw they couldn't turn with the little fighter. Some of what they'd thought would work, didn't. Generally, however, they'd been right on the mark.

"We had to stay fast," was an often heard refrain.

With the '21, the situation was different. The fighter was almost as fast as the Phantom, so they couldn't run from it. But it bled energy faster.

"So what you do . . . is keep him turning [until] he finally gets his airspeed down. Keep him turning nose high 'till pretty soon he gets down below a certain speed and then he really bleeds it because he's a big delta wing. [Then] what you do is keep him moving and pretty soon you hope that with your increased G—it takes a long time, it's not a quick process—but pretty soon you work yourself into an offensive position [where] he's slow enough and you're far enough away that you can turn around and shoot him in the head with your Sparrow."

It helped them tremendously to practice on the real thing, not only in lessening any "buck fever" accompanying a first encounter, but also in enabling them to fine-tune their tactics.

RIOs got to observe the MiGs in different profiles, sharpening their abilities to "visually acquire" the plane and, from greater distances, being able to recognize the MiG's "footprint" on their scopes.

Later, in a special dogfight session against the Air Force, the Navy demonstrated the superiority of its pilot–RIO teamwork philosophy. "The Air Force had pilots [not RIOs] in the back. . . . We got contacts at greater distances and entered on the offensive. They got less kills than us."

As a result, the Air Force instituted specialized backseater training.

On any given day, during the war-lull days of 1969, the best fighter pilots in the world were in the skies above the American desert fighting each other in Phantoms and MiGs, though only a handful of people in the country knew of the training. Not unexpectedly, there were clashes and disagreements.

VX-4 was staffed with former F-8 pilots, who flew without an RIO. Not all of them were convinced they needed a backseater to help them fight. Many pilots involved felt they had to uphold their reputations. In addition, the Air Force and CIA tugged at the Navy program's control. Arguments over who won dogfights led one Top Gun instructor to later say, "I'd fly into the ground before I'd lose to one of [the VX-4 pilots]." A VX-4 pilot countered, "I'd been told to watch out for some of them, but I wasn't impressed." On at least one occasion, say those who witnessed it, McKeown and Pedersen almost came to blows.

Ultimately, however, VX-4 and Top Gun enjoyed a remarkable partnership. Despite their differences, they appreciated one another. Teague and Foster sometimes took enormous risks to see that the information they discovered about fighting the MiGs got out to the fleet, and the Top Gun instructors gave of themselves to the same end. More often than not, pilots put the brakes on their egos for the sake of the mission.

Eventually, so those who could not go through Drill or Top Gun could benefit from the secret program, a 30-minute film about it was produced entitled "Throw a Nickel on the Grass" (from an old drinking song—". . . save a fighter pilot's ass"). It featured Teague as an on-camera narrator. The film was shown to every Navy fighter squadron in the fleet.

"The most important result of Project Have Drill," says Teague in the film, "is that no Navy pilot who flew in the project defeated the Fresco [the MiG-17] in the first engagement. . . ."

Some of the Top Gunners dispute that—but the point was well taken.

☆ ☆ ☆

"Once the school got rolling, it gained its own energy," says Pedersen. "The students went back to their squadrons, and their squadron mates found out, and guys came banging on the door, every day, all day, wanting to come over as instructors. [They'd say,] 'I can whip your ass. Let's go out and fight.' That kind of thing. . . .

We had to tell them, 'Sorry—don't have any openings. We'll keep your name in the bank. . . .' "

An elitism, now bolstered by real accomplishment, developed. "Top Gun meant 'ace of the base,' " remembers a junior officer who eyed the Top Gun patch worn on pilots' sleeves as a symbol to be envied. The little trailer at Miramar was now the place to be assigned.

"We never [told others] we were attached to 121, which we were," remembers Holmes. "We'd have our own suite at Tailhook. . . . Everywhere we went we tried to be first class, really pushing the Navy to recognize us."

They dropped bombing from the syllabus entirely (although it appears to have come back several times). The pilots, whenever and wherever they could, preached loose dcucc strategy and created fighter pilot slogans in the Miramar Officer's Club bar. "One was a Richthofen saying," remembers Holmes—" 'Find the enemy and shoot him down. Anything else is rubbish.' We had [officer's wives] calling the base and saying how despicable it was for us to display an enemy saying. . . . The wives didn't understand he [Richthofen] was a fighter pilot. We admired his capability."

The instructors invited aces to Miramar to give talks, culminating in a showdown of sorts with veteran pilot Robin Olds, although no one played it up as such. "My God, he was an ace several times over [in World War II]," recalls Holmes, and the leading American Vietnam fighter pilot with four kills at the time. "We wanted information from him. See what he thought of our ideas."

Olds was a brigadier general and commandant of cadets at the Air Force Academy. J. C. Smith was assigned to his backseat in a dogfight during Olds' stay at Miramar. "Olds was putting on his gear, and he's a big guy and was having trouble getting a harness over his shoulder," says Jerry Sawatzky. "J. C. said something like, 'General, if you'd get rid of that star you'd have an easier time of it . . . ' The general just stopped and looked. I think he was going to laugh, but then he didn't." Their relationship didn't improve in the air.

Smith recalls, "We went up there and I started screaming and hollering at him. . . . But he's not listening. Finally, he told me to shut up. So I said, 'Go ahead. Get your ass waxed.' "

"Olds was a very aggressive pilot," Mel Holmes remembered. "He had not been in a Phantom for nearly a year. I was surprised how quickly he jumped in. The first engagement was two-versus-two . . . relatively simple. I used him as bait and shot down the bogey. The second fight was completely different. We had two bogeys. . . . He went back to his own tactics and went off on his own to engage the bogey while I was trying to protect him. [Later, on the ground,] the only reaction I got from him was about J. C. He said, 'In my airplane, [the backseater] only does what I tell him to do.' J. C. said, 'Well, we don't do that here.' Robin got very upset."

Jim Ruliffson was involved in his own harrowing ejection shortly afterwards. One day in August 1969, while instructing a senior officer in how to do a rolling scissors in the Phantom, Ruliffson nearly became a fatal statistic himself. Sitting in the backseat, he found himself trying to talk the commander out of a departure—not once, but three consecutive times, with the third time ending in tragedy.

The commander, J. J. Chambers, had been picked to become a CAG; as a result, he had been assigned to take some refresher flights at 121. He was a graduate of Patuxent River and a former F-4 squadron skipper; but as others mentioned afterward, in those days, the only thing the pilots practiced with the Phantom was intercept.

Chambers and Ruliffson were flying against an instructor and an instructor-in-training, when, flying upside down, the plane departed. Ruliffson explained, "It's common for the airplane to depart in the maneuver because you're flying it right there to the edge."

The Phantom started falling uncontrollably, its nose approximately 30 degrees down and its wings not catching the air. This is technically termed an "accelerated stall." The recovery procedure was to roll the wings level with the horizon and start flying again.

"We had gone through the procedures in the brief [on the ground], and he had recovered the plane nicely," Ruliffson explained. But as they started to fly again, Chambers pulled the stick a little too hard and the plane departed again. Once again they were flying upside down, the nose now perhaps 60 degrees down.

There was a limit to the amount of the sky they had in which to maneuver.

"I started talking real hard. 'Unload the airplane [accelerate]. Use the rudder to roll the wings level, and start pulling out. Be easy with it. Get your eye on the gauges.'" He could use the angle-of-attack instrument to make sure he didn't go into another accelerated stall.

They recovered for a second time when "damned if he didn't do it again," said Ruliffson. "Now we're in our third consecutive departure, and we're now upside down passing through 5000 feet with the nose about 85 degrees down. There's no way in hell anyone could get out of that one in a Phantom. . . . Now that we're already vertical, it would take 6,000 to 7,000 feet just to get the nose back to level."

Chambers never said a word to Ruliffson, and Ruliffson did not have a clue as to why the commander continued to pull too hard on the stick, other than to speculate that he was probably overanxious.

"I said something like, 'Jesus Christ, commander. Get out!' I waited for a count of about two, and then I ejected."

Chambers never did.

Ruliffson ejected at about 2500 feet. Tumbling end over end, he caught a glimpse of the Phantom hitting the water. His chute opened just before he landed in the wreckage. A board of inquiry later found "pilot technique" as the cause of the crash.

The accident was an example of one of the problems the school was attempting to address: veteran Phantom pilots who were ignorant or fearful of the plane's performance edges.

By September, 121 and its parent, Air Group 12, both had new commanders. Dick Schulte and Lou Page respectively became the first RAG authorities who actively supported the new school. This was a major development for Top Gun. It meant it no longer had to beg, borrow, and steal planes and other equipment. Both Schulte, an attack pilot, and Page loved to fly the A-4 like a fighter, and they took every opportunity to fly adversary.

"I wanted to be associated with what they were doing," said Page. "If I came back with film of a Phantom in front of me, those guys weren't doing their job."

In hopes of getting even higher active support, Page flew his boss, Vice Admiral William "Bush" Bringle, commander of all the

Pacific Fleet's Naval air forces, smack into the middle of a Top Gun dogfight. Bringle had spent a lot of time off Vietnam and knew the F-4 problem first-hand.

"He was absolutely amazed," remembers Page, "at what we were doing with those airplanes."

Bringle's subsequent support was crucial. It meant that for the first time all the commanders in the chain of command up to Washington—121, Air Wing 12, and Air Pac— were actively supporting the school. They weren't just agreeing to requests by Pedersen, but making requests on behalf of the school themselves—a fact that must have made Gorder, Ault, and the other Pentagon supporters very happy.

In a speech made later at Schulte's departure from 121, Bringle singled out Top Gun as one of 121's major achievements: "During Commander Schulte's tenure . . . the . . . Fighter Weapons School . . . has become a reality. To date, this advanced weapons school has graduated over 50 aircrews. Not only have the Atlantic and Pacific fleet squadrons benefitted, but the Marines and Air Force as well. . . ."

Probably as a result of this support, in October 1969 Pedersen and his staff were ordered to fly to Washington and give a briefing to the Pentagon. They did so, and the result was official approval of the Top Gun syllabus by the chief of naval operations himself, and a message from the commander of naval air forces at North Island saying the approval was another step in the "ultimate goal" of the school becoming "a Weapons System School command" —a permanent, independent command.

But even as they savored the growing support, the instructors worried. The school had not yet passed the ultimate test: not one of its students had shot down a MiG.

"It gnawed at us," says Pedersen, who, by now was preparing to leave. "It gnawed at *all* of us."

☆ CHAPTER 21 ☆

Jerry Beaulier felt the sweat pooling around him. Little droplets ran down his arms, neck, and legs. It was steaming in his open cockpit. The *Constellation* was traveling downwind on Yankee Station; the course eliminated any cooling breezes and caused deck smoke and vapors to hover in the broiling sun.

It was March 28, 1970, almost one year to the day since Beaulier had graduated from the first Top Gun class. He and his RIO, Steve Barkley, were manning one of four "Alert 5" Phantoms on the forward deck. The bombing halt over the North was still in effect, but the U. S. was carrying out operations over Laos and South Vietnam, and the carrier had to be ready. Two Phantoms were already out on BARCAP, and those on alert would assist or relieve them, if necessary.

There were two kinds of alerts. Alert 15 meant the crews had 15 minutes to launch. They could wait in the ready room; there was enough time to run out and jump in their planes. But Alert 5 meant they had only five minutes to launch, barely enough time to do a quick startup as mouse-eared crewmen attached the Phantom to the catapult. In an Alert 5, the pilots had to spend their watch in the cockpit, ready to launch.

And so Beaulier and Barkley sat in their open cockpit, sticky with sweat, passing the time talking. Despite the conditions, both were where they wanted to be. BARCAP was usually a boring assignment, but, today the atmosphere seemed charged.

"Boy, there was a lot of activity going on on the flight deck," remembers Beaulier. Already on one catapult, sweating with the others, was his squadron's skipper, Gene Gardner. And on another was the new CAG, Paul Speer.

CAGs never sat Alert 5, and because of that Beaulier "damn well knew something was up." What he didn't know was that a scheme to shoot down some MiGs was being hatched.

In the past weeks, North Vietnamese MiGs had been making incursions down past the Thanh Hoa Bridge and Vinh. It had been the furthest south they had flown in some time. They had shot down a rescue helicopter, causing its six crewmen to be captured or killed. Fleet admirals were worried that they might attack ships or unarmed monitoring planes just off the coast.

Unprovoked attacks by U. S. planes were still prohibited by Washington, but Admiral Fred Bardshar, on board the *Constellation*, thought he knew of a way to trap the MiGs: he'd place BARCAP below the Vietnamese radar, at 500 feet off the water. The MiGs wouldn't make their incursions if they knew that Phantoms were in the area, or at least that had been the pattern. This way they wouldn't know Phantoms were in the area until it was too late—or so Bardshar hoped. The Phantoms could then claim self-defense.

"We tried it the day before," said Phil Craven, part of Bardshar's staff, "but the MiGs had been too far away—about 25 kilometers. Two F-4s off the *Coral Sea* had given chase but we were worried about their fuel, and so we called them back."

CAG Speer, a large, personable man, was a former single-seat Crusader driver who'd recently transitioned to Phantoms. On May 19, 1967, while flying escort for a surgical strike on a Hanoi thermal power plant, he'd shot down a MiG-17 in a wild, treetop battle involving as many as a dozen enemy planes. Already a veteran of two combat cruises, he'd been sent back out for a third, although Navy policy normally forbid that. The previous air wing commander had been killed and they needed Speer's experience.

Jim Ruliffson had been Speer's FAM instructor during his transition to the Phantom at the RAG. On a two-versus-two tactics hop, the second Phantom in Speer's section had failed to show. Rather than reschedule, Speer, with Jim Laing in his back seat, had taken off, talking over the radio as if the second Phantom was there.

When Ruliffson figured out the ruse, he'd abruptly headed back to Miramar, letting both Laing and Speer know how mad he was.

At the debrief, Speer said, "Jim, I know you're mad at me. What we've got to avoid is me getting mad at you."

Ruliffson, he says, "calmed down."

It was a short while later that CMDR Chambers died, as Ruliffson ejected from the backseat. Walking into his board of inquiry, Ruliffson had found Speer heading the inquiry. "He said, 'Oh, shit,' " recalled Speer, "but it wasn't his fault. Chambers thought he could bring the plane out and he couldn't. Jim had been right to punch out."

Now Speer was far from Miramar, hoping to get his second MiG. "The admiral had told me he thought [the MiGs] might come down again about this time of day, so I managed to get myself assigned Alert 5," said Beaulier "which is not a nice job. . . . People were wondering why I volunteered."

If he and Barkley did get launched, Beaulier knew he'd be either Speer's or Gardner's wingman—third position, but better than nothing. He watched the deck activity with increased anticipation.

Graduating from Top Gun, Beaulier had returned to 142 as its weapons training officer. "You did a series of lectures and briefings and things like that to try and bring up the levels of expertise . . . Munitions use, . . . airplane capabilities, and the bad guy's capabilities. . . . You run through all of it," Beaulier stated.

"In all fairness, it was such a new thing that [the quick ACM fix] was slow to develop. . . . It would be presumptuous for me to say I saw results [in the squadron] right away. . . . What you can hope for is that [the other pilots] became more aware."

VF-142 returned to Yankee Station and became involved in the bombing of Laos and Cambodia. "We were hauling bombs around to the passes over there," said Beaulier. "I was a flight leader then . . . I would take a two-ship flight. On occasion I did a three and then a four. You'd find the odd truck that had broken down, or the FAC's [Forward Air Controllers] would put you in on areas they thought were good. At night, they'd put logs in a kind of impregnated wooden thing that they'd kick out of the airplane." The logs, or moonlight, lighted the target.

Beaulier's most memorable mission had occurred one night when they had been bombing a river crossing and he made the mistake of making three passes at the target. "It's stupid to make that many runs. Really stupid." The enemy had anti-aircraft guns with special sights on them. "They just opened up. Holy Christ. I've never seen so much flak. It was everywhere. In front of us, above us, below us, behind us. . . . They shot something like 100 or 150 rounds just as we were pulling out. They were firing at sound because we didn't have any lights on. So instead of pulling up, like I normally did, I went straight ahead."

Beaulier was flying in total darkness—"Scared the living bejesus out of me."

The trees or mountains could have snuffed them in an instant.

Born in Michigan's remote Upper Peninsula, Beaulier was a loner. He preferred hunting and archery to team sports, and he had developed, while stalking game in the woods near his hometown of Kingsford, a kind of sixth sense for marksmanship.

"I didn't aim in the traditional sense. Just kind of shot with both eyes open. They call it instinctive with the long bow, but I did the same with a shotgun."

These abilities carried over to his ACM. Despite the fact that missiles did their own tracking, being able to lead shots, having an eye for relative motion and angle off, gave him an edge as a fighter pilot.

Suddenly Beaulier heard the Air Boss on the bull horn: "Launch Alert 5."

The planes flying BARCAP had left station to refuel, and the directors of the operation were sending the backup to take their place.

On the catapult, there was a malfunction in CO Gardner's plane. They pushed it off the catapult and started wheeling Beaulier's in. "Christ sakes," he remembers, "my plane captain is trying to get us to go through the checks and all that, and I'm trying to wave him away because we know something's up. We don't know what the hell it is, but you're better off being airborne than sitting tight to the goddamn deck."

Moments later Beaulier launched. But Speer was having trouble with his plane, too. "They're telling me my airplane is down . . . my ramps are open," Speer recalled. [Located inside the Phantom's side air intakes] "They're only supposed to be open when you go supersonic."

Gardner's plane was fixed, and he finally launched. But not far out it developed trouble again and he had to return to the carrier. By that time, Speer was launched.

"As I was proceeding," Speer remembers, "Jerry called me and said 'Stoke it, CAG,' meaning hurry up." They met near the *Piraze*, an enemy monitoring cruiser call-signed "Red Crown." They both switched to Red Crown's frequency, skimming low over the water, as Bardshar's strategy was designed.

Just as they were turning north, toward the Chinese-owned island of Hainan—almost due west from Vinh—they received their first transmission from Red Crown: "Your vector 280. Your bogey 280, 87 miles and you're cleared to fire."

"You don't usually get such a clearance," says Speer. "Here we are barely out of our turn and we're already cleared."

They both knew what the message meant: MiGs.

Their course was head-on. They spread out into loose deuce, staying low and powering into minimum burner in order to leave no smoke. They were still hoping to surprise the MiGs.

But they couldn't find the bogeys. "We were absolutely head-on. [vector] 280. 58 miles . . . 280. 45 . . . 280 and 30 . . . Our closure was astronomical, . . . but we couldn't find them," Speer recalled.

They were now well inland. They started climbing, not wanting to make themselves a target for SAMs. Suddenly, Beaulier spotted two MiG-21s. They were gleaming dots in the sunlight. By this point in the war, VX-4, through Top Gun, had been bringing in fleet pilots to fly against Drill's MiGs in the Nevada desert. But Beaulier's class had not been privy to Drill or Doughnut. This was the first real enemy airplane he'd ever seen.

"They were high, at about, oh, maybe my own one o'clock position" and about 15,000 feet above them. "One of the things I'd learned in Top Gun was that whoever's got the bogey in sight can assume the tactical lead. I did that."

It was classic loose deuce and exactly what Top Gun had taught. Although Speer was the senior officer and flight leader, as well as a MiG killer, Beaulier had sight, and therefore, he took the lead.

"If you are reluctant for a minute you might lose advantage," says Speer. "You gotta make that turn right then. You can't hesitate. . . . [Beaulier] called the 'Tally ho' and it was automatic. I might have said, 'You got it.' "

Although Speer had downed a '17, it was his first face-to-face meeting with a '21. "That '17 had banana wings . . . but these '21s were beautiful . . . silver . . . they looked graceful, like long-necked ducks," Speer related.

"I don't think their GCR [ground control radar] knew what altitude we were at," recalled Beaulier. "I called for a hard climbing turn and up we went."

There was no reason to conceal smoke anymore. They lit full burner. They had the advantage of surprise, but the disadvantage of having to climb, where they'd lose speed.

Seeing the Phantoms, the two MiGs split, one arcing high out to the left, and the other one diving in a hard right turn. Beaulier went after the diving MiG. Speer began defense against the other.

They didn't know it at the time, but later intelligence indicated that Beaulier's opponent was a squadron leader, an experienced pilot, possibly a colonel. The other, the next few moments would indicate, wasn't so experienced.

"It got kind of hectic for a while," Beaulier remembers. "Barkley kept the other guy in sight and a running commentary on what he was doing, which freed me. I got kind of slow in the beginning [as he reached altitude to confront them], and I thought, 'Goddamit, you're going to die because you don't have speed.' Speed is life [but] I don't think he had any energy either [so he went down]. So we went down low too, I mean well down below 'em. [As we bottomed out] we were back up around 700 knots indicated. We were smoking . . . 7 Gs on the airplane . . . and I was back in the fight. I've got my energy back now."

Now he had a new concern, as did Speer: his extra fuel tanks, they were slowing him down. But neither he or Speer could just jettison them. "It's not like in the World War II movies where they just come off the belly," Beaulier remembered. "In real life they'll do funny things . . . like come back into the airplane. . . . You get flow effects . . . they'll go through tails and stuff." He had to wait until he was at a relatively slow speed, approximately 475 knots, to dump them.

As he came back up, Barkley, who was also concerned about the tanks, told him, "Airspeed's good" and "we blew the tanks." He was now rounding out the first of two, huge, nearly vertical eggs that he and the MiG-21 would trace in the sky. They were immense, elongated circles with diameters approximately 15,000 feet across.

As they rounded the first egg, probably just after they'd dropped their tanks and had climbed to a higher altitude, the MiG fired a heat-seeking Atoll at Speer.

Realizing that the other MiG had taken himself out of the fight with his sweeping turn away, Speer had been coming back counterclockwise across the top of the circle to help Beaulier. The Atoll was fired at him head-on.

"Doesn't have a chance," he shouted to his RIO. The heat-seeker would have to make a 180-degree turn to come back on their tail. "I guess it made him feel good."

Beaulier was driving the '21, "keeping the pressure on him. I think the other guy actually lost sight." All he could think was, "I want to shoot the bugger. You're trying to be cool, but it's not a conscious thing. You're after this guy. You're trying to keep your energy up, trying to get yourself in a position where you can shoot. But you don't really think about it, because when you get really excited or really afraid, your brain is atrophied. . . . You're running on basics."

Barkley, his eyes on the other bogey, was still keeping up the commentary: "He's no threat! . . . No threat!"

Going into his second big turn, Beaulier started arming his switches. The vertical climbs were enabling him to gain on the '21, which was bleeding more energy than the Phantom each time they went up.

"I remember consciously thinking that I'm going to make damn sure my switches are right, 'cause there had been a lot of folks that have [tried to shoot] airplanes or drop bombs with the nose landing gear button [which was close to the firing button on his control stick]."

As they completed the second turn and went down into the third, Beaulier started getting close enough for a shot.

"You're not thinking about Top Gun per se, but I was saying, 'Hey, I know I'm getting close. . . . You recognized you were in range. I'd shot so many missiles at Top Gun that I was just aware."

The '21 knew he was close too. Its pilot made a desperate turn to the right, then reversed to the left. Beaulier thinks the MiG pilot lost sight and probably thought the Phantom had overshot.

The distance was rapidly closing now, Beaulier's Phantom perhaps 2000 feet behind the '21, which was about minimum range for a successful Sidewinder shot. Just an instant before, as the MiG had turned to the right, Beaulier had thought of shooting but had held back. As he would describe it later, the MiG was moving at a right angle in front of him. If he'd fired at that instant, the Sidewinder would have had to turn 90 degrees to track the angling MiG, a hard maneuver at best.

"But when he reversed left, I was suddenly looking right down his tailpipe. He'd solved my tracking problem."

Barkley, who'd been looking elsewhere and didn't realize how close they were, suddenly heard the Sidewinder's armed homing tone go from low growl to high-pitched whine—as did Beaulier. "Shoot! Shoot! Shoot!" he said, in the practiced manner.

Beaulier did.

The missile was true. But when it went off "underneath the guy," nothing happened. "In all my thoughts, in all the World War II movies I'd ever seen, you shot the guy and he explodes. He's a fireball. History. But nothing happened. Just a puff of black smoke. I thought, Jesus, I missed him."

He roared up over the MiG to prevent an overshoot, "Then the guy just burst into flames." Speer explained: "It's the Sidewinder's expanding-rod warhead. . . . It sends out a bunch of rods in an ever-increasing circle, slicing into the airplane. . . . It may take a nanosecond for fires to start. . . . To Jerry, it seemed like an eternity. If it hits him right, it might take a tail off." The same thing had happened to Speer on his 1967 MiG kill.

But Beaulier wasn't taking any chances. Although the '21 was now "wing-rocking . . . 50- to 75-foot flames shooting out the back of it," he came back over the top and shot him again. "I would have shot that sucker a third time," Beaulier insisted, "if he hadn't gone into the damn undercast."

The first MiG destroyed, Speer now lit out after the second. But it was already heading back north. "It [the MiG] becomes a very small target when he [the pilot] is trying to get away from you," said Speer.

Back at the *Constellation*, says Craven, they got word that the retreating MiG was going to run out of gas, which meant Speer could have pursued him with a good chance of getting a kill. "But we couldn't get the word to Paul." Out of fear of revealing that they were listening to enemy transmissions, Red Crown decided not to relay the information.

Beaulier remembers, "I was really beside myself. . . . I'd done my thing. But then, you know, I realized I didn't know where my wingman was. I called CAG. 'Where the hell are you?' 'I'm chasing this other guy.' Then he said he was turning back, and as I looked back [to where the fight had taken place], you could see all these smoke trails from the missiles that were shot. He [the '21] had shot one. I'd shot two. There was smoke from him going down. It was absolutely incredible—all the goddamn trails . . . [and] the afternoon sun . . . all backlighted by a reddish sky. We headed back for water, CAG a minute behind us."

In the aftermath of the fight, Beaulier reflected on what he'd just been through. "The initial part was just like being out there in Southern California, in Whiskey 281 or 291, or whatever it was. You're on a vector from the local GCI. But when you get up close, hey, it's real. . . . What the training did for me is it kept my feet on the ground. It kept me thinking properly. I didn't get buck fever. . . . It seems kind of funny that you could train a person to be a, you know, put him in a pretty sophisticated airplane and an arduous, harsh environment like a carrier, and that he'd get buck fever. But they do . . . it's excitement. Everybody's going to get excited. . . . But it's a shooting man's game, and it's the quality of training we see in Top Gun that makes you ready. You know all the things that are going to happen to you before you get there. You got a whole bag of tricks, you're not working from the book of Genesis."

It had been a classic shootdown and textbook Top Gun. They landed to a movie scene celebration; Speer literally picked up the smaller Beaulier in a hug, then the two of them skipped across the deck to cheers from the crew. Down in the ready room, it was like post-Super Bowl Sunday. Champagne was poured over the victors' heads (the captain breaking out vintage stash) and the admiral led the toasts.

The kill was immediately classified, and a doctored press release was issued, saying, "in the first such action reported since the November 1968 bombing halt . . . a U. S. Navy F-4 Phantom jet shot down a North Vietnamese MiG-21 while flying reconnaissance escort near Thanh Hoa. . . ." The release did not name the pilot.

Back at Miramar, those in the Top Gun trailer were as much in the dark as anyone.

"We heard that the Navy got a kill," says Steve Smith, "but we didn't know who." Bits and pieces were coming in. "We were trying to get the guy's name. . . . You're sitting there—and it's a really small club, because between all of us, we've got to know 90 percent [of the crew] in both squadrons on that ship . . . and we're saying, well it could have been him or him. Naw, shit, he'd of never gotten a MiG. . . ."

"It really came down to 'Boy, wouldn't it be sensational. We got two grad crews on that boat—wouldn't it be bitchin' if one of our guys was the one.' " When they heard the victorious crew were Top Gun graduates, the school closed for the day and everyone went to the base club and got drunk.

The kill was a testimonial to Top Gun, said Pedersen, who learned about it in the Mediterranean. (Pedersen had left Miramar in late 1969 to join Teague in Drill and then had been assigned as senior aviation advisor to the admiral commanding Task Force 60.2, the battle group then cruising off the Middle East. The admiral was one of the first non-aviators given a carrier group, and Pedersen had been singled out to help him.)

Pedersen's replacement as director-ONC of Top Gun was J. C. Smith, an NFO, which was fitting recognition of how far he and "backseaters" had come.

Other original Top Gun instructors were leaving as well: Holmes went to J. C.'s old squadron, VF-21; Nash would be leaving in June; Steve Smith and Sawatzky would be leaving in May. A new cadre was forming—the second generation of Top Gun instructors.

With its first kill now registered, the future of the school seemed stronger than ever. But that was an erroneous assumption.

PART IV

Triumph in the Skies

☆ Chapter 22 ☆

Jerry Kane, one of the new instructors at Top Gun, was worried. He often had a gnawing, gut-wrenching fear in his stomach. He was drinking more, and he couldn't sleep at night.

He wasn't alone. The other Top Gun instructors were worried too—Bjerke, Dave Forst, Dave Lortscher; and Roger Box, the new ONC who'd replaced J. C. Smith.

It was 1971. With the exception of Jerry Beaulier's kill, there had been no air war in Vietnam since the school had started. The new CO of the RAG, Don Pringle, was a protege of the new chief of naval operations, Admiral Elmo Zumwalt, whose "Z-Grams" were changing the Navy, was giving priority—as was his responsibility—to turning out fleet pilots. Top Gun was in danger of dying.

Pringle, said Kane, was a "creased and polished" aviator, "great with the rank and file . . . totally goal-oriented." But it was "our opinion that his intention was that 121 produce more [pilots] for the fleet than his predecessors, and if it was necessary to sacrifice Top Gun to do it, that's what would happen."

Kane seemed hardest hit. Since he and Bjerke had gone through the second class and graduated, they had been the first in the Navy to actually receive written orders to the new school. His dedication to the school had soared.

"You've got to understand how they primed us," Kane remembered. "First they select you for the class, make you feel elite. Then they select you to teach there. You feel more elite. . . . They've got you believing you're the best. And because you're the best, you believe it's a job that has to be done.

"And you could see the value of it, because we could see what was happening. We could see the level of accomplishment between when these guys would come in and when they would leave. Sometimes it was the difference between night and day. They'd come in and flail around—I mean obviously a candidate to get his butt shot off in the first melee he got into. But when they left, they were skilled. I mean really good."

Of all the things he'd been involved in in his life, "this was the one thing I totally, truly believed in. . . . I [Kane] was totally inspired to put everything I had into it. Guys were dying. . . . I saw it in the rawest, basic terms of saving people's lives."

Yet what Kane and the other instructors feared most *was* happening. Not since Dick Schulte had headed the RAG had Top Gun enjoyed strong support. Under Schulte—with help from Washington—the school had scored its first major administrative coup: the acquisition of four A-4 Mongooses, souped-up, single seat Skyhawks to replace the slower, less-agile TA-4s as MiG-17 adversaries.

The Mongooses were transferred from Lemoore, an attack base north of Miramar, with considerable protest from the air group that lost them.

Getting such airplanes during a war showed real priority. Everybody needed more airplanes, including 121. The acquisition was an "illegal borrowing," remembers Pete Kellaway, who had had a hand in starting the school from the beginning while serving on Phil Craven's 121 staff. "We kind of went out of the chain a little bit and went right to the guys in Washington [Naval Air] who had the assets and funds."

With the Mongooses, the instructors had expanded the Top Gun training to the fleet under what they called the "Fleet Adversary Program," which were ten-day detachments in which the Top Gun pilots would fly against entire fleet squadrons about to go on combat cruises.

"We were making the training available to the guys who were most likely to get into a melee with MiGs," remembers Kane. "We'd give them a brief series of lectures, and what I think was probably the best we had to offer: their first nonegotistical debrief [emphasizing not who won, but why]. We scheduled the time and made it available to them."

It taxed the school and its members to the hilt. "We would get like three hops a day," says Mike Guenther, one of the few who flew his way into the second cadre without a formal set of orders. "Each hop meant about six engagements; some were getting eighteen dogfights a day as an aggressor."

Nobody complained. They all loved it. But now Kane was seeing that even though they'd willingly work the longer hours, arrive home later, they were being assigned so many 121 duties that there was no physical way they could attend to Top Gun work.

"I can remember checking the flight schedule every night. If it said Kane would be on such and such a hop as instructor with a 121 student, it didn't make a damn bit of difference what my [Top Gun] skipper told me. 121 took priority.... And sometimes you'd find out you had a 4:30 A.M. brief and it was 8 o'clock [P.M.] and you still hadn't been home. In fact, some days I'd find out I was scheduled all the next day at 121.... You had a Top Gun class the next day.... It just couldn't be done."

They had meetings with the 121 staff. Discouraged, they began trying to get friends in high places to help them. "We had several meetings with people around the base whose opinions we respected and who believed in us and had seniority, about how we could save Top Gun and at least make the program available to the fleet if we didn't survive ... But we didn't have the 'graduation exercises,' nothing to show that we were killing the enemy in greater numbers than we had been before."

One kill—Beaulier's—wasn't enough. They needed more. But due to the political talks and a subsequent lull in the fighting, the MiGs had stopped flying as they regrouped.

So Kane decided to write a book about the Top Gun school. "I'll be honest. Part of it was therapeutic because I thought maybe [Top Gun] would not die if [the story] was in writing. I was going to give it to some people in Washington if I had to. In fact, I even at one time had thought maybe if [Top Gun] didn't survive, I would put it in some kind of form after I had left the Navy and make it available to members of the press ... to make people realize how important it had been."

Kane began interviewing all the old fighter pilots he could find, dating back to Korea. His idea was to trace how FAGU, the old fleet gunnery school, had gone out of existence. He wanted to trace what had happened because it could happen again.

"I began calling these guys up, making notes," recalled Kane, "Sometimes I'd tape. . . . It was important to me to find out how, when they truly were gunfighters, how it all had been lost and we had gone to the Buck Rogers mentality of just standing off and shooting a missile.

"And I was told repeatedly by the Pedersens and the Leeds and the Ruliffsons, who had done their homework, that there had been no perpetuation of this body of knowledge because technology had been thought by then to have eradicated the need. The more I got into it, the more I thought, 'Goddamn, how could they have just brushed all this aside because we'd gotten a radar missile?' We had this body of knowledge which was bearing fruit and if we lost it it would be tragic. . . . I'd seen what happened to the Air Force. . . . They got big and bureaucratic and really weren't doing [the best thing] for their people over at Nellis. And the more I looked into it, I'll be honest with you, the more easily I saw how these things could be lost. . . . When the war was over and Vietnam was forgotten, we'd be terminated and the same thing would happen again. . . ."

So he continued interviewing and worrying.

"The morale at our place had never been so low."

☆ Chapter 23 ☆

Randy Cunningham couldn't sleep. "I knew I was going over North Vietnam [the next day. It was] one of my first times. I was like those guys in the World War II movies about to go on their first amphibious landing. What's going to happen? What is tomorrow going to bring?"

Cunningham, a tall, lanky, ex-swimming coach with thick brown hair and a grin that squinted his eyes, was destined for stardom. But right now, as January 19, 1972, dawned, he wasn't even regarded by his squadron mates as their best pilot, at least as far as such judgments could be qualitatively made.

There was no question that he was one of VF-96's "tigers" — the most aggressive, ACM-oriented pilots; he was also a knowledgeable veteran of an earlier combat cruise and a respected flight leader. But VF-96, as its awards would soon show, was one of the best fighter squadrons in the fleet. Cunningham hadn't been among its pilots selected for Top Gun, a distinction which had gone first to his blond roommate, Jim McKinney, an academy graduate, and then, just before they'd left for this second cruise, to Steve Queen, with whom he'd gone through the RAG. (Queen was to attend when they returned.)

It was true that Top Gun wanted only career officers—those they could count on to be in the Navy after the war—and therefore pass on the knowledge the school gave them to others. But Cunningham had already been turned down several times for a regular commission.

"He was a hell of a pilot," remembers his skipper at the time, Al Newman, who would become an admiral, "but he hadn't really matured enough to be the rest of the things that people expect of naval officers . . . flying was just one little mark on his fitness report. . . . But if it didn't concern flying, Randy wasn't interested."

Randy was on his way, he probably knew, to a mediocre assignment after this cruise; the best assignments went to regular officers. But that didn't dim his enthusiasm.

Cunningham ate, slept, and lived fighter flying. He had a fighter library on board. McKinney remembers Cunningham kicking him from his bottom bedrack, saying, "Did you realize Richthofen did this or that? He could quote them verbatim. . . . He read intensively on World War I and World War II. . . . He was a true scholar of the air."

But not much of a diplomat. Once, when a previous skipper insisted that the squadron carry only wingtanks in combat, Cunningham marched in ready to do battle.

"The airplane doesn't perform as well [with wingtanks]," he told his skipper. And the skipper's excuse was, 'Well, we get a thousand pounds more fuel by using wingtanks instead of centerline.' He added, 'We're not going to use centerline because our sister squadron is using centerline. . . .' "To me that was ludicrous. I told him he was fucked up. I went to him and proved it. . . . I showed him even in Korea when they blew off their wingtanks [if both didn't release] you'd have a heavy wing plus the induced drag. The . . . actual usable fuel you got was only a couple hundred pounds. . . .

"I was a maverick and a purist." But, he admits, "That was wrong. . . . You don't walk up to a skipper and tell him he's fucked up."

Cunningham didn't fit the classic fighter pilot mold—suave, cool, understated. He was unpolished and unbridled in his enthusiasm for what he was doing. Some likened him to "a bull in a china shop." His single-mindedness irked more than a few in the squadron. "Every second of my life was devoted to [flying and fighting]," Cunningham said, "It was like I was training for the Olympics."

Even when they were bombing in South Vietnam, hundreds of miles from an enemy airplane, he'd always set his missile switches to "ready" after releasing the ordnance and had demanded that his wingman do the same.

"He certainly went about it much more methodically and aggressively than the rest of us," remembers Queen. "He was aboard the ship to do one thing—shoot MiGs. I guess he had a better ability than a lot of us to focus that energy. A lot of us would get distracted with the long at-sea periods. Maybe even lackadaisical. . . . On more than one occasion people chuckled [about it] and made jokes in the off hours. . . . It caused him [Cunningham] some grief. . . . But he took it good-naturedly. He had a very thick skin."

Cunningham had marriage problems too. "I was a coach and teacher before I went into the service," Cunningham stated. "Now I was gone for six or seven months [at a time]. There was a war going on and there were lots of pressures."

But little of this, if any, was on his mind this early January 1972 morning. Cunningham was thinking about the real possibility that in the next few hours he might encounter a MiG—something he'd trained for, it seemed now, all his life.

☆ ☆ ☆

Born in Los Angeles the day after Pearl Harbor, Cunningham had grown up in Shelbina, Missouri. He was a fairly good high school athlete and weekend hunter. "From the time I was old enough to walk, I was with my Dad and all my mother's brothers hunting deer, quail, and pheasant." He credits that and the spatial disorientation he got used to in diving with helping him in the cockpit. "I've read stories about other aces and they've enjoyed the hunt and were good shots. They knew how to stalk."

When he was a baby, a soothsayer, following an accident, told his mother he was going to make a name for himself in the air. "I don't believe in soothsayers or destiny or anything, but she said he came up to her and said, 'This boy is going to be a very famous pilot some day.' She told me this when I was a young kid."

After graduating from the University of Missouri with a master's degree in education, he became a successful swimming coach at Hinsdale (Illinois) High School; between 1965 and 1967, he produced 36 high-school All Americans. Some of them went on to the Olympics. Then the urge to fly came over him.

He started taking flying lessons at a little field outside Chicago. "The [instructor] was an old Air Force guy. He said if you really want to fly you should go in the military. . . . I remember thinking there are all these people who sit around and wish they had done something. . . . When I watch TV and say 'I wish I could do that,' I go out and try it. [I] never worked harder in my life than to get those gold wings and become a fighter pilot."

Cunningham had come to the RAG just as Top Gun was starting. "They were the hottest guys around. . . . You wanted to learn everything you could from them. . . . You wanted to be like them." Among his 121 tactics instructors were Jim Laing and J. C. Smith, who taught Cunningham when they weren't working with their Top Gun students.

"Randy was aggressive, enthusiastic," remembers Laing. "I think what stood out most was that you couldn't give him enough information. He always wanted more. 'What should I read? Where do I study more?' "

J. C. Smith remembers, "Not a fear in his [Cunningham's] head. He'd put the airplane where you told him. . . . But he was a bit slow. He tried to ingest too much at one sitting, put too much crap into his head. He wouldn't go home after a flight. . . . [He'd] want to stay there and talk about it more, head down, fussing at himself for making a stupid fucking mistake. That's what he'd call it even though it was just some trivial shit.

"I'd tell him, 'I don't care who you are, you can't become a pool shark overnight. . . . It takes time. You got all the makings, the desire . . . confidence. But, son, give yourself time . . . have patience.' He didn't have patience. That was his problem."

But in a stroke of good fortune, "the fighting Falcons," as VF-96 was nicknamed, weren't ready to receive him when he graduated. The squadron had suffered heavy losses and a terrible carrier fire. It was limping home. During the wait, he was assigned temporary duty at Top Gun.

"They said go down to the trailer and be a 'gofer,' which is essentially what I did. . . . Best thing that ever happened to me."

Ruliffson put him to work making up exams for the incoming first class. "As a student you study about missiles, but you don't really learn. It's like coaching football. When I was swim coach I [also] coached freshman football. I learned more about football then than I ever did playing."

Whenever he could, Cunningham bummed rides in the adversary back seats, getting an insider's look in the process.

"That's when I really learned tactics. When you're a student, you think you're flying the airplane to its limit. But at Top Gun you find out you're not." For instance, "if you want to turn fast, like in a rolling scissors . . . there's a certain timing involved. You want to pull power, jam rudder, then slap it and come around. You've seen the moonshiner snapping his car around 180 [degrees]. It's the same kind of thing in an airplane. . . . There's a lot more to it than you'd suspect."

Cunningham finally began "to get the three-dimensional thing. . . . I'd watch and listen to them and when they'd split the bogeys, they'd say, 'Okay, Duke. I'm going after the guy [in front]. You watch the guy behind us.' Right then you'd learn, 'Okay, I've got a 3-D picture of two different airplanes trying to come in and fight me. . . .' "

Cunningham would write the lessons down on 3×5 cards—"mistakes I don't want to make; good things I wanted to remember."

When VF-96 finally arrived home, his new CO, Early Winn, a proponent of the new tactical doctrine, who was going on leave with the rest of the squadron, told him to "go out and exercise" the squadron's Phantoms that otherwise would be idle for a month.

He jumped at the chance, putting the plane through all its paces, trying out what he was learning from the Top Gun instructors, testing the plane's limits.

"I'd go to 10,000 feet at 420 knots and see how many Gs I could pull until my airspeed started bleeding. . . . You know you can get the graphs in the books but they're all a little bit off, depending on what kind of ordnance you have and so on. . . . I'd write everything down. . . . I'd start out at 250 knots and split-S, think to myself, 'Okay, how much airspeed did I have coming out? How much altitude did it take?' In the back of my mind there's [a MiG] behind me.

Could I get away from him by flying into the ground? . . . zooming up?"

When the VF-96 squadron returned from leave, it became the first to go through the Fleet Adversary Program, which, in effect, was a mini-Top Gun class. It was an eye-opener for all of them.

Cunningham's first combat cruise had been relatively uneventful—bombing in South Vietnam and Laos—but he got the reputation of a man on a mission.

He was like a "born-again Christian," says McKinney, "Read, read, read . . . train, train, train." He'd give threat lectures to the squadron and write slogans on the blackboard, and not care that it rubbed some people the wrong way.

"There was a war on," says Cunningham. "I knew the better we trained, the better the odds of surviving."

He gave himself the call sign "Duke," after John Wayne. In Hong Kong, he says, he had a black flight suit made. "I wanted the enemy to know I was flying a death truck."

McKinney said, "He liked the Hollywood shot too—big guns, knives. . . . I always accused him of carrying so many weapons . . . that if he ever ejected, he'd sink."

Despite being a "nugget replacement," he was made a flight leader.

Returning to Miramar, the VF-96 had another Top Gun work-up, thus becoming the first fleet squadron to have gone through two Fleet Adversary Programs—a fact which would soon underlie the squadron's coming success.

☆ ☆ ☆

Cunningham and the squadron were going to Quan Lang in southern North Vietnam that morning. It was a settlement in a valley between Than Hoah and Vinh, near the Laotian border. The last MiG kill by an American pilot had been Jerry Beaulier's, nearly 20 months before. MiG sightings had been scarce. But since Christmas, the MiGs had begun to reappear and to attack B-52 bombers going into Laos. It was only a matter of time before they'd get one of the huge planes. So the planners in Saigon—Air Force and Navy—had begun to organize what they were identifying to the press as "protective reaction strikes."

Protective reaction strikes, or "Blue Trees," as they were code-named, were controversial attempts to start a fight. The U. S. pilots were tired of being at a disadvantage. The rules of engagement at the time prevented U. S. planes from attacking unless fired upon. To comply with the restriction, large Alpha strikes were organized around photo-reconnaissance missions. A single reconnaissance plane, usually a twin-seat, unarmed RA-5 Vigilante, was sent over a suspected MiG area with escort. If the "Vigi" was shot at—as was hoped—the strike force, waiting nearby, could pounce.

On one of the last Blue Trees, which did not bring up any MiGs, the Vigilante's cameras had recorded MiG-21s being wheeled into caves in the ridges surrounding Quan Lang. This morning's strike had been quickly organized.

The plan was to take 35 to 40 airplanes: A-7 Corsairs—which looked like plump F-8s—and bomb-laden F-4s as the attack airplanes; F-4s with Rockeyes as flak suppressors; and Sidewinder and Sparrow-loaded Phantoms as escorts. Cunningham and his nugget wingman, Brian Grant, would be part of the forward MIGCAP.

Grant, from Ipswich, Massachusetts, was a short, slightly built Tufts University engineering student who'd decided to fulfill his military obligation in naval aviation because he thought it would be more "challenging." That night, Cunningham had kept him up making preparations.

"All I was concerned about—knowing it was such a big strike—was going to bed and getting as much sleep as I could," remembers Grant. "But Randy probably spent the better part—until two or three in the morning—talking with Norm McCoy."

McCoy, who was also on the mission, had shot down a MiG-21 in an F-8 near Quan Lang in 1967.

"I [Cunningham] had gone to Norm's to go over in my mind every little detail. What his [the MiG's] weapons were? Capabilities? How fast could he go on the deck? Did he have any buzz problems at night?. . . . Not only that, but also what were the problems in the area that could hurt me? What about the SAM sites? Where were the potential MiGs coming from?"

He got up and made his way out to the ship's rail, overlooking the ocean. As dawn broke, he saw that he was not alone. Others had come out too.

"There were a lot of guys who couldn't sleep. . . . We weren't that far from the coast. You could look over and see the outline of the shore and knew that over there were people waiting to kill you. It was just those thoughts, you know, thinking about what was going to happen. . . ."

☆ ☆ ☆

Back at Miramar, Top Gun officer-in-charge CMDR Roger Box decided he had to do something about the low priority and lack of assets the school was experiencing.

"There were pressures from every corner to do away with the school," says Box, a Naval Academy graduate who later would become an admiral. "I was having to work my tail off to keep it alive."

It wasn't just that they were having to fight for airplanes, maintenance, and all the other things they needed. In addition, Top Gun "could put 121 in a secondary role of just teaching people how to fly the F-4, as opposed to being the premiere fighting organization."

A lot of it was just plain old-fashioned jealousy about the unit.

Box, a Detroit, Michigan, native and graduate of Navy test pilot school, traced his skills back to a FAGU instructor he had, Royce Williams. Box had come to the RAG after two combat cruises in VF-21, J. C. Smith's former squadron, and had fought his way into the tactics department, taking over Top Gun in May 1971.

He had served on Captain A. B. "Chick" Smith's staff, and it was Smith who had sent him to Top Gun. Now Smith was Commander, Fleet Air Miramar, which the RAG was under. Box decided to go over the 121 skipper's head and see Smith about the problem.

"I said we've been fighting this battle to become a [separate unit]. We're not even an official detachment—just a department. We depend on [121] for everything. Now they're starting to trade our people, and I am worried about our airplanes. We're going to need replacements as some come due for overhaul and what-have-you, and I don't know where we're going to get them."

Smith, a former World War II ace with eleven confirmed kills, had the power to correct the situation.

Box remembers "He turned to his chief of staff and he said, 'You know, the way you lose a pile of sand is not all at once, but a grain at a time.'"

It was an obvious reference to Top Gun losing a plane here, a man there until nothing was left.

"Make Top Gun an official detachment," Box says Smith instructed his deputy.

The order was carried out in mid-January 1972. While Top Gun had unofficially been called a detachment before, now it was a *"permanent* detachment," says Box, "officially constituted. . . . Now, instead of begging for everything, you could say 'I need somebody to replace this man. . . . I need my own operating allowance for gas'— and get it."

More importantly, he says, it would now be harder to eliminate the school. "Previously, it would have been easy without anybody having to sign a piece of paper or do a damn thing to wipe out Top Gun. All they would have had to do was just say, 'Okay, everybody go home.'"

But Box, Kane, and all of them knew that still could be done, even if it were a bit more difficult now. They needed a shot in the arm—something to unequivocally prove the school's effectiveness.

☆ CHAPTER 24 ☆

Cunningham's backseater was Bill "Willie" Driscoll, a big, square-jawed Irishman from Boston. Driscoll was an iconoclast. "Totally irreverent," remembers Steve Queen. "When the pilots would wear ballcaps, Willie would wear an umpire's hat. . . . [He had] no love lost for the military." Nonetheless, he loved to fly.

Taught by the Top Gun instructors in their fleet adversary and 121 instructor roles, Driscoll had a street-toughness that came out in his speech. It was a toughness that would serve him well in battle.

The mission force of 35 planes launched at noon. The plan called for them to fly over northern South Vietnam, making it appear they were headed for Laos, then veer northward in Laos until they were opposite Quan Lang, and suddenly swing back east and hit the target—*if* they could draw fire.

The force maintained radio silence as it entered Vietnamese territory. It was the first time many of them had been that far north. Below, the terrain was lush green, pock-marked with bomb craters from B-52s. Reaching the Ban Nape and Mu Gia mountain passes, the force commander, Gus Eggert, broke silence to call the first check point, "Point Alpha."

It was the signal to arm bombs and set the weapons switches at ready. Since their section was strictly MIGCAP, neither Cunningham or Grant had bombs. They'd already armed their missiles. Their mission was only moments away from the target.

The force began to split up, as planned. A number of the planes headed southwest for a spot below the target; another group flew north, for a position above it. They were setting up stations around the target, so that they could converge from all sides. Cunningham's section was to fly over a nearby airfield, looking for MiGs, and then set up in the north to cut off any MiGs that might head down in response to the strike.

The reconnaissance Vigilante drew fire, and the force converged, their radios coming alive with radio traffic and directions as the A-7 bombers and F-4 flak suppressors dove.

Cunningham and Grant roared low over their nearby field, but couldn't spot any MiGs. Zooming out northward, he suddenly realized he'd made a mistake as his SAM detection equipment came alive. Either the SAM sites had been missed by intelligence, or Cunningham hadn't been as thorough in his preparation as he'd hoped. The route he'd selected to their northern MIGCAP station had placed them directly over a nest of SAM sites, all taking bead.

He glanced down and saw two SAMs lifting, dust and dirt swirling behind the 35-foot "telephone poles."

"There is nothing, absolutely nothing, to describe what goes on inside a pilot's gut when he sees a SAM get airborne," he wrote in his book, *Fox Two*.

The SAMs rocketed toward them at better than three times the speed of sound. Cunningham ordered a hard turn, and managed to evade his SAM, but the other almost hit his wingman's plane. Luckily, the SAM was defective, or inside its minimum range, because it did not explode as it went by Grant.

Two more SAMs were launched, and then two more. The two Phantoms roared back over the field trying to escape. The attack nearby seemed to be at its height, with the bombers drawing most of the flak.

Still more SAMs were launched—a total of 18 in all, according to Cunningham. The Phantoms were zig-zagging frantically. MIGCAP was all but forgotten, and survival was the only thing on their minds.

Breaking into a missile that he knew was on him, Cunningham yelled to Grant, "You're on your own!" Driscoll yelled to Cunningham from the backseat, "Get the hell outta here!"

Outmaneuvering the SAMs took all the skill and courage Cunningham had. He'd wait till the last possible second with "panic [rising] in my throat," then wrench the Phantom toward the missile in an eight-G turn, causing it to break lock and veer off course.

But after a number of such breaks, he'd lost so much energy that he was slow and highly vulnerable. At 15,000 feet, he dumped the Phantom's nose down and lit burners for a dive, hoping to regain his speed.

The SAMs, he could now see, were also being launched at the A-7s over the target. The air was full of the deadly poles. Driscoll pointed out a SAM chasing an A-7 in a dive at their three o'clock. At the last second, the A-7 pulled up and the SAM exploded on the North Vietnamese runway.

As his eyes left the A-7, Cunningham saw two more jets. At first he thought they were other A-7s exiting the target to the north behind him. Then he realized that A-7s don't have afterburners.

He reversed after them, not sure yet what they were, but alerting Driscoll. "I thought they were MiG-21s, but for two years, I hadn't seen a MiG." Two days before, a pilot from their sister squadron on the ship, VF-92, had called out, "MiGs!" and it had only been a Vigilante.

When he'd first seen them, the bogeys were three and a half to four miles away, and flying low, obscured by ground clutter. Regaining his speed now in the dive, and closing on them at approximately 650 knots, he confirmed that they were delta-winged '21s. They were in "fighting wing," the leader about 500 feet off the ground in a canyon, his wingman abreast of him and to the right, about 700-1000 feet higher.

"Bandits! Blue Bandits [the code for a MiG-21]," radioed Cunningham. "North of the field!"

Grant and Sullivan, still dodging SAMs, heard the call and came after him.

Cunningham had been taught by Top Gun instructors that the '21 had a blind spot behind and below it. He purposely came in low and fast behind the leader, about 200 feet above the ground, still at 650 knots. He was looking up at the tail.

In the dive, he'd checked his switches. Driscoll now told him the leader was locked up on radar. "Shoot! Shoot! Shoot!" called the RIO.

But Cunningham didn't trust the Sparrow. In training back at Miramar against drones, he'd had several misses, while scoring constantly with the Sidewinder. So he'd already switched to "heat" and was listening for the tone. He got a good one. He squeezed the trigger and called, "Fox Two!"

But the MiG pilot, warned either by his wingman or tail radar, did the only thing he could to evade the missile just as it was launched. He broke right in a hard turn, which gave Cunningham his first full-plane view of the aircraft (as if looking from directly overhead). It was a streaking silver dart with red stars on the wings; its afterburner was scorching the treetops.

To match the MiG's turn, Cunningham performed a lag-pursuit maneuver, rolling up and to the outside of the MiG, then tucking under and ending upside down behind it with a view of the MiG's belly. The MiG continued to try to evade the Phantom pursuing it.

Cunningham's Phantom was only 200 feet from the ground, mountains but a blur around him. "I'm no Blue Angel," Cunningham later said of himself. He thought they were going to crash. He jammed in full left aileron and rudder while smashing the stick forward. The Phantom snap-rolled right side up, still saddled behind the MiG.

The MiG pilot must now have sensed the imminent danger, because Cunningham, watching the aircraft's right wing knifing toward the ground, saw the pilot's helmeted head "thrashing" from side to side, trying to see behind him. The other MiG had run away and the enemy pilot was on his own.

Driscoll called out their altitude; he advised Cunningham that their tail was clear.

"Get 'em, Duke!" he encouraged.

The MiG completed its right turn and now started rolling its wings to the left in preparation for a turn to the other side. Cunningham knew that if he waited to fire until the MiG had completed its turn, he'd probably miss again.

He called out, "Stand by. Stand by. Stand by. Fox Two. Op Away." It was almost verbatim the sequence he had learned on the practice range at Point Mugu. It was a conditioned response his squadron mates would later kid him about.

The MiG was approximately 3,500 feet dead center in front of him; it was a perfect envelope for the Sidewinder. Cunningham fired, and just as the MiG's wings leveled in the movement toward the left, the missile hit. The effect was spectacular, with the tail coming off and the tail-less fuselage and wings cartwheeling into the ground, sending up a large, debris-filled fireball that the Phantom flew through.

Cunningham dropped a wing and called, "Willie. Look at that!"

Grant, who by this time had arrived and had been watching their six, yelled, "You got him, Duke! Where's the other one?"

Cunningham's excitement was beyond description. For the first time in 18 months a MiG had been sighted and destroyed by a fighter pilot of the United States, and *he* had been that pilot!

Driscoll was "screaming . . . with exhilaration" in the back seat, when Cunningham saw a glint of sunlight from the fleeing wingman. The MiG was in afterburner, racing north and already out of missile range.

He lit out after it, commencing a near-treetop-level chase, weaving through canyons and over rocks at supersonic speed, his afterburner gulping gas.

"What's our fuel state?" yelled Driscoll.

Cunningham did not want to take his eyes off the MiG.

"Don't bother me now!" he yelled back.

"Duke! What's your fuel state!" Driscoll demanded. Driscoll already knew the answer, and he was trying to get his pilot to realize the seriousness of their situation.

"I was astounded to find we only had 7,500 pounds left," Cunningham stated. Five thousand pounds was required optimum for landing on the carrier.

Cunningham realized that he had to break off. But before he did, he decided to fire a Sparrow, on the off chance that it might get lucky and hit.

He squeezed the trigger but nothing happened. He later found out there was a short in its ejector cartridge which caused it to remain on the rail. He'd been right not to trust it. The Sparrow remained a Navy problem.

☆ ☆ ☆

The victory party for Cunningham and Driscoll broke all the rules. For such parties, Al Newman remembers, "I would invite the

CAG to the party and I would say, 'CAG, come on down and have a drink with us and celebrate the MiG that was downed today.' He'd say 'No, I can't do that.' Well, the party was in jeopardy when he said that because I was attempting to get somebody senior there. Finally, he would relent and come, and he'd be the first guy there and the last one to leave."

The liquor flowed freely. While before there had been an undercurrent of resentment toward Cunningham's gung-ho attitude and insistence on preparedness, there was now, at least on the surface, only backslapping and well-wishing. He'd done it. He was now, at least on this day, the best.

He described over and over how they'd fought the MiG, crediting his training and preparation for his success. Then one of his crewmates walked over and casually asked, "Duke, what's it like to kill another human being?"

The question stopped Cunningham cold. "It was like someone flashed a slide up on a screen. . . . I could visually see the [MiG pilot] again," Cunningham recalled, frantically turning his head from side to side, trying to evade the death behind him."

There had been a lot of talk about "Gomers" and "Gooks" — as some of them called the North Vietnamese—but basically for the air crews it had been an "impersonal" war. If you "release a bomb at 18,000 feet . . . you feel, well, 'I just bombed three monkeys, or roads.' [But] when you are up close and see somebody die, it's suddenly different. . . . I wasn't that religious at the time . . . but I had lived all my years without taking a human life . . . my parents were devout Christians.

"We'd flown [several] times that day. All of us were in a state of near exhaustion, wound up like a banjo drum." With the party and the drinking, "When it hit, it was almost like somebody pulled the plug out of the tub."

Cunningham shrugged off the question, but amidst the hoots and hollers he kept flashing back to the death scene: the crash, the fire, the pitiful thrashing of the doomed pilot in his cockpit.

"I had killed him. What did it mean?" Cunningham had asked himself. "Was I going to spend the rest of my life in purgatory?

What does the Bible say? What do men of war say? All this was racing in my mind. I was drawn pretty thin."

Cunningham finally left the party and went back to his quarters. "Then I really couldn't get it out of my mind. It just kept coming back." He wanted to talk to somebody. "But I couldn't go to my friends. . . . Fighter pilots aren't supposed to have this happen. I wanted to be what I demanded of my backseater and those I flew with—not heartless, but a pure professional in everything I did."

He was not the steely eyed warrior that he'd always thought he was. "It was a hard blow," he recalled.

At approximately 2 A.M., Cunningham was still awake. He'd been brought up Baptist, although he hadn't been to church in years. The Catholic chaplain was only a few doors down. It didn't matter what faith the man was, Cunningham decided—he needed to talk. He got the priest out of bed.

"[The priest] stuck with the lines in the Bible . . . David and Goliath. Joshua and Jericho. At times of war, our Bible condones an eye for an eye, a tooth for a tooth. And in that state we are not violating God's law. . . . I felt better."

He left the priest with the understanding that what they had discussed was confidential. He now felt that he could go out and perform aggressively again; shooting down MiGs was his duty. Although he'd suppressed some of his feelings to get where he was, he now knew it wasn't all glory when you get the brass ring. But he could handle it—at least he felt he could.

Cunningham awoke in surprise the next morning to learn that the chaplain had informed his CO of his problem. The breach in confidence angered him almost to the point of "going after the chaplain."

Newman, Cunningham's CO, was understandably concerned over the report. Would Cunningham falter next time he was in combat? Put his own life in jeopardy? Someone else's?

"All of a sudden it became very personal to Randy," remembers Newman. "He'd killed somebody. . . . Nobody at that time had thought of him like that."

The skipper ordered Cunningham and Driscoll to the Philippines for a rest. The next morning they were on a COD landing at Cubi

Point. A delegation of officers met them with congratulations, including a telegram from Admiral Zumwalt himself.

At the first chance he got, he went looking for the man "I patterned myself after" —Jim Ruliffson, who he says taught him everything he knew about the weapons system and knowing the enemy.

Ruliffson, who had been made the unofficial XO of Top Gun, had left Miramar in January 1971. He and Jim Laing had been assigned to a former F-8 squadron, VF-111, to aid in its transition to Phantoms; they were now on the *Coral Sea*, which was docked at Cubi Point while its crew took a week's shore rest from combat.

Cunningham found his teacher in the Cubi Point BOQ. Ruliffson remembers, "I had him go through the story of the kill several times in excruciating detail so that I could understand the tactics and the level of training that the MiG had displayed. . . . I tried to take him through it to a greater degree than any other debrief so I could use it to prepare my squadron."

Cunningham was feeling a lot better already. They went to the infamous Cubi Point Officers Club where Cunningham instantly became the center of attention. "Newman was right," says Ruliffson. "Randy comes in and sees all these guys from the other ships saying, Hey, by God, that's our business [to kill MiGs]. You did great. He gets reinforced that way."

Soon there was a group at their table, and Cunningham was telling Ruliffson he'd get two MiGs before the others got their first. Ruliffson wondered if he'd ever get his own.

☆ CHAPTER 25 ☆

Approximately a month and a half after his reunion with Cunningham, on March 6, 1972, Ruliffson and his wingman, mustachioed Gary Weigand, a young nugget pilot, sat perched on the deck of the *Coral Sea*, their roaring Phantoms "hot fueling": taking on gas as fast as they burned it, in order to be "topped off" when they were launched.

The strike force, which had left a few minutes earlier, was on its way to Quan Lang. It was another Blue Tree mission, designed specifically to hunt down MiGs.

In the prestrike brief, Admiral James Ferris had told the *Coral Sea* pilots, "Gentlemen, we think you're going to see MiGs today." When Tooter Teague, now CO of the *Coral Sea*'s other F-4 fighter squadron the VF-51 "Screaming Eagles" had asked, "Admiral, what if we bag one?", the admiral had raised his fist in a gesture of triumph and responded, "Whoever does gets a trip to Paris."

Technically, Ruliffson and Weigand were part of "Force Cap," the fighters to be vectored to a spot north of the carrier to intercept any MiGs attacking it. But the way the mission was planned, if the reconnaissance plane spotted any bogeys, they were to be sent in immediately to try and cut them off as they sped back north. They were going to be the ambush at the pass.

Weigand, born in Norfolk, Virginia, was new to the war. But the recent Ohio University graduate was a special pupil of Ruliffson's. Joining the "Sundowners," as VF-111 was nicknamed, in turnaround, Weigand had been one of two new pilots Ruliffson was considering for his wingman. At the time, Ruliffson was partial to the other pilot, who was a Phi Delta Theta fraternity brother, although from a different school.

Weigand remembers, "We were just about to deploy to Fallon [Nevada] for our [overland tactics and bombing] buildup prior to leaving for Vietnam. . . . [Ruliffson] sat me down, gave me a stack of books, half of which he'd written himself—the tac manual and all his Top Gun stuff—and said, 'Know this and know it cold. If you don't, I don't want you as wingman. . . .' That was his attitude. . . . I knew his reputation. I wanted more than anything in the world to be Jim Ruliffson's wingman."

After several flights, Ruliffson said, "I wanted the other guy, but, man, Gary's got a lot more natural talent." He tapped Weigand and began "pounding tactics into his head," just as Hernandez had earlier done to him. Soon they were flying as a unit.

The *Coral Sea* had arrived at Yankee Station in late 1971. The two flyers had been on other protective reaction strikes, but this was the first with real promise of seeing MiGs. "This was about as far north as we were allowed to go," recalls Ruliffson. "If anybody was going to see action, it should have been us—at least that's what we thought."

The main force, as with the force launched from the *Constellation* earlier, was again approaching Quan Lang through the "back door" route, across the top of South Vietnam to Laos and then north until they were opposite the target. Ruliffson and Weigand had spent hours the night before making preparations: "How much fuel were we going to have once we were over the beach? What do we want for airspeed?"

They'd flown into the area the day before and thus were familiar with the terrain. They figured they'd stay low to avoid SAMs and be able to use some of the ground clutter as camouflage. They had designated some of the ground configurations around the target as checkpoints and given them names such as "Parrot's Peak" in case "we get separated somehow and want to get back together quickly."

They were told that the strike force was getting close to their target. The ground crew disconnected the fuel hoses and they were moved up to the catapults. Weigand took the port cat; Ruliffson took the starboard. The catapult cables were attached, and the pilots gave the planes full throttle; the Phantoms strained against the cable.

Their noses were extended hydraulically high to give the planes their best angle as they were launched. The two Phantoms looked like winged rockets about to blast off.

They listened to the strike group breaking radio silence, as the photo plane turned back into North Vietnam to make its solo pass over the airfield.

Suddenly Ruliffson was being signalled by his plane captain. Something was wrong. The mouse-eared crewman ducked underneath the straining Phantom, came back up, leaned into the wind, and showed his hands. They were dripping with oily red liquid.

Weigand remembers, "I looked over at Jim's plane and it had this huge puddle of hydraulic fluid beneath it." The Phantom's hydraulic nose extension began to recede. The airplane drooped. "You could tell something was seriously wrong."

Having a failure at this stage wasn't uncommon. They always had a spare airplane ready and crew briefed in case of trouble. Hotfueling behind them was Lieutenant Jim Stillinger. "Yosemite," they called him, because of an exceptionally bushy, overhanging mustache.

Stillinger had been through the most recent Top Gun class. He was signaled up; Ruliffson was off.

"I just about cried," remembers the disappointed Ruliffson. "We wanted this mission so bad. But it just wasn't protocol to run across the deck and lift the spare guy out bodily from his airplane." He moved aside.

"I sort of waved at him and gave him the high sign—you know, go do it if you see anything." His sense of disappointment, however, weighed him down.

☆ ☆ ☆

Tooter Teague was among the MIGCAP for the Blue Tree. When Drill had concluded over the desert skies of Nevada, he and Dan Pedersen and Jerry "Devil" Houston, an F-8 tactics instructor and old football friend, whom Teague had also brought into Drill, had toured the Pacific Fleet, briefing squadrons on the lessons learned at Drill. Mugs McKeown, who was also now out at Yankee Station on Midway, had done the same in the Mediterranean. Between them and the two to four Top Gun graduates who by this time were in every fleet squadron, the news about how to fight the MiG was spreading throughout the Navy.

In a briefing after a mission in June 1972, Teague summarized how he felt: "I think the 121 crowd here [at Miramar], especially the Top Gun school, [is putting] an aggressive attitude back into the fighter community. . . . You've got to be aggressive. I just can't say that enough. . . . I went hunting a lot of times before I got to see a MiG. This attitude that there's nothing worth my ass is wrong, that I'd rather be back in a bank in Kansas City. If you're gonna kill MiGs, you gotta go trolling. You gotta get out there and get among them."

And this afternoon, that was exactly what Teague was doing in the clouds over Laos.

Almost as soon as the reconnaissance Vigilante got sight of the Quan Lang field, its pilot called out, "Bandits! Bandits! Two Blue Bandits [MiG 21s]!" Then after a pause, "More! Red Bandits! Red Bandits [MiG 17s]! Two . . . no, I think I see three Red Bandits."

The waiting strike group roared west, with Teague in the lead. He came streaking in at 8,000 feet, his backseater, Ralph Howell, almost immediately calling out, "I got one, eleven o'clock low. Going away." Teague looked below him. It was a '17 at approximately 5,000 feet, going in the opposite direction.

Teague made a yanking hard turn back into the MiG, accelerating after him. He fired a Sidewinder when he felt he was within cone.

"It guided like a champion," according to Teague, exploding high and just behind the MiG. "All sorts of crap came off the guy." He pitched straight up in a maneuver that Teague felt was certainly a death throe. "I don't think even Tom Cassidy could make that airplane pitch up that violently."

Teague climbed after it, but the MiG seemed to stop in midair. Teague had to overshoot to avoid hitting it. Before he could look back, he saw another MiG right above him.

"Second one at twelve o'clock high!" he shouted to Howell. Howell shouted back, "Look out left!" Two more MiGs were closing to their side.

They were surrounded.

Teague yelled for his wingman, Dave Palmer, but got no response. He didn't know it at the time, but Palmer's radio had gone out, and Teague's own stated procedure for such an occurrence was "to get the hell out."

All around them other Phantoms and A-6s were bombing, fighting, or dodging MiGs. "[The MiGs] were spaced around in a circle," Teague later told a debriefer, "and every time you started to move in on one, one moved in on you . . . They had their stuff together."

Teague and Howell were alone. Nonetheless, he had speed and the knowledge he'd gleaned from Drill.

The MiG above him seemed vulnerable. He pickled off another Sidewinder. "Really dumb shit thing to do. I was too close . . . the Phantom in afterburner, going like a spring goose. . . . I didn't recognize the closure rate. By the time I fired I was only about 1000 feet away. Didn't give it time to arm."

The missile whistled by the '17.

"I had buck fever. No question. . . . I've hunted deer all my life and it never stops for me. When somebody is in your sights . . . it's probably the most massive amount of adrenalin you'll ever get."

The MiG dove and Teague dove after him. Howell piped in, "You got a MiG at three o'clock coming in."

The MiG's angle was "bad, but they fire at any angle," recalled Teague. "Dick Bellinger [an F-8 pilot] had been shot down in '66 by a guy firing a high angle off [shot]. So I said screw this."

Teague turned hard right, breaking off the chase and climbing. When he came back down, all the MiGs had vanished. They arced back over the field. The sky was clear.

They believed they had gotten one, but neither he nor Howell—or any of the others—had seen the MiG hit.

Later, it was decided that he hadn't killed the MiG; he was only credited with a "damaged" MiG. The debris he'd seen, they told him, was mostly the MiG jettisoning tanks. Still, he told a debriefer, "One versus four you're not supposed to win. . . . We didn't get killed and we stayed in there and fought them until they left, and at least we put a hole in one of them. . . . Every time we looked like we were in trouble we just followed the book. . . ."

But the real book to Teague was Drill—how to kill MiGs. He had written it, and no matter what he told the debriefer, he was disappointed. "Mad . . . angry . . . pissed off. Words like that come to mind," he now remembers.

☆ ☆ ☆

Stillinger and Weigand raced to their ambush station as soon as the reconnaissance plane had begun calling bandits. Their station was an orbiting point inland, 50 miles north of the battle and south and east of Than Hoa.

They had scarcely arrived when Red Crown, monitoring them, told them they had two "bogeys" on screen, 50 miles south. The controller cautioned that he did not know the identity of the unidentified aircraft. They decided to drop down to 4000 feet and intercept.

The two Phantoms streaked south with their distinctive "Sundowner" markings gleaming in the sunlight—tails painted with red and white rising suns, and noses bearing angry shark's faces.

Suddenly the controller radioed urgently, "I have a confirmed bandit bearing 190 for 15 miles." "This [the bandit] was somebody different," remembers Weigand. "The others could have been a couple of our fighters. These were confirmed bandits."

They turned into the new heading. The bandit was approaching from the direction of the battle—and approaching fast.

The controller called off " 'Twelve miles at 220 degrees . . . eight miles 260 degrees.'. . . It got down to three miles bearing 310 degrees and we still didn't see anything. Then he came up and said, 'Merge plot.' Boy, that meant we were right on top of each other. We didn't see him. We said, 'No Joy! No Joy!' He came back with, 'Look low! Look low!' "

They were in a starboard turn. They both banked back to port and looked down. Simultaneously we saw this red star going through the tree tops."

It was on the wing of a green and brown camouflaged MiG-17. Blending with the ground cover, it had snuck beneath and behind them and was preparing to turn up.

Stillinger was the closest of the two planes. He called, "I'm engaged," and snap-rolled down into the MiG. Weigand shot up. The fight was on.

The MiG pilot, starting with an advantage and anticipating where the Phantom would come down, turned horizontally into Stillinger, forcing him to zoom back up in a high yo-yo maneuver to avoid an overshoot. When he came back down again, the MiG, waiting for him, did the same thing. Stillinger was on the defensive.

Meanwhile, Weigand was having his own problems.

As he and Ruliffson had practiced it, he knew he was to keep sight of the MiG as he went up, as well as to defend for other MiGs and to wait for an opening. But somehow, in his first real fight, he had lost sight.

"I was very concerned that there might be another MiG," Weigand stated. "But I also wanted to see what was going to develop. . . . I had a sense of impending danger. . . . That there was not a lot of time and I had to get things moving or it's going to be all over."

Weigand's backseater, Bill Freckleton, was turned completely around, glued to their six. He did not know what was happening up front.

When Weigand finally did regain sight of the fight, his heart dropped. Stillinger was in serious trouble.

"Jim was keeping the MiG busy, which was exactly as we trained," but because the MiG had the advantage and kept turning into him, "Jim couldn't get enough nose-to-tail to shoot." And the MiG was gaining on him.

Weigand verged on panic.

"The adrenalin kicked in and all of a sudden it hit me, 'Hey, this is for real. Somebody is going to die here if you don't get your butt in gear and start doing what you're supposed to . . .' "

He snapped out of it and lit his afterburner. He found himself on the fringe of the fight, which had drifted south, about a mile and a half away. He saw Stillinger turning away. Just as the Phantom's nose went up, Stillinger fired a Sidewinder.

"I could tell from Jim's attitude . . . the relative position of both airplanes, that it wasn't going to work. . . . You kind of feel from the training when you're losing. . . . I think he felt 'This is my chance. I'm not going to have a better shot.' "

As the Sidewinder missed, Weigand radioed, "I'm coming in." Stillinger rogered his agreement, "I've got to get out of here."

Weigand knew he needed a tail shot with a Sidewinder. Because his radar was down, they weren't carrying any Sparrows.

"Drag him south!" he shouted, taking charge, sending Stillinger in a direction opposite his own pursuit. If the MiG followed, it would give him its tail.

The MiG, in a right turn in front of him, appeared to spot Weigand. "I'm probably 200 knots faster than he is, but I still don't have a shot." He was afraid of overshooting.

He yanked his nose up, "did a real hard, high-G roll," going up and over in a tight circle, coming back down "at probably two hundred feet of the ground," still aimed at his prey.

But the MiG apparently *hadn't* seen him—or didn't care—because it had completed its turn and was taking Stillinger's bait. Weigand had a periscope view of the MiG's exhaust.

Stillinger, although going faster and already opening a gap, screamed, "Shoot him! Shoot him! For Christ's sakes, shoot him!"

Weigand was in the MiG's blind spot—as he knew from Drill briefings. He was below and directly behind the MiG, about a quarter of a mile. Trying to catch Stillinger, the MiG pilot lit his afterburner. (Later model '17s had them.) Weigand couldn't have asked for more. He fired.

"Seemed like an eternity for the missile to come off. . . . I was going to fire another when it came off the left wing station. It did a little sort of snake dance, which is where it gets its name Sidewinder. . . . Then it took off straight as an arrow and flew right up his tailpipe."

At first nothing happened.

"We were real close. . . . I thought, 'My God, couldn't have missed. I'd better fire another one.' As I started to . . . all of a sudden I saw a little bit of debris come off . . . then the entire aft section. The aft third of the airplane, tail and all, just flew off. It looked like somebody just chopped it with a meat cleaver."

The MiG flew into a hill, "tumbling into a million pieces" (oil, smoke, fire). "Of course we were so close we flew right through it. My immediate thoughts were, 'My God, I'm going to shoot myself down because of all this debris.' We were very low. . . . I'd estimate 150 feet above the ground when we shot him."

A relieved Stillinger started yelling, "You got him! You got him!" Then Red Crown cut off their celebration; the fight had not gone unnoticed. Six MiG-21s were no more than 15 miles away and closing fast.

The two Phantoms were low on fuel. They lit their burners and headed for the water as the MiGs tried to cut them off at the coast.

Back on the *Coral Sea*, Ruliffson had been on an emotional roller coaster. He had "stomped down to the ready room and basically stomped around mad" when he realized he couldn't be part of the attack. "Then I start cooling down," Ruliffson remembered, saying, 'Well, what the hell, let's see, I guess I get to take Stillinger's place on the flight schedule.'. . . So I start in . . . 'What was he scheduled for? . . .' Then CIC calls our ready room on the squawk box and says our Sundowner section is engaged with a MiG. . . . The whole ready room just went wild. Of course, I threw my helmet down. I said, 'Goddammit, I knew it! I knew it!' "

When the fight was over, it was mistakenly reported that Stillinger had made the kill. "Then I really flew off the handle." At least if Weigand had shot down the MiG, Ruliffson could have taken a modicum of credit, since Weigand had been trained by Ruliffson. But "five minutes later they corrected all that and said that it was Gary."

Ruliffson, at last, was ecstatic.

Weigand and Stillinger beat the six MiG-21s to the water by seconds. "They were about five miles from us when we hit the coastline," he says. "They were reluctant to come out after us because of the ship's missiles." A ship-to-air Talos had recently shot a MiG down.

Refueling from an airborne tanker, Weigand requested and got permission to do a victory roll. The kill was the first for the *Coral Sea* and the entire crew was on deck to meet him. "I landed and shut the airplane down right there. They towed me out a little ways . . . and 4,500 were on deck. The captain of the ship was the first one up the ladder and he pulled me out of the cockpit, shaking my hand and congratulating me. . . ."

The kill would become part of a classic Top Gun lecture that Weigand still gives today. The reason, says Ruliffson, is that in the beginning of the fight they did everything wrong. But when they started operating as they should have—as a team—"all of a sudden the MiG instantly becomes predictable. Gary takes control, tells Stillinger to go west . . . and the MiG gives Gary his six o'clock. It could have been over three or four passes earlier . . . but they were both too excited."

The next day, Admiral Ferris had Weigand and Freckleton to lunch. He told them he'd been rash in promising Paris. They got a week in Bangkok instead.

☆ CHAPTER 26 ☆

For several weeks following Weigand's kill, there were few, if any, MiG encounters. Then, with the breakdown of the Paris peace talks in 1971, North Vietnam launched an all-out invasion of the South, the largest since the 1968 Tet Offensive. Enemy soldiers and supplies poured over the Demilitarized Zone. President Nixon's response was to step up the bombing of the North, dropping geographical restrictions.

The *Constellation*, in Hong Kong on its way home, was abruptly called back to Yankee Station. So, too, was Randy Cunningham. His cruise ended, and thinking his combat days over, Cunningham had caught a plane to Miramar and taken his family to Shelbina to visit his parents.

Midway, *Kitty Hawk*, and *Saratoga* joined the *Connie*, *Coral Sea*, and *Hancock*, bringing the number of carriers off North Vietnam to six—the largest concentration of the ten-year-old war.

On April 28, as part of the escalation, Tooter Teague and Ralph Howell, flying MIGCAP for a bombing mission on the supply routes in the south of North Vietnam, took a vector from Red Crown with their wingman, Lieutenant Al Molinare, a junior pilot, and LCDR J. B. Souder, a senior RIO and graduate of 1971's second Top Gun class. The sea-based fighter control center had a MiG on its radar coming down from the north.

The two Phantoms, with Teague in the lead, set out after the bogey. Minutes later, Molinare and Souder's Phantom was in flames; the two crewmen ejected but became POWs for nearly a year. The MiG-21 had eluded all of them and had gotten behind Molinare's Phantom, which was about 1,500 feet abeam of Teague's, and shot it down with an Atoll. Nobody saw the MiG until after the Atoll hit.

What exactly happened in the engagement differs, according to the person asked. Souder says Teague was recklessly aggressive in going after the MiG, they were low on fuel, and they were too high for their radars to be effective.

Teague flatly denies the accusations, saying the situation wasn't any more precarious than is likely in combat. The disagreement, he says, is a personal one between himself and Souder that goes back a long time. The shootdown, he says, a later investigation showed, was the fault of a Red Crown controller who mistakenly flip-flopped the Phantoms and MiG on his shipboard radar as they closed in the last moments. The controller, thinking the Phantoms had passed the MiG, ordered them to turn around, thus giving the MiG, which was actually still in front of them, an easy—and surprise—tail shot.

Teague's tape of the engagement supports what he says, as does a tape that he sent home to his wife the night after the shootdown, which expresses his remorse and frustration at what had happened. But Souder never heard the tapes, and the shootdown is still a source of bitterness between the two.

Devil Houston, who was on the mission but was sent to refuel by Teague when the section went after the MiGs, says, "If they'd gotten the MiG, they'd be heroes. Since they didn't, it went the other way. I think both of them should have been horse-whipped for keeping their heads in the radars instead of checking their sixes. [Both agree they were trying for a head-on Sparrow shot, and thus a radar lockup, since they didn't have enough fuel to do much turning with the MiG.] But it was a two-edged sword."

☆ ☆ ☆

There were three senior flight leaders in the "Screaming Eagles" squadron besides Teague. They were Houston, "Black Jack" Finley, and Chuck Schroeder. All were Teague's contemporaries, and each was as eager as Teague to get a MiG. To be equitable, Teague set up a system that rotated MIGCAPs so each would have an equal chance.

On May 6, exactly two months to the day after Weigand's kill, it was Houston's turn for MIGCAP. The target was Bai Thuong airfield, which was 25 miles west and inland of the Thanh Hoa bridge, near the location where Molinare and Souder had been captured. Intelligence indicated that there was a large contingent of MiGs at the airfield, and an Alpha strike of Coral Sea planes was planned to bomb the airfield and do whatever damage they could.

The squadrons themselves were rotating missions, which was another reason Houston was pleased. It was VF-51's turn to act as pure fighters. Most of the Sundowner Phantoms were going as bombers, along with Intruders and Corsairs. Ruliffson, in VF-111, was tapped to be the strike leader, while the ship's new CAG, Roger "Blinky" Sheets, was to go in low with three other A-6s, five minutes ahead, and try to catch the airfield's anti-aircraft guns by surprise. Under the new engagement rules, there was no more need to draw fire before attacking.

Sheets, a tough, little commander, described by one pilot as "very macho, egocentric, professional," but who looked like "Don Knotts," had impressed everyone aboard by coming in barely two weeks before and restoring effectiveness to the Intruder squadron, which had been in disarray due to casualties. Despite never qualifying for a night carrier landing in an A-6, Sheets nevertheless had led the carrier's first big strike that period on Haiphong Harbor. It was a 4 A.M. mission, and it was barely 36 hours after his arrival. It was Sheets' idea for the four A-6s to go in first and alone.

Ruliffson remembers, "I can recall arguing vehemently with him, saying, 'I think this is dumb. You guys are exposing yourself. I think we ought to put a couple of fighters in there with you.' He said, 'No. We're going to do it my way.' " He felt the fewer planes, the better chance for surprise.

As they were manning up on the deck, just before getting into their planes, Ruliffson says Sheets cautioned him: " 'Ruff,' he says, 'don't go chasing MiGs. If you see them, leave them alone. You're the strike leader. Lead the strike group to the target.' "

☆ ☆ ☆

At VF-51, Houston was having his doubts about the mission. The weather was bad and for a while he didn't think it would go ahead. He was also skeptical about the MiG reports.

"We'd heard this kind of crap before," Houston remembered, ". . . we'd been knocked down so many times by poor intelligence, I didn't really have any faith in it."

But there was always the chance that the report was accurate, and "we thought there might possibly be a transport down there to take [Molinare and Souder] to Hanoi, and if that were the case, that would be a possible target, too."

Both Teague and Finley "came down and in so many words said they'd be willing to fly my wing." But Houston picked his long-time roommate Schroeder. Two Sundowner Phantoms would fly CAP on the other side of the strike.

The weather finally lifted. Just prior to hitting the coast, the four A-6s, led by Sheets, split off at low altitude and went directly west for Bai Thuong. The main strike force kept traveling south until just below Thanh Hoa, where it turned inland to the karst, a jagged, grooved landscape, where they turned north toward the target. The karst provided a protective alley.

They hadn't even reached the karst when they heard radio shouts of "MiGs everywhere!" from the A-6s approaching the field. "There were MiGs in touch-and-go patterns," says Ruliffson. "MiGs overhead waiting to come down."

Hearing the calls, Houston and the other CAP began to move out ahead of the main force, which was gathering speed for its run.

As the Intruders dove in on the airfield's defenses, the MiGs "scattered like quail." Apparently they were in training and had few experienced pilots.

Sheets' Intruders caught the enemy defenses cranking up and pelted them. As the A-6s came off the target, each turned 90 degrees to the left and exited south, one after the other. They were low and in single file, fleeing down the same karst valley that the main force was now coming up.

Ruliffson was leading the main force. "They passed directly underneath us. I looked down and started counting. One. Two. Three. . . ."

There were *five* airplanes—not four. The fifth, Ruliffson quickly realized, was a MiG-17. It was further back than the others, rushing up to get on the last A-6's tail.

Ruliffson almost went down. "It was just laying there for me. Piece a' cake. All I had to do was split-S and I had a free MiG. But the last words I'd heard on deck were Sheets' saying, 'Don't chase the MiGs.' "

So instead he went to his radio. "Okay, TARCAP, there's a bandit right below us, behind the A-6s. Go get him!"

He and the other F-4s he was leading accelerated straight ahead, heading for the target.

Everybody in the group heard the call, including Sheets, who now realized he had a MiG behind his exiting flight. Houston, along with the other CAP, was already speeding in preparation for fighting.

At first, Houston couldn't see the MiG or the A-6s. But his RIO, Lieutenant Kevin I. Moore, called out, "There they are."

The MiG had black, white, and gray camouflage, and it was at Houston's lower two o'clock. It had been going so fast to catch up that it had overshot the last two A-6s in the line of four, scattering them, and had settled in behind the second A-6, the one behind Sheets.

As Houston reversed to go down after him, punching off his centerline tank, the MiG began firing. Ruliffson said the A-6 pilot later told him he saw "big golf balls coming across his canopy" as the 37-millimeter cannon spat out its bullets in deliberate relatively slow-paced precision.

Sheets now did something unexpected.

"Blinky was fighter-experienced, a former fighter squadron CO," says Ruliffson. "By this time, he knows about the MiG-17's terrible rate of roll. He's understood the tactics that by this time Top Gun and the RAGs were all teaching." He wheeled back around in an S-turn and flew between the MiG and the A-6 it was shooting at, "actually dragging the MiG off of number two. He was offering himself as a more attractive target. It was an absolutely courageous thing to do."

Enticing the MiG away, Sheets now kept it at bay by rolling and turning whenever the MiG prepared to shoot. To compensate for the speeds, it had to draw a bead slightly ahead of Sheets. The roll wasn't anything fancy—just a quick rotation along the A-6's longitudinal axis, like swiveling a pencil periodically between thumb and forefinger. But the MiG couldn't match it. Sheets was always ahead of its sights at least for a few seconds each time.

Houston hadn't seen Sheets' ploy. All he knew when he came out of his 180-degree dive-reversal and got ready to fire was that there was an A-6—pilot unknown—in front of the MiG drawing its bullets. Houston was low, only about 100 feet off the ground, and was speeding toward the MiG at approximately 600 knots. Sheets and the MiG were doing around 500 knots.

Houston got a good Sidewinder tone. The heat-seeker was tracking—but which airplane? They were both in his sights.

He called for the A-6 to break. It stayed in front.

The problem was that Houston was flying an old Marine Phantom, a retread that VF-51 had renovated but without frills. The radio wasn't functioning properly and had transmitted his Sidewinder tone, when he was tracking, blocking out any other transmission. All Sheets heard on his radio was a high-pitched whine. Sheets wouldn't have moved anyway. He knew—as Houston knew—that the MiG-17, as Drill had revealed, had little control response at 500 knots. He was going to keep dragging until the Phantom loosed its missile. Then he would break, leaving the MiG driver—apparently new to his profession—to realize, as Houston phrased it, "his stick was locked in cement."

So Sheets remained in front, rolling each time the MiG got ready to shoot.

In the adrenalin of the moment, Houston forgot about his radio transmission problem. "All I knew was that I had some deaf son-of-a-bitch out there who wasn't listening."

Time was running out. In a matter of seconds he'd be too close and out of envelope. He reached minimum range and fired.

As has happened to others in the same situation before, time suddenly compressed.

"Something mentally and physically happened. It had to be the result of the adrenalin, I guess. But my goddamn body-clock just quit. Everything went into extreme slow motion. From the time I pressed the trigger . . . I had time to think a thousand times, 'For Christ's sake, it's not going! It's not going! The goddamn thing's not going to go. I mean it was just an eternity, but you're only talking about a three-quarter-second delay. . . .

"It was just phenomenal. . . . All of a sudden you've got more time to do everything than you've ever had before in your life. Every second lasted a minute and a half. Your mind's running a thousand miles an hour but everything's in slow motion. Even today I've not seen enough explanation of this. [In Drill] I'd fought [MiGs before] and flown 'em. There's nobody alive that's fought against more, and I was always personally relaxed. . . . But this was different. Something in your brain or body just takes over. It's the most important moment in your life. . . . You just can't believe it."

The missile finally came off, went up and down in its snake dance, and then homed straight for the MiG's exhaust. Sheets saw it and broke hard right, but the MiG pilot, if he saw it—and Houston, who was in what he knew to be the MiG's blind spot, thinks he didn't— couldn't break. The Sidewinder entered his tailpipe, blowing off the tail. Almost instantaneously, because they were so low, the MiG hit a ridge and exploded; the MiG pilot did not have time to get out.

A second MiG settled on Schroeder's tail. He eluded it by flying through the jagged karst at high speed. When Houston came back to look for more, the only MiG still around was the MiG which had been pursuing Schroeder. It was racing back north.

They decided, finally, not to chase it. Houston and his RIO, Moore, who had played a decisive part in the shoot-down by spotting the bogey and directing Houston to it, wanted to get back to celebrate.

The *Coral Sea* now had its second MiG, and VF-51 had its first.

☆ CHAPTER 27 ☆

The Bai Thong mission was deemed a complete success. The *Coral Sea* raiders had cratered the runway and returned certain they had left several MiG-17s with no way to take off. The MiGs were "meat on the table" if Task Force 77, the overall carrier command, could get a strike in fast enough.

It was late in the day and the only carrier available was *Kitty Hawk*. The mission fell to Air Wing 11, for which Pete Pettigrew, one of the second generation of Top Gun instructors, and later an advisor to the Top Gun movie, was CAG LSO.

Pettigrew remembers "We were in the middle of cyclic Ops [normal small-scale, round-the-clock bombing] so they cancelled the cyclic Ops and went to the big Alpha strike." The strike was ordered to get airborne as quickly as possible.

☆ ☆ ☆

Pete Pettigrew had gotten into Top Gun the only way a pilot without orders to the school could: he had so impressed the instructors that they had invited him.

"I wanted to become the best air-to-air tactician who ever lived," the tall, former Stanford University water polo player remembers about his 1970 arrival at Miramar, after nearly two years of combat.

"On our first cruise we lost a third of the squadron [VF-151] in two and a half weeks—two to MiGs and three to SAMs," Pettigrew recalled. But he'd survived, eventually learning the important skills, gaining new confidence—sometimes foolishly so.

"You did very dangerous things. You'd come out of burner right away off the catapult, trying to save gas when you probably should have kept it for four or five seconds. You'd do campy rolls on your wingman or buzz a junk to see if you could explode it with your afterburner."

He'd had a friend who liked to go north to the railroad coming out of China into Hanoi and strafe trains at night: "low, in the mountains, five-hundred-miles per hour in the dark. . . . Your odds of flying into the ground are about eighty percent. . . ."

It was thrill-seeking, plain and simple.

"Ruins you for Disneyland and Knott's Berry Farm. . . . The first thing you have is intense fear. But then you get used to that. Then getting shot at doesn't bother you any more. You go further and further. Pretty soon you're wondering 'how far am I willing to go for the reward?' "

He had actually dueled with radar-controlled flak, calculating where the next burst would explode, then yanking just in time to miss it.

By the time he got his assignment as a RAG instructor he wanted to learn ACM. When he found out about Top Gun, he asked Jim Ruliffson, with whom he'd gone through flight training, how he could get in. Ruliffson "outlined it for me."

Soon, whenever he got the chance, Pettigrew was fighting Holmes, Nash, and Ruliffson. "I can remember fighting John Nash a bunch of times. Every chance I could, I'd look where he was on the schedule and go jump him just to see what he did. It was the best way to learn from him. He used to kill me. . . . Even if I had a big advantage he'd still come back and kill me."

Holmes showed him moves he'd never seen before. He put them in his own bag of tricks.

When Nash left, he'd been given Nash's slot, and with the others of the "second cadre" —Bjerke, Kane, Dave Frost, "Goose" Lortscher—he'd helped them put their own mark on the school by modifying tactics, by teaching Israeli pilots brought in on the QT (who had also taught them), and finally by moving the school out of the little trailer into larger hangar offices.

But like the others, he had a burning urge to try out what he'd been teaching. "I hate to say it, but combat is such fun. . . . I mean there's nothing like returning from a particularly rough mission.

You've had your ass shot off, missiles fired at you, been engaged. . . . It's just like after a big game. You pat each other on the back, everyone's laughing. . . ."

Pettigrew was an LSO and loved it. "You get a real feeling of accomplishment. . . . You get crippled airplanes, shot-up airplanes . . . people screwed up in the night, people scared to death. You're the guy who gets them aboard safely. . . . It's not delayed reward. It's right-now reward."

When they offered him his "dream" job—Air Wing 11 LSO on the *Kitty Hawk*—he hadn't been able to turn it down, even though he'd promised his wife that he'd leave the Navy when his RAG tour ended.

He wanted to be an ace.

☆ ☆ ☆

The rush to launch a quick strike caused problems: Planes configured for other missions couldn't be completely reconfigured. Briefings had to be short. But this was nothing new. The carriers were always improvising.

As air wing staff, Pettigrew was usually able to pick his missions. But this time he had accepted BARCAP, the position least likely to encounter a MiG. The fact was that Pettigrew didn't really expect the launch group to run into any MiGs. He had been on too many missions before that had ended without sighting a single MiG.

Because he was scheduled to fly BARCAP, Pettigrew's plane did not get a full complement of missiles. He had only two Sidewinders and two Sparrows, instead of the normal four each. His additional missiles were given to other planes flying in the MIGCAP group.

The force rendezvoused over Red Crown. But early into the mission, one of the MIGCAP planes, piloted by CDR John Pitson, lost its radar. Without radar he was blind. He asked Pettigrew if he wanted to swap.

"Of course," said Pettigrew.

So Pettigrew and his backseater, LTJG Mike McCabe, joined up with Pitson's wingman, Lieutenant Bob Hughes, a junior officer, despite the fact that they were missing half of their firepower.

Darkness was rapidly approaching as the strike group headed north. There was now a sense of urgency among the group, because the pilots needed to be able to ascertain how many planes were on the enemy field. They decided to by-pass the normal air refueling and to continue on with what they had.

The force sped inland. Pettigrew and Hughes left the main group as they went "feet dry" below Than Hoah and headed for their MIGCAP station.

Almost immediately after separating from the main group, they received indications on their Electronic Counter Measures gear of an enemy plane behind them tracking them on radar. They swung back around, but found no MiGs. After a short distance, the indications reappeared, behind them again. Again they found nothing.

Red Crown came on with a vector a short time later. The vector was near the strike group. They veered south, but three miles away realized the "bogey" was one of their own F-4s.

They had already consumed a great deal of gas, and they still hadn't reached their MIGCAP position. As they started to turn back, they received another vector from Red Crown. This one was northwest of them, in the corridor coming down from Hanoi.

Suddenly they heard a new voice on the air from Red Crown. They now had a new controller. To Pettigrew it was a great relief.

"He really knew what he was doing. . . . He had taken the [earlier] controller's seat and . . . all of a sudden everything changed. Instead of just saying he had bogeys, he said, 'Bandits. I have two bandits. Three three zero at 30 [miles].' You could tell immediately that it was serious."

Although they didn't know it at the time, Chief Larry Nowells, the head Red Crown controller (who would become an ace as a result of his work this day), had taken over. (Controllers were credited with the kills on which they'd vectored planes. Eventually, Nowells would be credited with 12 MiG kills.)

When advised of the MiGs, Pettigrew thought of dropping their wingboard fuel tanks, but decided to wait until one of them had spotted the bandits. They nosed down and gunned north at 500 knots.

Almost immediately, Hughes' RIO, LTJG Joe Cruz, got a lock on one of the MiGs. It was an unusual lock given their radars: velocity only, a tough one to hold. Since McCabe, Pettigrew's RIO, didn't have one, Pettigrew gave the lead to Hughes, becoming—as he'd taught so often at Top Gun—Hughes' wingman.

The bandits were about 25 miles away, closing swiftly. Suddenly, Cruz lost lock.

"What happened is that they had gone to beam, and you don't get any closure. If you don't get closure, you'll lose the lock," recalled Pettigrew.

Apparently worried that the MiGs would arrive at the U.S. strike group too quickly, the enemy controllers had directed their pilots into a "defensive pattern"—a full circle—to eat up time. They wanted to hit the strike planes as they went into their bombing patterns.

When the MiGs had completed the circle, Cruz picked them up again. They were again closing.

"We got another lock at around eight [miles]." The MiGs continued to close, but neither Cruz nor Hughes could spot them visually. They were well aware that whoever caught sight first had an enormous advantage.

Suddenly, controller Nowell piped, "Check left. Ten o'clock."

Everyone saw the *four* MiGs at the same time. They were in what Pettigrew called a "box" formation. The number one and number two MiGs had been so close together that they had shown as a single "paint" on the Navy radars, numbers three and four were together in trail. They were almost in a "wing" formation, which looks like a "V," with only a quarter mile separation between the two sections.

The MiGs came in low, passing beneath and to the side of the Phantoms and emerging from the setting sun. They were now easy to spot against a low haze layer. Oddly enough, it didn't appear that they had seen the American jets.

Pettigrew, eyeing the MiGs, had two distinct impressions. One was that it was a very beautiful airplane. "I said, 'God, that's the most beautiful airplane I've ever seen in my life.' The second was . . . this isn't like a surface-to-air missile which doesn't have a brain.

This is a man and he wants to kill me. . . . It was not so much fear of the man as a great fear of failure. . . . This is your chance. You don't want to screw it up. There were a lot of people who screwed it up. . . . You don't want to be in the history books as the guy who got bagged." In Pettigrew's case, the fear of failure was even worse, because he had been a Top Gun instructor.

Pettigrew's and Hughes' Phantoms were in optimum position to press the attack. They were high and to the rear of the passing MiGs, and they were looking back at the MiG exhausts.

Pettigrew felt that the four MiGs were probably all there were. "If it had been two, I would have thought there might have been others around . . . but they usually traveled around in fours or fives. . . ."

They were above a picturesque and remote area known as Banana Valley. Surrounded by mountains and carpeted with lush greenery and gentle rivers, it contained, as far as they knew, no SAM or Triple-A sites. All they had to worry about was fighting the MiGs.

Pettigrew saw that Hughes was going to have the best shot as they came out of their left-turn dives. He told Hughes, "You're shooter, I'm cover." Since they had the advantage, he was going to go high. "I had a theory at the time that if you're in a stern area and both airplanes are offensive, there's no reason to split."

He was going to cover Hughes' tail. "Let's engage," he said.

The two F-4s wheeled left and down.

Suddenly the MiGs saw them and reacted with a hard turn into the Phantoms. But Hughes and Pettigrew had the jump. They were after the rear two MiGs, hoping the forward pair were too far in front to be any immediate threat.

Hughes was on the outside as they came around. The MiG he was nosing for, the number four bandit, was on the outside of the two.

Although he was at a 45-degree angle and not yet in position for a good shot, he nevertheless fired one of his four Sidewinders. Neither of them thought it would guide. They were wrong. "The thing cranks this giant turn," remembers Pettigrew, "hits the MiG, and knocks a little piece off it."

It immediately fell out of the formation.

"He's smoking a little bit," remembers Pettigrew, "but still in one piece and flying. . . . So I thought to myself, 'Well, I gotta confirm this MiG. We got a guy who's hurt and I want to make sure he ejects or hits the ground or something.' "

But then Hughes crossed under him and started aiming at the remaining MiG, which Pettigrew regarded as his.

" 'Well, now,' I say to myself, 'wait a second. I'm going to confirm his MiG and he [Hughes] is pulling to the inside and going to shoot mine?' . . . I said the heck with it. I can't follow this guy any more and keep sight of what's going on in the fight. So I pulled very, very hard."

He hadn't intended it, but his swing outside—with the wrenching pullback—had given him room to cut the turn radius of the other MiG, which was turning into them. As he yanked back into the fight, he had less angle off—and a better shot coming up—than Hughes, who was now on the inside, also pulling hard.

Hughes fired a second Sidewinder, missing. He then fired a third, with the same result.

Meanwhile, in the same few seconds Pettigrew had his own problems. Because of the hasty launch, he didn't know the arming circuitry of his Phantom. The older circuitry demanded that a green light flash on, showing the system was "tuning," before a lock could be made. Although he'd flicked the switch earlier, he had not seen the light.

If the plane had new circuitry, the lack of the light wouldn't matter. His Sidewinder would lock without problem. But if it had the old circuitry and it really wasn't tuned—rather than having a malfunctioning light—he'd be locking the missile outside its envelope with no chance of adjusting it. The same would hold true for his remaining Sidewinder.

He had to make a choice: it was now or never. "All the [unforeseen] things we talked about in Top Gun all of a sudden were happening to me."

Pettigrew threw the switch. "I got a horrendous tone."

The missile *had* tuned.

He was now almost out of the envelope. He squeezed the trigger. "Just as I did," recalled Pettigrew, "I saw out of the corner of my eye—that's how close Hughes and I were—a missile come off Hughes' rail."

As he waited the interminable milliseconds for his Sidewinder to launch and track, he watched Hughes' missile take off.

"It hit a little bit off to the right of the tail along the elevator. . . . I couldn't tell what happened because almost immediately my missile, a half a second later, went all the way up the tailpipe to the turbine blades and blew up, absolutely disintegrating the airplane aft of the cockpit."

Pettigrew had to roll his Phantom to miss hitting the debris. "There wasn't a piece larger than a postage stamp."

As he flew by he saw the MiG pilot come out of the tumbling cockpit.

Two forward MiG-21s had curled back and were now at approximately Hughes' and Pettigrew's eight o'clock position.

"We're going through this left-hand turn, shooting like mad and our RIOs are saying 'No threat, no threat,'. . . which is allowing us to prosecute."

But the two planes were both very low on gas, and they had only one Sidewinder (Pettigrew's) left between them. The best they could hope for, given the relative positions of the MiGs, was a minimum of two passes before they would be in position for a good shot. And the first pass would be a head-on taking them west—further inland.

"I suppose I'm not proud of it," adds Pettigrew, but, "you know, there is this tremendous urge to get feet wet because you've got this tremendous story you want to tell, and where you are you're not going to be able to tell it. . . . I think we just said, 'Hey, we've got two of 'em . . . we're running out of gas . . . one missile left . . . let's get out of here.' "

They turned and streaked toward the water, and the two MiGs gave chase for about 20 miles. The entire engagement had lasted only about a minute and a half.

It was almost dark by the time Pettigrew and Hughes refueled in the air and made it back to the ship. Pettigrew's long-awaited victory roll, unfortunately, took place in the middle of a storm cloud hovering above the *Kitty Hawk*. In the end his roll wasn't as visible as he had hoped. In fact, in his excitement he forgot to defog his windshield, and suddenly, in the midst of the cloud, he found himself flying blind and in danger of not living long enough to enjoy the celebration.

Later, there was deliberation about who was to be credited with the second MiG kill. Should it be split by both crews? Pettigrew was willing to take what he got.

"Hughes hit him first," but, "we were able to determine that it was my [Pettigrew's] missile that destroyed the airplane. . . . When I researched it, if you go back to World War II and, if you put a bunch of bullets in a guy, you wouldn't get credit for him if another guy came in and finished him off. . . . Hughes was perfectly happy with that . . . The way I resolved it when I wrote the awards and sent them off, I described what occurred rather than try to say I claim the kill."

The Navy decided the matter by crediting Pettigrew and McCabe with the MiG.

☆ CHAPTER 28 ☆

Several days after Cunningham and Driscoll had gotten their first MiG kill, they witnessed, with quite a different reaction, an American plane being shot down. It was the the first U.S. plane they had ever seen shot down. The downed plane was an Air Force fighter–bomber, hit by a SAM.

"My first reaction," recalls Cunningham, "was like I was watching a baby carriage going across the street. You see the cars and you know it's going to hit."

He screamed for the jet to break, but it didn't.

"It just kept going. You feel helpless . . . the fireball . . . the horror . . . the rage. At that point, I would have killed anything that moved."

In the months that followed, Cunningham got wound tighter and tighter. His quick callback from the states after thinking his Vietnam days were over drained him, and the strain on his family was even worse. His relationship with his wife had deteriorated as a result. His spirits were at an all-time low.

But Cunningham had willingly returned to Vietnam, exhilarated by the thrill of flying. He had disregarded his fear and had held his rage for the heat of battle, when, it became in some ways an advantage.

During a strike on Haiphong, as he related in a book that he wrote, he and Driscoll found themselves the only plane with enough gas to defend a downed A-7 pilot in the harbor's waters. The pilot was being threatened by shore batteries, and two Russian freighters attempted to run him over.

The situation so enraged Cunningham that he dropped to 200 feet and began a jinking, daring run at the freighters, hoping they'd fire on him so he could "blow them out of the water." He radioed the threatened pilot, "Blue One, we have you in sight and will kill anything that gets close."

Tracers streamed by their plane and at least one SAM was launched. But the freighters backed down. Brian Grant, jinking behind his leader, put a bull's-eye into an artillery battery, and the A-7 pilot was rescued by an equally daring helicopter crew.

"You vent your anger. . . . [until] you think you're invincible," Cunningham states today.

All through April, he and VF-96 participated in the pounding of the North, especially the Ho Chi Minh Trail, through which the enemy offensive was being supplied. When Houston, Hughes, and Pettigrew got their MiGs on May 6—a record three in one day for the new, heated-up U.S. air war—several of the "Fighting Falcons" threw a party on the *Constellation*. They were celebrating not only to relieve the tension of their round-the-clock missions, but also to anticipate their own next mission.

The May 8 schedule had Cunningham and Grant flying in the MIGCAP for a multicarrier strike on a big truck staging and driver training area near Son Tay, approximately 25 miles west of Hanoi. Located near the Red River and Thud Ridge, Son Tay, at the base of a mountain, had been the site of a prison camp. It was now believed to house approximately 300 to 400 trucks. It was in the heart of what Cunningham liked to call "Indian Country." There were MiG bases all around the area. The MIGCAP was going in ten minutes ahead of the first wave of the strike. Their job was to help clear the skies above the trucking area before the bombers arrived.

As usual, Cunningham prepared meticulously. They launched without hitch and headed for the Red River Valley, with its notorious defenses. They entered the coast at the mouth of the beautiful delta, its hourglass rivers splayed like fingers before them.

The two Phantoms hadn't been inland a minute when two SAMs were launched. They swung into a valley, and they were met with more SAMs, as well as 85 millimeter fire. They ducked behind the mountains for cover.

Red Crown came on with a vector for "unknown bandits, 340 [degrees] at sixty miles." The bandits were coming from the direction of Yen Bai, further northwest, which they knew was being hit simultaneously by the Air Force. They headed for Yen Bai while arming their switches and preparing to jettison their centerline fuel tanks.

But Red Crown lost the bandits on radar along the way. Cunningham figured they must have dropped down below the ridges to avoid detection.

Suddenly a glint of metal below caught his eye. But it turned out to be only a flight of A-7 Corsairs. Then Driscoll picked up two radar contacts at ten o'clock. Who were they? There were two fighters from *Kitty Hawk* also in the area, as well as Air Force jets. They couldn't fire a Sparrow without positive identification.

They were now 20 miles up the Red River Valley from their assigned area. The distance from the target area and the peekaboo nature of the contacts was making Cunningham very nervous. He was aware of what had happened to Souder and Molinare just a week and a half before, and he figured his own strike group was just about arriving at Son Tay.

He told Grant they were going back.

Just as they turned around, Red Crown came on again: "You have a bandit at six o'clock . . . closing . . . Twenty miles."

They turned again, headed back toward Yen Bai, flying at about 10,000 feet. There was a haze layer below them that obscured the ground—and anything below the haze.

Suddenly Grant radioed for Cunningham to make a left turn.

"Go!" shouted the wingman, urgency in his voice.

Cunningham was confused and leery. This was exactly the same kind of thing that had happened to Teague and Molinare right before Molinare and Souder took a surprise Atoll.

If he went left and the bandit was still approaching head-on, he'd be giving him a shot at his six.

He jerked the Phantom nose high, flicked in afterburner and went straight up. Just as he did, a MiG-17 popped out of the haze and started to shoot its nose cannon at Grant from Grant's rear.

From his vertical observation point, it took Cunningham a second to realize what was happening.

"You do a double take, and then, 'Goddamn, it's a MiG.' Even though you're expecting it, your mental processes still need to click in."

"I said, 'MiG, Brian! . . . Mig-17 at seven o'clock!' He instructed Grant to use the MiG disengagement maneuver."

Just as they had been taught by Top Gun instructors, the two planes began working as a team, Cunningham taking charge, directing what was to follow.

They also had some luck going in.

The MiG pilot behind Grant apparently was new, or at any rate not very good in gunnery. He wasn't pulling the correct lead, and his shells, the "size of grapefruits," fell behind Grant. Cunningham told Grant to get rid of his wing tanks, to increase his speed and maneuverability. "Get rid of your tank," he told Grant. "Unload" —extend out away from the bullets—"I'll call your turns."

Cunningham had seen this kind of situation before when VF-96 had trained with Top Gun in its precruise workup. Grant's job was to drag the MiG, using the Drill-developed, Top Gun-polished tactic to keep the MiG at bay.

Grant lit out straight and to the right—away from the tracers. Suddenly something came off the MiG's wing that looked like a missile. Intelligence had been telling the U.S. pilots that '17s didn't carry heat-seekers. But the projectile the MiG fired started to track.

"Atoll!" screamed the surprised Cunningham. "Break port!" He had to send Grant back into the MiG's guns trajectory. But, luckily, again the bullets were going behind Grant.

Cunningham, completing his vertical climb, was now starting down. Driscoll, in his backseat, yelled, "Duke. Look up!"

Two more MiG-17s, passing head-on on either side of him, roared by. They were no more than 200 feet above them.

He knew they had to turn around to come back, and he therefore decided that the MiGs were no immediate threat. "My exact words to Willie were, 'Don't worry. They're out of the fight.' "

His concentration was on the MiG below him, and he sensed it was about to fire another Atoll. He was not yet in Sidewinder envelope, but he felt he had to do something quickly. He decided to fire a Sidewinder anyway, hoping it would scare the '17.

Just then Driscoll yelled that the two MiGs that he'd disregarded were zipping up behind them. "I said, 'Bullshit, Willie. They can't be' . . . about this time I saw cannonball tracers coming by the canopy."

They were only 4000 feet apart when they'd passed over. The two MiGs had turned inside on dimes without even crossing each other's flight paths, and they were now blazing away from behind his six. Cunningham didn't yet have the speed he needed to out-maneuver them.

"I'd made a mistake with that vertical pull-up. . . . I was much slower than I really wanted. . . . I've only got about four and a quarter knots when I wanted 550."

Nonetheless, his Sidewinder, although it had missed, had done what he'd wanted it to. It had caused the MiG behind Grant to break away. And in its sudden turn it had unwittingly given Cunningham a shooter's view of its exhaust.

He wondered briefly whether the two MiGs behind him were setting up a drag, but he squeezed off another Sidewinder, simultaneously telling Grant "to pitch up and go vertical."

Cunningham's missile hit the MiG perfectly, and it crashed into the top of the mountain. But he still had the two '17s firing at him from behind.

He attempted the Drill tactic again, although the situation was a little different from the one for which the tactic had been devised. One MiG on either side wasn't the same as having one MiG behind you.

When he rolled to the right, the MiG on the right fired. When he rolled to the left, the other one had him in his sights. They didn't have to match his roll rate. He was sandwiched between them, and in serious trouble.

At one point, they crowded so close that he almost hit one, veering away from its belly and then looking momentarily into the face of the pilot of the other as he flashed by.

If he didn't do something fast, the tracers were going to find their mark. "If I pull pure vertical, they rendezvous on me." If he pitched down, what was beneath the haze layer? A rock? A mountain peak? The cloud layer was at no more than 3000 feet.

None of the choices were good, but there wasn't time to dwell on them.

He snap-rolled the Phantom "120 degrees," positioning it nearly upside down, and then pulled it straight down "just as hard as I could." The sudden tug put a phenomenal "12 Gs" on the airplane, "broke both flap hinges" and "pulled . . . rivets out of the wings."

As they plunged into the clouds, he radioed Grant that he was going to pop back out in a moment, dragging the pursuing MiGs so Grant could shoot them.

Inside the clouds, he lit his afterburner. He hadn't done so before for fear it would entice the MiGs to shoot an Atoll.

The cloud layer was intermittent and he could see the ground below every few seconds. "It gave you the feeling that there was a rock or something [there], so I called Brian that I was going pure vertical. I pulled it up. . . . I now had about 550 knots on the airplane and a ['17] can't follow that."

As he popped back out, Grant rolled in on the pursuers, "but they must have seen me, or their controller did," he remembers, because "they dove back into the clouds, breaking off the attack on Randy."

Cunningham wanted to go after the two MiGs, but when he and Grant reentered the clouds, they were gone.

It had been a fast and furious fight, with Cunningham and Driscoll emerging as the leading Navy MiG killers in Southeast Asia at the time. They were tied with several Air Force crews who had two. (Olds was now gone.)

When he and Driscoll landed to a tumult of congratulations, one of the first things Cunningham did was to send a message to Weigand and Ruliffson on *Coral Sea*: "I'll get number three before you get two."

☆ CHAPTER 29 ☆

A day after Cunningham and Driscoll's second kill on May 9th, the mining of Haiphong Harbor and other North Vietnamese war-supply ports ordered by President Nixon was completed. The mining was a major escalation of the war. The Navy had long been arguing for such a move, knowing that stopping the flow of guns, tanks, and gas from Russia and its satellites would severely limit Hanoi's ability to fight.

Simultaneously, a joint-service air operation called "Linebacker" was begun. Linebacker, so named because it was designed to back up the counterattack against Hanoi's Easter Offensive, would send hundreds of U.S. planes in massive strikes against enemy railroads, bridges, and storage areas. The plan called for the Air Force to fly in mainly from the west (Thailand and Udorn Air Force Base); the Navy would attack from the east, off its carriers in the Gulf.

As May 10th dawned, Air Wing 9 on the *Constellation* was already preparing to launch the first of three strikes planned for that day; 35 planes were targeted to attack the large port and storage facilities of Hon Gay, just north of Haiphong on the coast.

Pilot Curt Dosé, a graduate of Top Gun's second 1971 class, and his leader, Lt. Austin "Hawk" Hawkins, were assigned the northernmost MiGCAP station. They were part of VF-92, Cunningham and Driscoll's sister squadron.

"We expected the threat to come from Kep," remembers Dosé, "so we wanted to put ourselves between it and the strike."

Kep was located north of Hon Gay toward China, a very sensitive border. The attack was taking place on the eve of President Nixon's visit to China, the first such visit by a U.S. president since the Communist takeover in 1949. U.S. pilots had been warned to stay clear of China's borders.

The strike launched at 8:30 A.M. Dosé and Hawkins' first race-track pattern put them directly over a group of 100-millimeter guns, which started firing. They scooted five miles north and closer to China. In their new pattern, they watched the air strike group as it made its single pass over Hon Gay in the distance.

As the strike ended and the planes began exiting, Red Crown announced "Blue Bandits" 30 nautical miles northeast of Hanoi in the vicinity of Kep. The bandits weren't closing on the strike force, and according to John Gresham, a military systems analyst who talked to the air wing commander Gus Eggert, "Eggert didn't want them to go chasing after anything. He had a limited number of planes and two more strikes to go that day."

But Hawkins and Dosé, who had been flying together for over a year, had decided previously that if the opportunity "to go shopping" presented itself, "we'd go shopping." The strike was over and they had plenty of gas.

"Let's go," said Hawkins.

They joined in combat spread, descended into the ridged valleys that zig-zagged north, and sped away.

Back on the *Constellation* the controllers in the Combat Information Center (CIC) were immediately concerned. By dropping down, Hawkins and Dosé were no longer visible on Red Crown's radar. All CIC knew was that when last seen, the two Phantoms were streaking north—in the direction of the forbidden border.

Steve Queen, down in CIC, remembers "frantic calling on different frequencies" trying to raise the missing flight.

According to Gresham, "They were scared to death because they didn't know what was happening. On the other hand, Dosé and Hawkins and [their backseaters] couldn't hear because their radios were pretty much line-of-sight."

At Kep, the North Vietnamese were unaware of the approaching Phantoms. Two MiG-21s were readying to take off on one runway. Two other '21s were holding on an intersecting runway, preparing to turn and follow. There were numerous other MiGs—'17s and '19s among them—protected by walled and sandbagged revetments along the sides, with attendants working on them or nearby.

As Hawkins and Dosé got Kep in sight, they were flying at approximately 2000 feet, traveling at over 500 knots, and approaching from the southeast. They came in heading north, still descending, perhaps three miles abeam of the runway on which the two MiGs were readying to take off.

The runways were constructed of alternating cement and blacktop slabs, and at first Dosé and Hawkins saw only the two '21s holding. Dosé wondered whether they'd be giving off enough heat for a Sidewinder shot. But then Jim McDevitt, Dosé's backseater, saw the two MiGs taking off and called "MiGs rolling."

"I think when I first looked," remembers Dosé, "they were on the cement [and blended in] because when I turned back, they were really obvious. They were gorgeous, shiny silver with nothing but solid red stars on the wings and fuselage."

The wingman was "staggered right," and Dosé, in the best position, immediately called lead. Hawkins, with J. Tinker in his backseat, was now *his* wingman.

With a quick, descending turn, while kicking in afterburners as they pulled, the two Phantoms leveled out to no more than 100 feet above the runway. At the opposite end, the two '21s were near the end of their roll. Dosé hoped to get off a shot just as they were lifting, but he was still too far away.

The two MiGs must have seen them, or they were told of the Phantom's presence by controllers. Even as they began to pull in their wheels, they made hard left turns, one staggered behind the other. As they did, they jettisoned their centerline tanks, which exploded in orange fireballs on the green terrain beyond the runway. During their turns, the MiGs turned on their afterburners, trying to gain distance. The airborne MiGs were now at fighting weight and running.

The two Phantoms roared after them. "We were going about [Mach] 1.1, 30 to 50 feet above the runway," recalled Dosé. "I was sort of right on the edge of the runway. . . . I got this view of all these MiG-19s and MiG-21s in the revetments with all those guys looking up at me as we go by and jumping off the wings and things. . . ."

"I got a Sidewinder tone even before I looked through the missile sight," says Dosé. Hunching down to peer through it, he saw the missile was sensing on the trailing enemy wingman's exhaust. He called, "I got the one on the right. You got the guy on the left."

Hawkins acknowledged. He was right beside Dosé, two hundred or so feet to the left.

The MiGs stayed low in a hard left turn, weaving at supersonic speeds among the dips and highs in the hilly, tree-covered topography. At one point, Dosé's air-conditioning fogged the canopy, spitting out snow and obscuring his line of sight. "It does that every time you go real low [in that kind of humidity], and you've got high power on."

He was so close to the terrain, he says, that he actually had to lift his wing several times to avoid hitting tree tops.

The MiGs were zigzagging wildly. Because the Phantoms were going faster, Dosé and Hawkins had to lag out to the sides to avoid overshooting their targets.

"At about a half mile, I had my best shot," says Dosé. "I pulled the nose on, got a good tone and squeezed the trigger." He experienced a sense of time compression as he waited for the missile to launch. Finally, it took off. It pulled up high, cut back toward the MiG and did a 90-degree pass behind the MiG, its warhead exploding in a hill.

Dosé pulled in and shot off another Sidewinder, which came off the wing the same way. It looked like it was going to do the same thing, "except right at the end it sort of does a little straightening out, makes a final turn and I see it go right up the guy's tailpipe. There is this long pause. . . . Then just a huge orange fireball, and the MiG comes out the front going head over heels. It doesn't seem to have a tail on it anymore; just tumbling and immediately slams into the ground. No ejection, nothing . . . "

Hawkins now fired a missile at the lead '21, but his Sidewinder did exactly what Dosé's first one did. Dosé then fired on the lead, and watched his Sidewinder hit a tree enroute. "We were just so low."

He tried to fire another, but it jammed. He asked McDevitt if they could get a lock with a Sparrow missile, but their radars were nearly white with ground clutter.

Dosé was now so close to the leader that he could see his flippers moving. "I can see the individual fires in his afterburner plumes, about twelve of them around his engine." Hawkins and he had separated a little bit. "I decided that the best thing to do is to try and get [the MiG] to reverse in front of Hawk."

To do that he wanted to fire a Sparrow ballistic (without electronic guidance) in front of the MiG, hoping it would veer. But as he moved to get in position, he glanced over his shoulder, and found two more '21s coming in from his four o'clock in a descending turn.

"Either they were coming back into a pattern, or they were those two MiG-21s that were holding short."

Both Phantoms broke defensively, causing the two new MiGs to overshoot badly. They'd flown back now almost full circle to the field. A new MiG-21 was lifting off and coming after them. They decided it was time to leave.

Having been briefed that the '21, because of control problems, couldn't fly supersonic below 5000 feet, Dosé didn't feel the enemy plane was an immediate threat. "But that wasn't so, because this '21 just came sailing up behind Hawk." The '21 may have been a new version called the "J." "It had to be going [Mach] 1.2, 1.3, and he wasn't having any trouble flying.

"We were back in good combat spread now. I called Hawk, 'In place. Turn now! MiG-21 at your six o'clock.' As soon as he started turning, [the MiG] fired an Atoll. It came tracking up, but couldn't hack the turn."

Dosé swung around after the MiG. McDevitt shouted, "What do you plan to do with this guy?"

"We knew we were out of 'Winders," remembers Dosé. "Sparrows are no good at this point, and so I said, 'Rog,' and the MiG kind of continued on straight ahead. Maybe he couldn't control himself very well, because he didn't follow Hawk in his left turn. So I just pitched up and swung back around to the east."

The MiG kept powering toward the south, and Dosé started looking for Hawkins. But Hawkins was gone. They couldn't raise him on the radio.

"That was an uncomfortable situation; we got real low again and I started to pitch back [into the vicinity of the MiGs] and [McDevitt] again asked 'What are you going to do?' We were down to about 4,000 pounds of gas by this time, and I said, 'Okay,' so we started heading out."

He didn't want to leave, but by this time, a relieved Red Crown back at the carrier had again picked them up, and had started calling bandits behind them.

"There is no way to look behind you in a Phantom and you get real uncomfortable if you don't have your wingman with you."

They were beside a ridgeline that led back toward the Gulf and decided to use it as a shield as they sped out.

"We just went faster and faster ... hold your breath kind of thing. They [whatever bandits were behind them] trailed them out, and as we approached the coast we needed to go up and over the gun batteries—the coastal batteries. So we pitched up to about a 40-degree climb, and as soon as we pitched up, bang, from the other side of the ridge here comes Austin!"

It was almost a scene out of a movie. The euphoria of their lone victory—the first for VF-92 in the new air war—marred by the loss of their section mate, suddenly and spectacularly resurrected by the sight of Hawkins' Phantom climbing beside them.

With elated chatter, the Top Gun graduate—now another of the growing number of Navy MiG killers—roared out to sea with his leader in place.

CHAPTER 30 ☆

Hawkins and Dosé had helped stir a hornet's nest that morning.

Exiting from the mob-scene celebration on deck, they were met by an intelligence officer who told them to report to CIC below immediately. Besides having to deal with a perturbed CAG Eggert, who didn't appreciate their leaving their station, they were informed that North Vietnamese radio traffic had suddenly skyrocketed.

"The general debrief," remembers Dosé, "was 'What did you guys do? Bomb a hospital? Violate the Chinese border?' " The North Vietnamese were moving every available MiG from outlying areas into the Hanoi–Haiphong axis.

Dosé now speculates that they had unknowingly shot down somebody important, perhaps a Russian. What Dosé didn't realize was that the same morning, as part of Linebacker, the Air Force had sent a large strike force against the Paul Dourmer Bridge outside Hanoi, a vital link in the Ho Chi Minh Trail and a continual problem to the Air Force, just as Thanh Hoa was to the Navy. The Air Force had destroyed it once before, in 1967, only to see it rebuilt. As Hawkins and Dosé had sped off for Kep, the advance Air Force MIGCAP for the Dourmer strike had engaged eight MiGs (four '21s and four '19s), shooting down three of them, while losing one. The bridge had been severed, and a meaningful chunk of the North Vietnamese Air Force had been knocked out as well.

"Though we didn't hear about it at the time," says Gresham, "the North Vietnamese air defense system must have been going bat shit. They'd lost Dourmer. They'd lost four MiG-21s that morning, which is probably close to between 10 to 20 percent of their [available] MiG-21 fleet. Even worse was that for the first time [in the resumed attacks], there'd been a major incursion on Kep Airfield."

The enemy was on the alert in a way that they had seldom been before.

☆ ☆ ☆

Randy Cunningham and Bill Driscoll were part of the *Constellation*'s second strike that day. The strike was targeted for the Hai Duong Railroad Yards, a large (by Vietnamese standards) marshalling area for supplies and transportation, roughly halfway between Hanoi and Haiphong. The MiGs, they knew, would be up in force. The yard was smack in the middle of North Vietnam's defense network, which was close to all its major MiG bases.

Leading the strike was the CAG himself, Eggert. MIGCAP consisted of both number two officers in the Air Wing's two squadrons: VF-92's XO, CDR Harry L. Blackburn, and VF-96's XO, Dwight Timm; their RIOs and wingman; and a third flight led by VF-96's Matt Connelly, who was considered by many of his squadron mates to be the best pilot they had. Connelly was cool and calculated. Called an "Iceman" by his crewmates, Connelly had gone through the RAG at the same time as Cunningham; that is, just as Top Gun had been getting started. Jim Laing had given him critical instruction on timing. Laing's instruction, says Connelly, had been a turning point for him as a fighter pilot. VF-96 also had Cunningham, as well as Steve Queen, who was to be working back on the *Connie* that day as squadron LSO; and Steve Shoemaker, a former Blue Angel, who was along as a Shrike escort. (Shrike is the name of the anti-SAM-site missiles carried by the A-7 that he was assigned to protect.)

Once airborne, the 32-plane armada flew in south of Haiphong, purposely skirting the port's heavy defenses. Then it moved north by northwest, above the widening delta of the Red River.

When Eggert reached the check point, he released his MIGCAP with the words, "Play ball. Play ball."

Timm and Blackburn and their wingmen took the cue and accelerated ahead toward Hanoi to set up between the target and Gia

Lam, Phuc Yen, and Kep. Connelly and his wingman veered south to guard against MiG threats coming from Bai Thuong.

There weren't any airfields around Haiphong to the east, but Shoemaker, who didn't have a wingman, throttled toward the harbor with his A-7 Pouncer to look for SAM sites.

Cunningham and Driscoll stayed with the main force. They had almost not been included on the strike because of a lack of planes, but Cunningham had protested and managed to get Eggert's ceremonial Phantom airborne. They were going in as attack bombers, which meant that only after unloading their bombs could they assume roles as fighters.

Because of a layer of haze, the bombers—codenamed "Boomers," "Jasons," and "Busybees"—overshot their target. Subsequently, they had to circle back, and they were just starting their single bombing dives or "looking like a column of ants," according to Cunningham, who was waiting his turn, when the northern MIGCAP arrived at its station.

"We were with Harry Blackburn and his RIO, Steve Rudloff," remembers Fox. "They were to our starboard, above us, and about a quarter of a mile. We got to our position, and I asked the XO [his pilot Timm], 'Where do you want to set up?' He said, 'Let's wait and see where [Blackburn] goes.' Just as I said that, [Blackburn] broke left in front of us—just cut right across us—swinging around in a loop toward the northwest."

Northwest was in the direction of Hanoi, and it seemed likely that Blackburn had seen what Fox was about to see:

"We broke starboard [toward Blackburn's break, which was port]," Fox recalls, "and our right wing went down. That's when I saw the first MiG." It was the first MiG the University of Oklahoma graduate had ever encountered. "[It was a] MiG-21, silver with a big red star. My initial thought was, 'What a beautiful airplane. . . .' It was diving almost straight down, about a half a mile away on the strike group."

Directly behind the '21—and so close that Fox said that it looked as if "it was trying to shoot the '21 down"—was a camouflage-painted MiG-17. "Right about that time," Fox recalled, "all hell broke loose."

Suddenly the air was alive with radio transmissions.

"Bandits! Bandits! Bulls-eye," called Red Crown from its position in the Gulf. "On guard . . . On guard!"

Another voice broke through. "MiG-17! MiG-17! . . . He's on my tail!"

It was the beginning of an air battle between as many as 20 or more MiG-21s, '17s, and '19s and a vastly outnumbered U.S. MIGCAP.

As Fox looked up from the two MiGs, he saw Blackburn and Rudloff fly right into a flak trap, which was a pre-aimed piece of airspace where enemy gunners waited for someone to enter. "The Phantom exploded into a fireball," Fox recalls, tumbling end over end."

South of Fox, Cunningham and Driscoll, about to dive on their target, witnessed the hit too.

Fox saw two bodies tumble out of the hurtling fireball into "good chutes"—but with nothing but North Vietnamese territory beneath them.

Blackburn's wingman, Rod Dilworth, and his RIO were also hit by the flak barrage, but managed to limp away on one engine. With the battle only seconds old, a third of the designated MIGCAP was out of commission.

Shaken by what they had seen, and leery of flying into a flak trap themselves, Cunningham and Grant dodged two SAMs, released their bombs, and came up ready to fight.

"I made a left turn," recalls Grant, who was approximately 1000 feet behind and to the inside of his leader, and then "it was like something out of a movie."

Two MiG-17s came flashing by him, no more than 500 feet to his inside; they were aiming for Cunningham.

Driscoll, too, saw the bogeys. They were "black dots . . . really coming up fast," he recalled. For milliseconds, it didn't register that they were a threat. "Then I noticed how fast they were coming."

"Break port!" he yelled to his pilot.

Cunningham was still looking down the opposite side at the building that they'd just bombed when the shouts unnerved him. He whirled around to see the lead MiG barreling in, shooting fire. "The muzzle flash," he wrote later, "seemed to jet out the length of a football field."

For a millisecond, Cunningham debated whether to turn, although he feared a repeat of what had happened in his last engagement, when the '17 had cut across and "rendezvoused" on him. But then he noted its high speed and how rigid its controls would be, and he veered.

The MiG pilot didn't have the strength to move the stick and overshot.

Cunningham reversed, bringing the Phantom's nose back to the MiG's exhaust, and launched his first Sidewinder.

When the missile exited the wing, the MiG was too close. But the MiG was going so fast that it quickly opened enough distance between them. The Sidewinder went up the '17's tailpipe and exploded.

Cunningham and Driscoll now had three MiG kills—the most of any U.S. flyers active in the war. But this was no time to celebrate. The two downed MiGs had actually been a part of a larger formation of four, and Grant, who had told Cunningham that he'd take care of the second MiG in the lead element, now found himself being attacked by one of the two MiGs in trail.

"My RIO started yelling, 'We've got a MiG on us.' And sure enough," recalled Grant, "I turned around to see the [muzzle] flashes."

Cunningham had reversed his direction, knowing that the second MiG would probably get on his tail, but decided to "drag" it for Grant. "Okay, I'm dragging 'em . . . get 'em, baby!" he said, right after shooting down the first MiG, according to a transcript of the fight, which was taped.

But Cunningham got no response; Grant was busy dealing with the MiGs behind him. So Cunningham said nervously, "He's on my tail. . . . Where is he?"

Grant's response, according to Cunningham, was "Can't help you, Duke. . . . Got two on my tail."

Cunningham snap-rolled in a VX-4-like disengagement and left the pursuing MiG "sucking air." Grant copied Cunningham's move and joined his leader in fighting wing, and the two zoomed up to a higher altitude to get a better look.

What they saw, according to a declassified Navy message written from their debrief, was an estimated eight MiG-17s in counter clockwise orbit, 10,000 to 15,000 feet above Hai Duong. In the middle of this "defensive wheel" were planes from the strike group exiting the target, and at least three F-4s, including Timm and Erickson, who had chased MiGs into it.

Around the periphery were more planes, and according to the message, a "column" of four MiG-17s "diving in . . . from the northwest."

According to Cunningham, it looked like a scene from *Dawn Patrol*. "Our guys should never have been in there. . . . They were down to 350 knots, which is a good speed at which to die."

Approaching at 550 knots, Cunningham and Grant jumped back in.

Another F-4 on the periphery, Matt Connelly's, came up from their station to the south in response to the radio calls and found himself above the others, perhaps 18,000 to 20,000 feet high, looking down.

Connelly says, "Somebody in the strike group started hollering, 'There's a MiG on my tail! There's a MiG on my tail!' Just screaming it, without saying who he was or where he was. I said, 'Where are you?' and at the same time started looking at the strike group," which was exiting below him.

"I looked way down at about maybe 8000 feet," Connelly recalled, "way below me, and here was an A-7 going along and two little black specks right behind him."

"I didn't hesitate," Connelly recalled, "I just rolled in on them," "telling my wingman: 'I got something. We're going down.' "

Unfortunately, Connelly's wingman didn't follow. The wingman could not be reached for comment through the Navy or through an independent search, but his RIO recalls, "We started [to dive] but then he said, 'Can't pull it through,' and straightened out. . . . He just said basically that he wasn't going to make it, and 'check six,' which means watch the airplane's tail." Moments later he had exited the area.

"I don't know if it was fear for himself," says the wingman's RIO, "as much as fear for his family. The wife and kids were the biggest thing in his life, if I recall correctly. . . . But when the real thing came along, that is, the possibility of losing [death] . . . it was just something he couldn't deal with. It's a disappointment I will carry for a long time."

Connelly wasn't immediately aware of his wingman's departure. His concentration at this point was on the "specks" below him. As he dove closer, the specks became enemy planes.

Unable to get a Sparrow lock because of a malfunctioning radarscope, Connelly fired a Sidewinder, even though he thought he was out of envelope.

"My philosophy right then," he related, "was this may be the only chance I ever get."

Almost as soon as the heat-seeker left the rail, the MiG—a dark blue '17—turned up and flew at them head-on, almost hitting them. "I mean we're talking, well, maybe a hundred feet or something," said Connelly.

A short time later, realizing the absence of his wingman, Connelly made his only taped reference to it. Calling the wingman by his first name, he asked, "Are you okay?" No response was recorded. Although he didn't know what had happened to his wingman, Connelly's concentration went back to the fight. After missing with his Sidewinder and bottoming out from his dive, he became aware of "a whole ball of airplanes" above him.

"Pete Pettigrew knows all this stuff . . . intelligence told him. . . . Apparently when there is a large strike coming in, [the North Vietnamese] launch all the MiGs and put them over a geographic checkpoint." [Then] "their GCI [ground controllers] vector them around behind you. . . . Maybe it's a mountain or a town or whatever. Well, this particular day they ended up sticking 'em right over the railyard we were bombing. So in actuality, they were probably as surprised . . . even more surprised to see us than we were to see them."

Connelly quickly went after a MiG-17. "I picked him up visually and started swinging in behind. He could see me coming and started to turn into me but I went to his six o'clock. . . . He reversed and I pulled back behind him again.

"The '17 has this big shield that goes over their head for the ejection seat. They can't see behind them. . . . I was pulling into that blind spot and in the meantime really closing in on him."

The MiG made another reversal and Connelly moved closer. Apparently, the MiG thought Connelly had gone, because he rolled wings level and started flying level.

"I was behind him maybe even less than a thousand feet . . . real close . . . trying to get the nose on him to shoot a Sidewinder, and I finally got it on him and the tone was good and loud. I squeezed the trigger and the thing went straight off and up his exhaust pipe."

The MiG burst into a fireball and started heading down, its pilot ejecting.

It was Connelly's first MiG kill—the second kill of the battle, which was still barely a minute old.

"Okay, splash one," Connelly said quietly over the UHF.

Meanwhile, amidst desperate calls from strike bombers of "He's back on your four o'clock! . . . Get the goddamn thing! . . . Break left! Break left!" Cunningham and Driscoll had roared down from their observation point and almost had their own mid-air collision, though it wasn't with a MiG.

Dwight Timm and Jim Fox had come barrelling out of the gaggle and missed Cunningham by a hair. The XO and his RIO had gone into the melee to help the bombers, but they found themselves running for their lives.

Timm had three MiGs on his tail: a '17, about 2000 feet behind; a '21, perhaps 1000 feet behind the '17; and a second '17, which came in from the right, "almost like he was joining up," recalls Driscoll. It hid beneath the fleeing Phantom's belly.

Timm was successfully escaping the two trailing MiGs, who didn't yet have an angle on him. But the hidden '17, Cunningham could see, needed only to swing in behind the Phantom to have the proper angle—and he was preparing to do just that.

Cunningham, accelerating in after the pursuing MiGs, immediately got a good Sidewinder tone. But Timm's afterburner was fully lit, and he knew the Sidewinder couldn't distinguish between exhausts. He screamed at Timm to break right so he could pull the trigger.

"F-4 in a port turn. Reverse starboard! . . . Reverse starboard GODDAMMIT!!!"

Timm and Fox heard him, but with their left wing mostly low in the turn, their cockpit blind to the nearby MiG, they were unaware of the most pressing danger. They thought he was talking about the two MiGs in trail.

Fox says, "I heard Randy yelling. . . . I yelled back that we couldn't because we had two MiGs on our eight o'clock position. If [we] broke starboard we'd set up a dead six for those two. . . . [They] were staying with us and the '17 was firing his cannons. I could see the sparkles coming out of his gun ports and the tracers going right over our canopy."

Driscoll called from the back seat, "Four MiG-17s at our seven o'clock." Above them, Cunningham looked up and caught the glint of sunlight off canopies rolling in above, then saw guns firing. It turned out they were newer, generally better performing MiG-19s.

Knowing he was in serious trouble, Cunningham reversed, leaving Timm and Fox for a few seconds but also putting the '19s out of range—except for the closest MiG, which was just about in firing position.

Luckily, he had speed at this point, approximately 550 knots. The remaining MiG on his tail couldn't close on him as long as he didn't turn too tight. But he *had* to turn to get back to help Timm.

He told Driscoll to advise him each time the MiG pulled lead for a shot.

"Now!" his RIO screamed, his neck craned back at their rear.

Bullets whizzed by, but Cunningham had already straightened the plane out and opened a gap on the MiG. Within a matter of seconds they were back behind Timm and Fox and screaming for them to reverse again.

Timm, feeling he'd escaped the two in trail and wanting to get back in the fight, finally did turn. The MiG, close astern, was going too fast to follow. At last, its exhaust was the only one visible to Cunningham's heat-seekers.

"Fox two!" Cunningham roared.

At precisely that second, Timm, who was now on the trail of his own MiG and had fired a Sidewinder too, saw to his right what

Cunningham had been screaming about. He later told Cunningham that his (Cunningham's) missile "traveled the entire length of the '17," exploding it into a tumbling fireball.

It was the third kill of the fight, Cunningham and Driscoll's second of the battle, and their fourth in the war.

They were now tied with the Air Force's Robin Olds, one kill away from being America's first aces of the Vietnam War. But the battle, barely minutes old, was still raging.

Underneath them—with Red Crown continuing to announce, "Bandits . . . Bandits . . . 052 [degrees relative] . . . 19 miles . . ." ("As if we didn't know," quips Fox)—Connelly had found another stray '17. The MiG was flying wings level, seemingly checking out the periphery of the fight for someone to jump. Using the advantage gleaned from Drill, Connelly flew to the MiG's blind spot.

"He was looking for me, and then he gave up. . . . I waited for a good tone, got one, and just as I squeezed, [the missile] dropped off. I went, 'Oh shit.' I thought it was going to miss. . . . It went along, I saw a black puff and thought, 'Christ, it did miss.' "

But then Connelly saw something fall off the MiG, and sliding by it, because of a lot of "overtake," he saw that the small jet didn't have a tail anymore. Shortly afterwards the MiG driver ejected.

It was Connelly's and Blonski's second kill—the fourth of the battle, coming at approximately the same time as Cunningham and Driscoll's second.

"Splash two! Splash two!" Connelly radioed, this time with discernible excitement.

Above them, Cunningham's Showtime-100 had narrowly avoided hitting the ejected MiG pilot from the second kill, when they found "two or three" MiGs behind them.

The pursuers were MiG-17s, one light purple, the other green and brown. "I'll never forget the nose with [its] slow white flash comin' [out]," remembers Driscoll. "The wings were . . . twinklin' real quick, and the two or three behind us were bouncing up and down . . . almost like they had wing overlap and one was gonna hit the other."

Four MiG-21s, who had seen them "smoke their buddy," as Cunningham put it, came at them as well. Showtime-100 dived, and

Driscoll remembers "the sensation of little bridges and stuff . . . very close to the ground." Cunningham was rolling and extending, trying to get away.

"Everywhere I looked there were MiGs," recalled Cunningham.

According to Driscoll, "We were right on the ragged edge. . . . We tried to maintain enough semblance of order so as not to [panic. . . . There was] a tremendous sick feeling in my stomach, like you're about to throw up. . . .

"I just didn't see how we were gonna get out of it. . . . In the combat environment, it's not the man who out-sophisticates or out-exotics the other. It's the guy who makes fewer mistakes who's gonna win, or at least not lose." Driscoll yelled to Cunningham "to break! Break! Give me all you got!"

Cunningham turned hard into the shooting MiGs. "As we did, we rolled the thing back and tried to unload a little bit, then broke in again."

Cunningham and Driscoll got away, miraculously, probably because the MiG's primary targets were the bombers. Gresham, who interviewed the attack pilots (the bombers), says, "I [documented] five or six MiG encounters with [attack] aircraft. . . . Fred Baldwin and Al Junker from [attack squadron] 146 get in the middle of it, and they're 'thatch' weaving, back and forth, covering each other's tails. They're trying to work their way back to the beach because they've got two problems. One, they are many miles inland away from any help. Second, they're running out of gas. . . . If that isn't enough, the *Kitty Hawk* strike on the Hai Doung Bridge . . . is fifteen minutes behind this one [and] the advance elements have already started in. . . . We are talking a stack-up situation that's obvious to anybody around.

"So Baldwin and Junker are thatch-weaving out. Cartwright gets a MiG on him that he manages to dodge. Mike Gravely gets one on him that he manages to dodge. George Gorianick is chasing one around trying to get him with his cannon. . . . Bill Smith, XO of [attack squadron] 147, is chasing one. . . . The attack guys are dreaming of a Sidewinder at this point because they are so short of them . . . [and] Gus Eggert is yelling, you know, 'Jason's! Bombers! Get out of here!' "

Getting out of danger for the moment and seeing MiGs all around him, Cunningham did a 180 degree turn and started heading for the coast. He had second thoughts about leaving, thinking he might get some more kills. But he'd lost track of Grant in the melee and knew he was badly outnumbered.

He continued east at 10,000 feet and climbing. Driscoll was still very much "spring loaded," looking for MiGs to his rear. It was Cunningham who spotted the next one—a MiG-17 up ahead, coming right at them.

The Navy would later identify the MiG pilot as Colonel Toon or "Tomb"—the enigma, who was said to be North Vietnam's leading ace.

But to Cunningham, he was just another "gomer."

"Watch me scare this guy," he said to Driscoll, while preparing to use the fly-close-by technique that he'd learned at Miramar to insure minimum separation.

But as he powered forward, the '17s' front lit up like a Christmas tree.

"That proved to be my first mistake. A-4s [the planes he'd practiced the technique on at Miramar] didn't have guns in the nose."

Cunningham jerked right and then yanked the Phantom up into a vertical climb. He expected, he said, to look down and see the MiG start turning in the horizontal. Instead, Cunningham got the surprise of his life. Approximately 300 feet to his right, canopy to canopy, was the MiG, climbing with him.

"I could see the pilot clearly," Cunningham reported, "leather helmet, goggles, scarf. There was no fear in this guy's eyes."

The Phantom out-climbed the '17, but, in this case, it was to Cunningham and Driscoll's detriment. As the Phantom left the MiG, the MiG pilot executed a tough nose-roll toward them and, still climbing, fired.

Typically, said Driscoll, enemy pilots would shoot a steady stream, "walking it up to you," but this MiG pilot conserved his ammunition.

"It was like, who is this guy? He gave it a couple of squirts and took his finger off. . . . He knew exactly what he was doing."

Cunningham pitched over and started down to avoid the fire. The '17 went over, too, nearly treading air until Cunningham dove by him. Then it jumped in "behind us," says Driscoll, "in a very lethal gun position . . . just like he was tied to us on a string."

To break the MiG's tracking solution, Cunningham pulled the Phantom up and out into a loop, causing the '17 to overshoot. But as he followed it down, too close for a shot, the '17 pulled out to the side, making him overshoot. The two planes started ribboning around each other in a vertical rolling scissors that quickly plunged into a Death Spiral as they swirled toward earth. The MiG was the only one that could get a shot in such close proximity, and it was moving closer to the Phantom with each scissor.

The swirling was causing the Phantom to lose speed, giving the MiG more of an advantage.

Driscoll remembers, "There was tremendous tension and anxiety. . . . We were trying to do something to make sure he didn't shoot us, and trying to extricate ourselves from the situation."

It was just bravado, Cunningham says, when he told Driscoll, "This S.O.B. is really lucky. . . . we'll get this guy now."

But he did have an idea.

During training, Cunningham said, Dave Forst, a future Top Gun instructor, and "one of the smartest fighter pilots I've ever known," had surprised him in the same situation by suddenly running out of a scissors as the two passed each other.

Gresham feels that the time elapsed on the type of the fight was not sufficient for more than two climbs, but Cunningham says—and Driscoll confirms—that he started up again, just as he'd done previously. But this time he didn't want to be predictable. To be predictable, went the dictum, was to die.

As the MiG curled by him, the Phantom's airspeed down to around 200 knots, Cunningham lit burner and raced out, nose down, in the opposite direction, increasing his airspeed to over 500 knots.

He was now out of range and highly maneuverable with his new energy; he turned back to meet the pursuing MiG.

Again he went up, and again the MiG went up with him. And again, they came back down in a spiraling scissors.

The advantage changed continuously as they careened toward earth. Cunningham could never get enough of an advantage to take a shot. "Everything my airplane did, he reacted to instinctively. He was flying damn good airplane!"

Every time the Phantom would get out in front, the MiG pilot would squeeze off a burst. He had chances to run, but he didn't—as Cunningham didn't—although running, given the superior speed of the Phantom, would probably have been riskier for the MiG.

"The only way one guy was going to get away was to shoot the other guy down," says Driscoll.

They separated again and came back for a third pass with Cunningham angling so that the MiG couldn't use its guns.

Another idea occurred to Cunningham. "Your mind works overtime in a situation like that." Each time, he had out-climbed the MiG. Now, as they went up together again, facing off across cockpits as they'd done before, Cunningham yanked the throttles back to idle, popping out the speed brakes at the same time.

The Phantom, which had started the vertical climb at nearly 600 knots, suddenly slowed to 150. The MiG, nose to nose with him a second before, shot out in front of him for the first time.

Advantage Cunningham. But what to do with it?

He was now going so slow that he had to light his burner to avoid falling out of the sky, and he was still too close to shoot a Sidewinder. Deftly manipulating stick and rudder to avoid stalling, he nosed the Phantom toward the MiG's exhaust. The surprised MiG driver probably lost sight of the Phantom, because he rolled over on his back, which was a good way to take a look.

Below him, Cunningham was walking on air, teetering right, a situation that could turn on him should the MiG use its slow speed advantage and curl back.

But just as the MiG pilot realized what was happening and attempted to reverse, Cunningham thought that he departed. "His nose fell through," said Cunningham and he dove by the Phantom, which itself was now nosing downward. Later, they say, they learned that the MiG was low on gas, and its controllers were telling the pilot "to get out of there!"

But at the time, all they knew was that "this tremendously difficult, demanding opponent has just . . . peeled off," says Driscoll. "Why did he do that? . . . For a moment we couldn't believe what we're seeing."

The MiG was running! Cunningham pulled hard and they roared down after the MiG. "It was like . . . pardon the language," remembers Driscoll, "but motherfucker, you're gonna die!"

Cunningham and Driscoll closed the gap to firing range. Cunningham wondered whether the ground heat might spoil his Sidewinder's track. He fired anyway.

He probably experienced some time compression because he recalled that while the missile guided, he saw what he describes as "bees" coming off it or the plane. His mind might have been so focused that he actually saw the individual components of explosion. He started to fire another Sidewinder when there was an "abrupt burst of flame," black smoke, and the MiG flew into the ground. "At this point," says Driscoll, "we realized how low to the ground we were."

Cunningham pulled sharply up to avoid hitting the ground.

"All right, splash one bandit. Duke, you got another one," says Driscoll on the tape, giving little hint in his voice of what they'd just been through.

The two Navy fighters had just become the first American aces of the Vietnam War, the longest war in American history. They had gained their distinction in one of the longest sustained air battles of the war—approximately five minutes, and probably downed North Vietnam's best fighter pilot, whatever his name.

But deep in enemy territory, low on gas, surrounded by hostile fighters with over thirty miles to reach the Gulf and safety, they were not, by any means, out of trouble.

☆ CHAPTER 31 ☆

Steve Shoemaker, guarding the Shrike, didn't get overly excited when he heard the sudden radio traffic back at the target.

"I'd gone around so much . . . '66 through '68, that time frame, when the Navy was just so dry of seeing MiGs . . . that it kind of got my attention, but it didn't impress me that much. It could have been that they were getting painted by SAM targets . . ."

But then a MiG-17 "went right over my head, straight over my canopy!"

It was the first one the Iowan had ever seen. "I thought, Holy God." He radioed the Shrike he was escorting "to get the hell out of there. Go feet wet . . . which wasn't too smart. I should have stuck with him a little longer, but . . . I was like a mad dog in a meat shop . . . MiGs!"

He was probably the farthest north of any of the participants, and didn't arrive until the battle was well in progress.

"I'd never seen anything quite like it," Shoemaker remembers. There were missiles going through the air . . . contrails . . . quite a bit of talk . . . parachutes . . . Just a big dog-and-cat fight . . . "

He saw an F-4 exiting with a MiG on its tail. "For some reason," he remembers, "I knew who it was" [Dave Erickson]. "I jumped in but couldn't get a good angle."

He chased around for a few seconds and finally got a chance to shoot a missile ballistic in hopes of scaring the MiG off. Just as he loosed it, another F-4 came roaring out from underneath him, so close, that his just-loosed missile almost hit the Phantom.

It was Timm, who was doing the same thing he was—trying to

get the MiG off Erickson's tail. Neither of the crews had seen the other. They almost pancaked in mid-air, and it scared Shoemaker so much that he broke away.

By the time he got back in the fight, it seemed to be over. "I probably arrived around the middle of it. I have no idea how long it lasted, no sense of time there. But all of a sudden it was kind of over. Everybody was heading out. I heard people talking about leaving. 'We're low on gas,' or 'We're getting out of here.' I think I was pointing toward the southeast. . . . I saw an F-4 climbing out, just making a slow, straight climb-out toward the coast."

Then he saw something chilling.

"There was a MiG on its tail."

Pulling up from their third kill, Cunningham had asked Driscoll for a heading out. "I gave it to him," remembers the RIO, "east, southeast." They started their climb. "We were concerned about gas now," said Driscoll. "Everybody is over water. . . . We still got maybe 25, 30 miles to go. . . . We were five to six minutes behind everybody. We were the only ones there. . . . We have just been extricated from what seemed like a relatively impossible thing to get away from . . . We just wanted to get the hell out."

Climbing, they were purposely not jinking or using burner. "We were going maximum conserve power to conserve gas," says Driscoll.

Because of its markings, Shoemaker knows the F-4 he saw was a VF-96 Phantom, but he didn't know he says, [until later] who was in it.

"I headed down [toward it] and radioed, 'F-4 headed out of here. You got a MiG on your tail.' "

(His exact words on the tape are: "Showtime low about two-one zero, you got a MiG at your six. He's coming up after you . . . look out.")

He and his RIO, Keith "Cannonball" Crenshaw, targeted the MiG.

"Just about the time I jumped him, he [the MiG] saw me and started to break down left." Shoemaker went after him. The two planes swirled into a "descending spiraling turn. . . . I wasn't making any progress 'cause that '17 could really turn hard, and he was getting more angle off on me all the time."

Shoemaker knew the angle wasn't going to get any better. He fired a Sidewinder. Then, knowing he'd been vulnerable while concentrating on the MiG, he "broke right, pulled the nose up and turned back left" so his RIO could check their six. "I had the feeling I was the last guy in there and I was all by myself. . . ."

But they were clear. Bringing his nose back to where the MiG he'd shot at had been, the sky was vacant.

"I told [Crenshaw], 'Where in hell did he go?' "

Just then the RIO said, "Look at that!" Below them was a huge explosion. It was later determined that the explosion was the MiG he'd just shot at—the sixth MiG kill of the battle.

"I was still antsy about being there alone. I said, 'I'm getting the hell out of here.' And rightfully so, because the minute I reversed, here comes another MiG-17 across my tail. We kind of went into a scissors."

When we got the chance—the two planes passing each other "canopy to canopy" —he did the same thing Cunningham had done to disengage: "dumped my nose and torched the burner and just kept him a good angle off." He took off for home.

Cunningham and Driscoll were still climbing in minimum burner. If the MiG Shoemaker shot had been on their tail, as Shoemaker believes, they both say they were unaware of it, which is understandable given the confusion of such a battle and the fact that the MiG would have been in their blind spot.

But they soon encountered more MiGs, the number and position of which vary according to reports.

In his book, Cunningham says the MiGs suddenly converged on them from several points, just after Matt Connelly warned him, "There are four '17s at your seven o'clock."

But Connelly says—and he is backed by the tape of the fight— that he saw only one MiG near them, saddled in dangerously behind them.

Following their second MiG kill, Connelly and Blonski were moving at a very slow speed—"about 270 knots or something"—and were nearly hit by a MiG-17 making a pass at them from their three o'clock position.

"He slid underneath us . . . came out the other side," remembers Blonski.

The MiG pilot could have attacked them, but he ran instead, diving for the rice paddies. Connelly and Blonski, attempting to pursue, lost him among the paddies. Low on fuel, they decided to exit and head home.

"It was at this point, [when] I essentially came out of the dive and gained speed . . . that I ended up abeam Randy," said Connelly. "We were about a quarter of a mile away . . . climbing out in combat spread. He is at my three o'clock, right off my shoulder, so I can check his six o'clock and he can check mine. And it just happened that . . . there was a MiG-17 behind his airplane. *One* Mig-17. Not four."

The transcript of the fight, prepared by Gresham, has Connelly radioing, "Showtime headed about . . . 180 [degrees]. Heads up . . . You got a MiG behind you."

Cunningham: "Where is he?

Connelly: "Okay, he's right on your tail . . . just don't let him get guns. It's a '17. You can outrun him."

Cunningham: "Okay, we're alert."

Connelly says the F-4 was in basic engine. "I could see all the smoke [from the F-4] and the MiG was maybe two airplane lengths [behind] at the most [approximately 50 feet, he estimates.] I mean he was right behind [Randy], and I told him to light the burner and unload and he could outrun him. The F-4 didn't do anything. So I said again, 'F-4 headed . . . over a large river. You got a MiG on your tail. Unload!' "

The F-4, according to Connelly, continued climbing in basic engine. Connelly decided to try to scare the MiG. He was out of Sidewinders, and his Sparrow radar was still down; nonetheless, he turned his nose toward the MiG and shot a Sparrow ballistic without guidance.

It was at this time that Cunningham says he saw Connelly. "I saw Matt with his nose on us. . . . I thought 'Matt, Jeez, you're shooting at us!' His Sparrow went right over our tail and back to our seven o'clock . . . where four '17s were in pursuit."

Connelly and Blonski both say they sighted the MiG—not the F-4—and had no worry about hitting the Phantom. To Connelly's surprise, the missile started guiding, and Blonski told him the radar was back on. The Sparrow, says Connelly, went over the MiG. The MiG broke off and started descending. He chased it a few miles, but then with "everybody screaming for the tanker. . . . I wanted to get out of there real fast."

He lit his afterburners, turned around, and headed back out for the Gulf, passing Cunningham's lone F-4, which was still climbing without visible signs of trouble.

Driscoll, the backseater in Showtime 100, didn't remember Connelly or the MiG on their tail.

"We saw a couple of MiGs down on the left side [passing them], but nobody was chasing us. . . . We start[ed] to feel now kinda like, hey, it's all right . . . still nervous . . . but starting to realize what we'd done. . . ."

Then, heading toward the Gulf, all of a sudden, he says, they were hit by a SAM.

"We roll to the right and there is this long white exhaust track. . . . I see the orange smoke . . . and . . . I hear this stuff hit the side of the plane."

It sounded to him like "somebody took a handful of BBs and threw them against the side of your car. What it is . . . see a SAM's got about 4000 pieces of metal about the size of a .38 slug, and it [the metal] travels 10,000 feet per second, or Mach 10. It's real hot and they were hitting . . . some of them were hitting on the underside of the belly."

He asked Cunningham, "Hey, Randy. Everything okay?" [Randy replied] 'Yeah.' We continue to climb maybe 15 seconds, and then the thing kinda yawed to the left. It's kinda like a skid almost. . . . I said, 'Everything okay?' He said, 'Startin' to lose PC2.' That's one of the hydraulic systems."

Over his shoulder, he noticed fire on the fuselage. He alerted Cunningham, who replied, " 'I'm starting to lose the utility.' That's the backup system. . . . When you lose the main and the backup, the book says to eject. I know this and I'm thinking, 'Oh, shit. We still got maybe 20 miles to go to get over water.' "

The fire, enlarging beyond what they could see, rapidly engulfed the airplane behind the cockpit, destroying Cunningham's ability to control with hydraulics. But afraid of becoming prisoners, they elected not to eject until the very last second.

Cunningham now remembered a publicized account of how Duke Hernandez had used only his feet to "barrell roll" his way out of North Vietnam. Also with crippled F-4 hydraulics, Hernandez had instinctively jammed his tail rudder controls and the plane had slid to the side and up. As they rolled and were upside down, he had jammed the other rudder and they had rolled over. What Cunningham now attempted, recalls Driscoll, was the same "corkscrew type" maneuver. "The nose would come up . . . and he would start to put the rudder in . . . we'd roll through a 360-degree sphere . . ."

They continued spiraling toward the coast, both trying to talk calmly so the other wouldn't hear the fear in the other's voice. Land and sky blurred alternately in their rotating vision. Suddenly an explosion rocked the Phantom, shaking the plane violently. But still Cunningham kept going, eating up the territory between them and the coast. At last, they saw water sparkling ahead and finally beneath them.

"Eject! Eject! Eject!" screamed Cunningham, purposely repeating so there would be no mistake. Ejecting turned out to be a fight between crushing Gs and disorientation, but both finally got out. Cunningham injured his back when his deploying parachute jerked open, slowing his free fall.

Below, they saw North Vietnamese patrol boats, a large freighter, and some fishing junks moving out to pick them up.

"Oh, shit!" thought Driscoll, who had just experienced a "tremendous exhilaration" at getting out of the airplane alive over what he thought would be the safety of the Gulf. All they could do was begin broadcasting May Days on their hand-held radios.

But other members of the strike force, having seen the fireball from their plane when it hit the water, were already searching for them.

On the tape, a Corsair pilot says, "Do you see the chutes?"

Another pilot answers, "I saw a red chute a little bit ago . . . Ahhh, here we are . . . We're going right by them. . . ."

Several other planes came in, including a VF-92 Phantom. "Two good chutes . . . out at our three o'clock."

Eggert: "Okay . . . hold three hundred feet over them."

They were quickly encircled by friendly firepower.

As the North Vietnamese boats got closer, Eggert radioed: "Hit anything that moves. . . ." A number of SAMs were launched, but the fighters easily eluded them.

It wasn't long before Driscoll and Cunningham heard a rescue helicopter approaching. Fifteen minutes later they were picked up, and, rejoicing, they were on their way out to a hospital ship.

☆ CHAPTER 32 ☆

One other Navy Phantom crew shot down a MiG on May 10. The Navy's total score for that day was eight MiGs—without a single loss of a U.S. plane in a MiG dogfight.

The Navy's post-lull kill ratio rose to a highly commendable 14 to 1 (15 to 1 if Beaulier's 1970 MiG was included). Their kill ratio contrasted sharply with the Air Force's continued 2-to-1 ratio, which included two May 10 losses to MiGs.

For the first time in the war, the Navy's performance was back to what it had been in previous wars. The Navy brass, understandably, was ecstatic.

Cunningham, for becoming the country's first Vietnam War ace, received an on-the-spot regular commission, something rarely seen on U.S. Navy vessels and the first such commission of the Vietnam War. He and Driscoll, the first all-missile aces in U.S. history, were ordered home and assigned to Top Gun as instructors. But even before they'd assumed their new posts, they were crediting the school for their success.

"First words out of Randy's mouth—if not factually, then essentially," says Roger Box, who talked to those who talked to him, "were something to the effect that 'Everything I did I learned at Top Gun.'. . . They just stepped off the airplane saying, 'I owe my victories to Top Gun.' "

The Navy air victories did not stop there. On May 12, Mugs McKeown, with Jack Ensch in his back seat, shot down two MiG-17s in a wild dogfight over Kep, when as many as six MiGs surrounded them. That same day, according to a declassified "flash" to the CNO, a MIGCAP crew from the *Hancock* encountered a MiG whose pilot, on the first pass, elected to eject rather than turn and fight.

Navy strategists speculated that the North Vietnamese were becoming leery of the well-trained Navy pilots.

On June 11, Tooter Teague finally got his own confirmed MiG kill. He credited his RIO, Ralph Howell, as much as himself with the shootdown.

"For the record," the former F-8 single-seater told his debriefers, "I've changed my mind [about backseaters]. The squadron has been in five MiG engagements, four of which resulted in downed MiGs, and in all five engagements the RIOs have 'Tally-hoed' the MiGs . . . Plus . . . in two separate engagements, RIOs have called a total of four MiG-17s at somebody's six o'clock. . . ."

It was another validation of Top Gun doctrine, and coming from Teague, a former skeptic, it had special significance.

In late May or early June, Jerry Kane, back at Top Gun, remembers receiving a phone call from former Top Gun commander Dan Pedersen, who was in Washington. He told Kane, "As a result of these MiG kills . . . everybody here in Washington can see the value [of Top Gun]. It looks like it's going to be made an independent command."

For Kane, it was like hearing news about the birth of his first child. "It just made my whole day. Not until that call did I personally feel we'd accomplish the final goal of becoming a separate command."

Ten days after Teague's kill on June 21st, CMDR Sam Flynn, with Bill John in his backseat, shot down a MiG-21 while flying with VF-31 from the *Saratoga*. It was a fitting kill, for it brought the Vietnam fighter tactics story full circle. Flynn had been one of the first F-4 pilots to begin urging a change in tactics to accommodate the Phantom's advantages and to negate the MiG's.

With Flynn's kill, the Navy had now shot down 21 MiGs and lost only one Phantom in air-to-air encounters since January. It was an achievement the CNO himself called "phenomenal" in a message to the fleet.

Most of the credit had to go to Top Gun and Drill, which had been phased out.

On July 7th a special ceremony took place establishing Top Gun as a separate command. The ceremony was conducted on the Miramar parade grounds, and a three-star admiral, Tom Walker, made the address. Besides Jerry Sawatzky, who was in charge of the ceremony, few (if any) of the original instructors were in attendance.

In the next six months and until the war's end, three more MiGs were shot down by Navy crews, including the last MiG kill of the war by Vic Koveleski and Jim Wise on January 12, 1973.

Koveleski, too, was a Top Gun graduate, prompting Sawatsky, who had helped train him, to note: "For Jim Ruliffson, Mel Holmes, or John Nash it was understood that they'd get a MiG if they crossed paths with one. . . . But to me, Top Gun had done its job if the average pilot like Vic can be effective in combat. . . . That's the test. . . . Vic was no fire-eater. . . . He'd probably beat half the guys on a given day, and they'd beat him on another. . . . He was the guy next door, but he went out there and shot the fanny off one of those MiGs."

A Top Gun Marine crew also got a MiG in those last few months. The crew consisted of "Bear" Lassiter and his backseater, John D. Cummings, who both had graduated from the school in 1969. But a Top Gun graduate, R. I. Randall, was also shot down in a dogfight with a MiG, proving that even expert training doesn't make an aircrew invincible. The final post-Top Gun Navy kill ratio closed at 12 to 1 (counting Beaulier's kill).

By all accounts, both the school and the Navy's fighter pilot performance were a resounding success. The Air Force, which had made no significant changes in its air-to-air training since the Vietnam War's beginning, ended the war with the same 2-to-1 ratio with which it had started.

When the cease fire was signed on January 27, 1973, finally ending U.S. involvement in the war, Navy pilots were the only U.S. forces that could claim an unequivocal victory. Cannon-less Phantoms had ruled the skies in the war's last years.

"Two statistics stick out in my mind," says Jim Ruliffson. "One is the kills per engagement after the lull. They skyrocketed from about .2 to 1.0.... It meant that we knew what we were doing. Every time we met them—on the average—we shot them down."

The other statistic, he went on, "is that I believe that over 60 percent of the MiG kills from the time we went back north until the war ended were done by Top Gun graduates. It wasn't so much that Top Gun graduates were the only ones who could kill, but that they were acknowledged as the best crews in the squadron. When there was a tough mission, or one that looked ... like MiGs might be airborne, they sent those guys."

The air combat statistics helped to cause a virtual revolution in air combat training. As a result of their poor air-to-air record in Vietnam, the Air Force in 1975 initiated "Exercise Red Flag," a graduate level air-to-air course "much the same as the Navy Fighter Weapons School," according to *Tailhook* magazine in its review of the 1984 book, *Red Flag: Air Combat for the 80's*. Both the Air Force and Navy continue the training today, the first time in American history that war-level dogfight practice has been maintained steadily after hostilities have ceased.

A great victory had been forged in the little trailer at Miramar and in the secret skies above the desert. The former pilots and instructors in a remarkable gathering of eagles got together again for the Red River Fighter Pilots Association's "Welcome Home" dinner and dance for the newly returned POWs, held in the Las Vegas Convention Center, near Nellis and the desert where they'd spent so much of their time. It was a time for a celebration and reunion—a time to reflect on what they'd accomplished.

"Everybody was there," remembers Dan Pedersen. The instructors were there and the VX-4 people.

"We had reversed a trend," says Pedersen. "You can never quantify just how many ... but a lot of guys who were there that night were alive because of what we had done...." Their legacy, too, will live on, in the form of the most famous and distinguished fighter weapons school in existence—the school known as Top Gun.

☆ Glossary ☆

A-1 "Skyraider" Heavily armed propeller-driven aircraft resembling World War II fighter. Used for bombing, strafing, and rescue. (Also called "Spad.")

A-4 "Skyhawk" Light-weight, single-seat attack bomber used by Top Gun as MiG simulators because of their maneuverability. Training versions were modified to have two seats.

A-6 "Intruder" Two seat attack bomber with distinct bubble canopy. The crew of pilot and navigator-bombardier sat side-by-side.

ACM Air Combat Maneuvering or dogfighting.

Air-to-air Usually referring to missiles shot from one airplane at another.

Air-to-ground Bombing or shooting missiles from an airplane to a target on the ground. Sometimes called air-to-mud.

Alpha Strike Large offensive strike usually involving all a carrier's available airplanes.

Atoll A Soviet-built heat seeking missile much like the American Sidewinder.

BARCAP Barrier Combat Air Patrol, usually fighters positioned between the land and an aircraft carrier to defend the carrier.

Ballistic Unguided; following a trajectory determined solely by thrust.

Bogey An unidentified approaching aircraft usually assumed to be hostile. Also an opponent in a training dogfight.

Bolter Unsuccessful landing attempt on a carrier. Tail hook fails to engage arresting wires and the plane has to fly off for another try.

CAG Carrier Air Group Commander, a World War II term still used, although carrier groups are now called wings.

CAP Combat Air Patrol, of which there are several types.

Clock Positions Positions of objects outside an aircraft as if its nose were at 12 o'clock, the tail at 6 o'clock, the right wing at 3 o'clock and the left wing at 9 o'clock.

COD Carrier Onboard Delivery aircraft. Usually a propeller plane that shuttles between ship and shore.

CNO Chief Naval Officer.

F-4 Phantom Two engined, two seat interceptor-bomber used by both the Navy and the Air Force. Unlike the Air Force model, the Navy version did not have guns; it relied solely on missiles. Navy RIOs, unlike their counterparts in the Air Force, were not able to control the plane from the rear seat.

F-8 Crusader Sleek Navy fighter in the MiG-21 class. Had both guns and missiles.

Feet Dry Radio code indicating an aircraft or group of aircraft has crossed over land from the water. Usually used before a strike or action.

Feet Wet Code for having crossed over water from land. Usually used after a strike or action.

Fox Two Code indicating a Sidewinder missile has been launched. (Fox One is used for the Sparrow.)

G Force The force exerted on a pilot or crewmember by gravity and/or change in speed or direction, especially turning at high speed.

Jink Constant maneuvering in both the horizontal and vertical planes to present as unpredictable a target as possible.

Judy RIO term used to indicate contact with a bogey.

MiG-17 Single-seat, highly maneuverable Soviet fighter armed with guns and missiles. The name MiG comes from combining the names of the two Soviet designers of the airplanes, Mikoyan and Gurevich.

MiG-21 Fastest fighter in the North Vietnamese arsenal. Single seat. Armed with missiles.

MIGCAP Usually fighters with the specific mission of attacking MiGs.

NAS Naval Air Station

NFO Naval Flight Officer. A commissioned aircrew member other than the pilot. A RIO is a specific type of NFO.

Red Crown Code name of a ship providing specific threat information to pilots.

RIO Radar Intercept Officer. The NFO who occupies the rear seat in an F-4. He has specific duties in team with the pilot and is sometimes called a "backseater."

SAM Surface-to-air missile. In Vietnam, the most feared were Soviet built SA-2s, which looked like flying telephone poles.

Sidewinder A heat-seeking air-to-air missile.

Sparrow A radar-controlled air-to-air missile.

TARCAP Fighters stationed around an air strike in order to protect the bombers, either by intercepting them or discouraging their attack.

VA Prefix designating a Navy attack or bombing squadron.

VF Prefix designating a Navy fighter squadron.

XO Executive Officer, second in command of a squadron or ship.